VIGNETTES OF MANHATTAN
OUTLINES IN LOCAL COLOR

Books by Brander Matthews

These Many Years, Recollections of a New Yorker

———

BIOGRAPHIES

Shakspere as a Playwright
Molière, His Life and His Works

———

ESSAYS AND CRITICISMS

The Principles of Playmaking
French Dramatists of the 19th Century
Pen and Ink, Essays on subjects of more or less
    importance
Aspects of Fiction, and other Essays
The Historical Novel, and other Essays
Parts of Speech, Essays on English
The Development of the Drama
Inquiries and Opinions
The American of the Future, and other Essays
Gateways to Literature, and other Essays
On Acting
A Book About the Theater
Essays on English

———

Vignettes of Manhattan; Outlines in Local Color

"PEOPLE WHO THRONGED THE FLOOR WERE WELLNIGH AS VARI
OUS AS THE PAINTINGS"

VIGNETTES OF MANHATTAN:
OUTLINES IN LOCAL COLOR

BY
BRANDER MATTHEWS

WITH AN INTRODUCTION BY
W. C. BROWNELL

ILLUSTRATED BY
W. T. SMEDLEY

NEW YORK
CHARLES SCRIBNER'S SONS
1921

THE SCRIBNER PRESS

TO

THEODORE ROOSEVELT

My dear Theodore,— You know—for we have talked it over often enough—that I do not hold you to be a typical New-Yorker, since you come of Dutch stock, and first saw the light here on Manhattan Island, whereas the typical New-Yorker is born of New England parents, perhaps somewhere west of the Alleghanies. You know, also, that often the typical New-Yorker is not proud of the city of his choice, and not so loyal to it as we could wish. He has no abiding concern for this maligned and misunderstood town of ours; he does not thrill with pride at the sight of its powerful and irregular profile as he comes back to it across the broad rivers; nor is his heart lifted up with joy at the sound of its increasing roar, so suggestive and so stimulating. But we have a firm affection for New York, you and I, and a few besides; we like it for what it is; and we love it for what we hope to see it.

It is because of this common regard for our strange and many-sided city that I am giving myself the pleasure of proffering to you this little volume of vignettes. They are not stories really, I am afraid—not sketches even, nor studies; they are, I think, just what I have called them—vignettes. And there are a dozen of them, one for every month in the year, an urban calendar of times and seasons. Such as they are, I beg that you will accept them in token of my friendship and esteem; and that you will believe me, always,

Yours truly,

BRANDER MATTHEWS

New York, *May,* 1894

"When I came to my chamber I writ down these minutes; but was at a loss what instruction I should propose to my readers from the enumeration of so many insignificant matters and occurrences; and I thought it of great use, if they could learn with me to keep their minds open to gratification, and ready to receive it from anything it meets with."

—STEELE, *in "The Spectator," August 11, 1712.*

INTRODUCTION

FEW volumes of short stories published a generation ago remain in print to-day and fewer still either merit or would repay reprinting. But the case is different with the two volumes published by Mr. Matthews in the early nineties under respectively the title and subtitle now given to their contents combined in one and made once more accessible to the reading public. Whatever may be said of the progress made by current literature in the interval, the public for it has augmented at least correspondingly with the census, and it is permitted to hope that the interest of this wider public in work of such exceptional authorship, subject and quality has similarly increased. Mr. Matthews has himself a wider public, amply earned, and I should say that interest in New York has probably increased in pretty nearly equal measure with the change in its character. Its cosmopolitanism has grown prodigiously, yet its self-consciousness far from diminishing has distinctly deepened—if one may properly speak of depth in connection with it. No doubt the chameleon's changes, even shallower, quicken its sense of self. Vignettes of Manhattan should therefore appeal to such actual local pride and public spirit as we have, as well as to a historic interest in a previous epoch of their subject's evolution—as the pace of the day requires us to consider the aspect, character and manners of twenty-five years ago, when Mr. Matthews had the idea of fixing these in the framework of the short story. Besides, a good deal of the scent of those roses survives.

So far as I know it was a unique idea. It was certainly a happy one. Would it not be a pleasant thing if we had such series of analogous authorship systematically celebrating London, Paris, not to say Florence, Rome, Athens itself? Perhaps it was never attempted by any one before because it was too difficult of execution. To the pure fictionist it would necessitate irksome notation; the mere observer would hardly perceive its fictional value. Mr. Matthews fortunately was at home in both departments of writing. The result was that almost every essential phase of New York life and character, belonging to every quarter of the city, is veraciously pictured in these twenty-four proficient and polished stories. Each is composed with attentive art to illustrate its two-fold motive of interest as fiction and as portraiture. And the whole, the collection, constitutes a dramatic panorama of the metropolis a generation ago of great variety and point. "Little old New York" has never had so thorough-going and so diverting a historiographer. Are there any New York "types" omitted? I think of none. How

did the author come across some of them? How
get some of them to sit for him? Unlike a writer
with a reporter's record he has never been, as it
were, a prowler among the precincts and pur-
lieus of the town; yet clearly he knows his Mulberry Bend material as well as that of Fifth Avenue, the studios as well as the stage, the now ex-
tinct saloon as well as the still flourishing Salvation Army barracks, and portrays Lazarus and
Dives with equal familiarity—our kind, too, of
each and all. I suppose a writer must have been
born in New Orleans to have such a sharp sense of
New York, but it is true that he immigrated early.

Rich enough in material for plots and characters—in the right hands—Mr. Matthews shows
the metropolis to be in these twenty-four stories,
(though I wish he had also republished a volume of
Manhattan "Vistas" containing twelve more tales
belonging to the same period). But obviously to
have forced the fictional note would have been to
diminish that of portraiture and accordingly to
have minimized the motive of the stories. In order to keep New York itself in the foreground the
author's personages are of necessity types—not
individuals to be found anywhere. And their
stories are such as might have happened, since
their author's design is to convey an impression of
what does happen. Their representative qualities
and circumstances and adventures are therefore
those that are emphasized. They are not for this

reason less definitely depicted, though they may be less elaborately realized. If they were more highly complicated, however, their typical function would be frustrated. New York itself would recede too far into the background. As it is, Miss Marlenspuyk, for example, though a personally charming silhouette, is chiefly differentiated for us by the characteristic perfume of geniune Knickerbocker idiosyncrasy. Similarly of homely and low-life figures for supplying which the author never seems to be at a loss, any more than he is for supplying them with appropriate Manhattan adventure—drama and dramatis personæ, indeed, Manhattan to the core. Among them all they certainly create the illusion of a very palpable environment.

It was to be sure a little different from that which now surrounds us, and furnished a different theme for treatment different from current practice. Probably if ecstasies and excess, "psychoanalysis" and external melodrama had in the nineties been invented, or been deemed normal, Mr. Matthews would have picked his way through them, but in any case to be veridical the Manhattan "picture" of those days had to be, by contrast with ours, placidity itself. The crime-wave was unknown, the daylight holdup unprecedented. There was an occasional murder mystery, always more than a nine days' wonder; the public had not yet grown callous. One of the stories records an assault with murderous intent. There were

more fires. Our author has a fire story. Suicide
has always been with us and we have here a rather
notably well handled one—minus the horror, which
the fastidious artist must generally, one would
think, doubt his capacity to dwell on to advantage,
just as the sensitive painter leaves Niagaras and
volcanic convulsions to Nature. But incontest-
ably the life here mirrored was quieter than ours
and, being "slower," was correspondingly fuller.
People had time to devote to living.

It is furthermore incidentally to be pointed out
that the Vignettes have a technical interest quite
apart from that of their substance. Every one
nowadays is enormously interested in process.
One might almost say there was a "popular movement" of concern with the philosophy of technic.
If so, it could hardly be denied that Mr. Matthews
was one of its pioneers. Certainly of the philosophy of the short story he was the first analytic and
explicit exponent. Each of these tales is his
theory in action, so to say. Nor is it to be
doubted, in the case of so ardently systematic a
temperament and such a talent for argument and
organization, that this was in each case definitely
his design. He was not content to contend but
desired to demonstrate and we have here his
"philosophy teaching by example." Accordingly
the skeleton, the structure, the framework and
the filling of each little tale produce an effect
that at least is bound to have the merit of hav-

ing been intended. The hap-hazard and the desultory are avoided not only altogether, but, to analysis, quite obviously. For this reason indeed the Vignettes have also, I should think, a certain text-book or "collateral reading" value in the populous courses now offered by the Universities for the elevation of the short-story-writing masses. Nothing, one would say, could better inculcate by explicit example the measured and disciplined practice, the ship-shape and organic result which—plus, of course, literary talent—are the elementary excellences of this prevalent form of literary expression.

"Introductions," too, I may add, are in fashion, and fashion is, as is well known, inexorable. Otherwise I should not have been asked to write one about the lighter work of an author who in virtue of a shelf-full of books comprehending all varieties of literary activity—novels and tales, biography, autobiography, history, linguistics, literary and social criticism, the drama, versification and verse as well as prose, even juvenile fiction—is widely recognized both at home and abroad as one of the particularly representative men of letters of our time.

W. C. BROWNELL.

CONTENTS

VIGNETTES OF MANHATTAN

	PAGE
In the Little Church Down the Street	3
The Twenty-ninth of February	11
At a Private View	21
Spring in a Side Street	35
A Decoration-Day Revery	45
In Search of Local Color	57
Before the Break of Day	73
A Midsummer Midnight	87
A Vista in Central Park	107
The Speech of the Evening	117
A Thanksgiving-Day Dinner	131
In the Midst of Life	145

OUTLINE IN LOCAL COLOR

An Interview with Miss Marlenspuyk	161
A Letter of Farewell	175
A Glimpse of the Under World	189

	PAGE
A Wall Street Wooing	205
A Spring Flood in Broadway	225
The Vigil of McDowell Sutro	241
An Irrepressible Conflict	263
The Solo Orchestra	277
The Rehearsal of the New Play	295
A Candle in the Plate	323
Men and Women and Horses	337
In the Watches of the Night	357

ILLUSTRATIONS

People who thronged the floor were wellnigh as various as the paintings . . . . *Frontispiece*

FACING PAGE

Distracted by the crossing shouts of loud-voiced men 48

Two slim Japanese gentlemen 108

Coming from church 134

"Winifred!" he cried 234

"The air was thick and heavy" 278

Explanations 340

She almost shivered, the place seemed to her so cheerless 360

VIGNETTES OF MANHATTAN

IN THE LITTLE CHURCH DOWN
THE STREET

HE little church stands back from the street, with a scrap of lawn on either side of the path that winds from the iron gate to the church door. On this chill January morning the snow lay a foot deep on the grass-plots, with the water frozen out of it by the midnight wind. The small fountain on one side was sheathed with ice; and where its tiny spirtle fell a glittering stalagmite was rising rapidly, so the rotund sparrows had difficulty in getting at their usual drinking-trough. The sky was ashen, yet there was a hope that the sun might break out later in the morning. A sharp breeze blew down the street from the river, bearing with it, now and again, the tinkle of sleigh-bells from the Avenue, only fifty yards away.

There was the customary crowd of curious idlers gathered about the gate as the hearse drew up before it. The pall-bearers alighted from the carriages which followed, and took up their positions on the sidewalk, while the undertaker's assistants were lifting out the coffin. Then the bareheaded and gray-haired rector came from out the church porch, and went down to the gate to

meet the funeral procession.   He held the prayer-
book open in his hand, and when he came to the
coffin he began to read the solemn words of the
order for the burial of the dead :

"I am the resurrection and the life, saith the
Lord : he that believeth in me, though he were
dead, yet shall he live : and whosoever liveth and
believeth in me, shall never die."

Preceding the pall - bearers the rector led the
way to the church, which was already filled with
the dead actor's comrades and with his friends,
and with mere strangers who had come out of
curiosity, and to see actresses by daylight and off
the stage.   The interior was dusky, although the
gas had been lighted here and there.   The Christmas greens still twined about the pillars, and still
hung in heavy festoons from the low arched roof.
As the coffin passed slowly through the porch,
the rector spoke again :

"We brought nothing into this world, and it
is certain we can carry nothing out.   The Lord
gave, and the Lord hath taken away ; blessed be
the Name of the Lord."

Throughout the church there was a stir, and all
heads were turned towards the entrance.   There
were tears in the eyes of more than one man, for
the actor had been a favorite, and not a few wom-
en were weeping silently.   In a pew near the door
were two young actresses who had been in the
same company with the dead man when he had
made his first appearance on the stage, only three

years before; and now, possessed by the emotion of the moment, these two sobbed aloud. By their side stood a tall, handsome, fair-haired woman, evidently not an actress; she was clad in simple black; she gave but a single glance at the coffin as it passed up the aisle, half hidden by the heaped-up wreaths of flowers, and then she stared straight before her, with a rigid face, but without a tear in her eye.

Slowly the rector preceded the pall-bearers up the central aisle of the church, while the vestured choir began the stately anthem:

"Lord, let me know my end, and the number of my days; that I may be certified how long I have to live.

"Behold, thou hast made my days as it were a span long, and mine age is even as nothing in respect of thee; and verily every man living is altogether vanity."

It was for a young man that this solemn anthem was being sung—for a man who had died in his twenty-fifth year, at the moment of his first success, and when life opened temptingly before him. He bore a name known in American history, and his friends had supposed that he would be called to the bar, like his father and his grandfather before him. He was a handsome young fellow, with a speaking eye and a rich, alluring voice; and his father's friends saw in him a moving advocate. But the year he was graduated from college his father had died, and his mother also, and he was left alone in the world. As it happened, his father's investments were ill-advised, and there was little or no income to be hoped from them for years. In college he had been the foremost member of the dramatic club, and in the summer vacations he had taken part in many private theatricals. Perhaps it had always been his secret wish to abandon the bar for the stage. While he was debating the course he should take, chance threw in his way the offer of an engagement in the company which support-ed a distinguished tragedian. He had accepted what opportunity proffered, and it was not as a lawyer but as an actor that he had made his living ; it was as an actor that his funeral was now being held at "the little church down the street."

While the choir had been singing the anthem, the coffin had been borne to the chancel and set down before the rail, which was almost concealed from sight by the flowers scattered about the steps and clustering at the foot of the pulpit and in front of the reading-desk. The thick and cloy-ing perfume of the lilies was diffused throughout the church.

The rector had taken his place at the desk in the chancel to read the appointed lesson, with its message of faith and love. There were sobs to be heard when he declared that this mortal shall put on immortality.

"Then shall be brought to pass the saying that

is written, Death is swallowed up in victory. O death, where is thy sting? O grave, where is thy victory?"

There were those present—old friends of his boyhood, come from afar to give the dead man the last greeting of affection—who knew how high had been his hopes when he went upon the stage; and they knew also how hard that first year had been, with the wearisome drudgery of his apprenticeship, with the incessant travelling, with ambition baffled by lack of opportunity. Some of them were aware how the second year of his career in the theatre had seen a change in his fortunes, and how discouragement had given place to confidence. There had been dissensions in the company to which he belonged, and the tragedian had parted with the actor who played the second parts. Here was a chance for the young man, and he proved himself worthy of the good-fortune. No more youthful and fiery Laertes had been seen for years, no more passionate Macduff, no more artful and persuasive Mark Antony. He had the gifts of nature—youth, and manly beauty, and the histrionic temperament; and he had also the artistic intelligence which made the utmost out of his endowment. Before the end of his second season on the stage he was recognized as the most promising actor of his years. He had played Mark Antony for the first time only twelve months before; and now he lay there in his coffin, and the little church was filled with the actors and actresses of New York who had come to bid him farewell.

When the rector had finished the reading of the lesson there was a hush throughout the church. A faint jingle of sleigh-bells came floating down from the Avenue.

A few straggling rays of sunshine filtered through the windows on the right side of the little church, and stained with molten colors the wood-work of the pews on the left. There was a movement among the members of the vestured choir, and a large and stately woman took her stand before the organ ; she was the contralto of a great opera company, and it was with skill and power and feeling that she sang "Rock of Ages."

In a pew between the organ and the pulpit sat a slight, graceful, dark - eyed and dark - haired woman, young still and charming always, although the freshness had faded from her face. This was the celebrated actress with whom the dead man had been acting only a week before. She was the ideal Juliet — so the theatre-goers thought — and never before had she been aided by so gallant and so ardent a Romeo. Never before had the tragedy been produced with so much splendor, and with dramatic effect so certain and so abundant. Never before had "Romeo and Juliet" been performed for a hundred and fifty nights without interruption. And for once the critics had been in accord with the public, so potent was the glamour of youth and beauty and passion. It was a joy to all discerning lovers of the drama to see characters so difficult interpreted so adequately. Thus it was that the tragedy had been played for five months to overflowing audiences ; and its prosperity had been cut short only by the death of the fiery wooer—of the Romeo who lay now in the coffin before the chancel, while the Juliet, with the tears gliding down her cheeks, sat there by the side of the middle-aged merchant she was soon to marry. The young actor, to catch a glimpse of whom silly school-girls would watch the stage door, and to whom foolish women sent baskets of flowers, now lay cold in death, with lilies and lilacs in a heap over his silent heart.

When the final notes of the contralto's rich and noble voice had died away, the rector went on with the ritual :

" Man, that is born of a woman, hath but a short time to live, and is full of misery. He cometh up, and is cut down, like a flower ; he fleeth as it were a shadow, and never continueth in one stay."

The dead man had been the last of his line, and there were no near kindred at the funeral. There was no mother there, no sister, no wife. Friends there were, but none of his blood, none who bore his name. Yet there was a shiver of sympathy as the tiny clods of clay rattled down upon the coffin lid, and as the rector said " earth to earth, ashes to ashes, dust to dust."

Then the service drew to an end swiftly, and

the pall-bearers formed in order once again, and the coffin was lifted and carried slowly down the aisle.

As the sorrowful procession drew near to the open door and passed before the pew where the tall fair-haired woman stood, stolid, with averted head, and a stare fixed on the floor, one of the bearers stumbled, but recovered himself at once. The woman had raised her hand, and she had checked a cry of warning; but the coffin was borne before her steadily; and they who bore it little guessed that they were carrying it past the dry-eyed mother of the dead man's unborn child.

(1893.)

THE TWENTY-NINTH OF
FEBRUARY

THE Governor of the State and his secretary had just finished their lunch in one of the private parlors of the hotel. The Governor lighted his cigar and leaned back in his chair as the secretary went to the door and admitted an old man who had been patrolling the corridor impatiently.

"The Governor will see you now, Mr. Baxter," said the secretary.

The old man, tall, thin, and impetuous, strode past the secretary without a word of thanks, and came straight to where the Governor was sitting.

"At last!" he cried—"at last I've got a chance to talk to you face to face. If you only knew how I have longed for this, you would have let me in before."

"Take a seat, Mr. Baxter," said the Governor, kindly.

"Thank you, but I'd rather stand," replied the old man. "In fact, I'd rather walk. I don't seem to be able to sit nor to stand when I get a-talking about the boy. You know why I wanted to see you, I suppose?" he inquired, suddenly, fixing the Governor with a penetrating stare.

11

"You wish to urge your son's pardon, I take it," the Governor answered; "and I am ready to listen to you. I have all the papers here," and he indicated a bundle of documents at his elbow. "I have just been reading them."

"But the men who wrote those papers didn't know my boy as I know him, and they can't tell you about him as I can tell you. He's in jail, and he's been there nearly three years, and he's twenty-four years old to-day—for to-day's his birthday—but he's only a boy for all that. He isn't a man yet, to be judged as a man, and to take a man's punishment. I can't tell you that he didn't shoot the fellow, for he did; but he did it in his anger, and he was sorely tempted; and what's more, he did it in self-defence. Oh, I know that wasn't brought out on the trial, but just you read this," and he tore open his coat and pulled out a package of papers; selecting one of them, he thrust it into the Governor's hands. "That's from the man who sold Bowles a pistol and a knife on the 28th of February, the day before the fight. Then you read this too," and he picked out a second letter, and gave that to the Governor with the same impatient and imperious gesture. "That's from one of Bowles's friends, the fellow who was with him just before the shot was fired. He kept quiet at the trial, and said as little as he could. He knew that I was sick abed, and so he held his peace. But I've been at him ever since I got about again, and now I've pinned him down. And there's the result; the truth must prevail in the end always. There, in that letter, he says that Bowles had that pistol on his person on the morning of the 29th; and that if it wasn't found on the body, it was because Bowles dropped it as he fell. The pistol was picked up that night under a plank in the sidewalk. It was this same friend of Bowles's who found it then, and he said nothing—the cur! Even at the trial he said nothing! But I knew he had something to say, and at last I made him speak. He's telling the truth now, and the whole truth. Read the letter and see if it isn't. He hated my boy; and he said he wanted to see him swing; but I made him write that letter. And if that isn't enough, I'll put him on the stand, and I'll make him swear to every word of it."

The Governor adjusted his glasses, and began to read the letters thus forcibly placed in his hands.

In his eagerness to be heard, the old man could not brook even this delay, and as the Governor laid down the first letter, he broke forth again: "To-day's his birthday, the first he's had since the shooting, the first that he's ever spent away from me. He was born on the 29th of February, and he has a birthday only once in four years; and it was just four years ago to-day that he got into this scrape, and fired the shot that caused us all this trouble. He was twenty years old that morning, for he was born in 1864; that was the

year when General Grant was getting ready to
smash Jeff Davis and the rebels ; that's why we
called him Grant—out of gratitude for the saving of the country. Sometimes I think it's a pity
he hadn't been born twenty years before, so that
he could have died at Cold Harbor like a man,
without ever having seen the inside of a jail.
But it was to be, I suppose. Our lives are laid
out for us, I suppose. Maybe a boy born on the
29th of February is different from other boys ; I
don't know. He was loved more than most boys ;
I know that well enough. I was raised on Cape
Cod, and my father never gave me a caress ;
though I guess he loved me, too, in his way. But
I moved out to Lake Erie when I was married,
and out by the edge of the lake we waited, my
wife and I, for a man-child to be born to us. And
we waited a score of years and more ; and when
Grant came at last, he was our only child. Both
his sisters had died in their cradles. So he was
the son of our old age. Maybe we spoiled him.
Surely we spared the rod. Why, we loved him
too much ever to say a hard word to him. In
the main he was a good boy, too—wild at times,
and skittish — but always loving and easily led.
His mother had only to look, and he'd jump to
serve her. So we let him do as he pleased, and
most generally he pleased us. Perhaps I gave
him too much rope ; I've often thought so, now
I see how near he came to hanging himself. But
he was a good boy, and devoted to his mother

always.   And she loved him—oh! how she loved
him!—more than she loved her husband, I know,
fond as she was of me."

Here the old man paused in his vehement
speech, and turned away abruptly.

"Is Mrs. Baxter with you here in the city?"
the Governor asked, gently.

"Here—in the city?" cried the old man, facing
about sharply. "She's at home—in the cemetery!
That's where she is. She drooped as soon as ever
he was arrested, but she bore up till the trial was
over, hoping that he might get off somehow, not
believing that her boy could be found guilty.
But when he was sent off to Auburn to serve fifteen years for manslaughter, why, then there
wasn't anything left for her to live for any longer, with all the joy of her life locked up in a
stone cell. So she took to her bed, and she died.
She faded away; she had lost her interest in life,
and so she gave up. Now the boy's all I have,
and I want you to give him back to me. That's
what I've come down here for. That's what I've
been pursuing you for these six months. The boy
is all I have. I want to see him back at the old
home on the lake before I die — and I can't live
much longer, I guess. I'm seventy now, and for
all I look hale and hearty, there's something the
matter with my heart, the doctors say, and I may
go out any time, like a candle in a gale of wind.
Well, give me back the boy, and I'm ready to
die. Let me see him at home once more, a free

2

man, and I'll carry the good news to the old
woman whenever the call comes, and gladly."

He paused for a moment, and his impassioned
speech had lost a little of its fierce fire.

The Governor took up the second letter and
began to read it. The movement of the Governor's hand as he raised the paper aroused the
old man again.

"If the District Attorney had done his duty
by the people of the State it wouldn't have been
left for me to wring the truth out of that coward
whose letter you are reading. Sometimes I half
think this cur was at the bottom of the whole
thing. It was he who introduced Grant to the
woman. You know that the wedding was to
have taken place that very night — the night of
the shooting? Yes, it all came out on the trial.
Grant only had one birthday in four years, as
I've been telling you, and so he persuaded the
girl to set it as the wedding-day too. And he
was just twenty—a mere boy. It was no wonder
they took advantage of him. If you've read the
report you can see how she deceived him. Even
the District Attorney admitted that, bitter as he
was against the boy. Ah! if I could only have
been in court at the trial! If I had only been in
town the day when the boy discovered the truth,
he wouldn't have shot that villain, for I'd have
done it myself."

"Then who would have come to me to ask for
your pardon?" inquired the Governor, smiling

kindly. "I have read these letters, but they contain nothing that is new to me, and—"

"Nothing new?" interrupted the old man, violently. "That letter shows that Grant fired in self-defence, since the fellow had a pistol in his hand. Isn't that something new?"

"Not to me, for the District Attorney—against whom you seem to have a prejudice, Mr. Baxter —had already informed me of this."

"If you've been listening to him, I suppose there isn't much hope of my getting what I'm after," the old man returned, hotly ; "for no man ever spoke more unfairly against another than that man did against my boy."

"You do him injustice," the Governor said, firmly. "He did his duty at the trial in pressing for sentence, and he has done his duty now in laying before me this newly discovered evidence. He has even gone further : he has urged me to accede to your request for your son's pardon."

"The District Attorney?" cried the old man in surprise.

"Yes," the Governor replied.

"Then his conscience has pricked him at last."

"And it is chiefly in consequence of his recommendation that I have decided to pardon your son," the Governor continued.

"I don't care on whose urging it is, so long as it's done," the old man rejoined. "When can the boy come out?" he asked, eagerly.

"I will let you bear the pardon to him," said

the Governor, and he unfolded one of the papers
which lay on the table by his side and signed it.
"Here it is."

The old man seized the paper with a convul-
sive clutch. His knees trembled as his eyes read
the pardon swiftly.

The door of the parlor opened, and the secretary returned.

The old man grasped his hat. "Do you know
when the next train leaves for Auburn?" he inquired, hastily.

"There's one at four o'clock, I think," the secretary answered.

"I shall be in time," said the old man; and
then, the pardon in his twitching fingers, he left
the parlor without another word. He passed
quickly through the corridors of the hotel, down
the stairs, and out into the street. When he
reached the pavement he stood still for a moment
and bared his head, quite unconscious of the rain-
storm which had broken but a minute before.

A small boy came running to him across the
street, crying, "Evening papers — four o'clock
Gazette!"

Seemingly the old man did not hear him.

"Terrible loss of life!" the newsboy shrilled
out, as he moved away. "Riot at Auburn! Attempted escape of the prisoners!"

Then a clutch of iron was fastened on the
newsboy's arm, and the old man towered above
him, asking hoarsely: "What's that you say? A

loss of life in the prison at Auburn? Give me the paper!"

He seized it. On the first page was a despatch from Auburn stating that there had been a rising of the convicts at the State-prison, which the wardens had been able to repress after it had gained headway. The prisoners had yielded and gone back to their cells only after the wardens had fired on them, wounding half a dozen and killing the ringleader, who had fought desperately. He was a young man from one of the lake villages, sentenced to fifteen years for manslaughter; his name was Grant Baxter.

As the old man read this, the paper slipped from his fingers, and he fell on the sidewalk dead, still tightly grasping the pardon.

(1889.)

AT A PRIVATE VIEW

WHEN the Spring Exhibition opened, March had thrown off its lion's skin, and stood revealed as a lamb. There was no tang to the wind that swept the swirling dust down the broad street; and the moonlight which silvered the Renascence front of the building had no longer a wintry chill. Flitting clouds were thickening, and threatened rain; but the carriages, rolling up to the canvas tunnel which had been extemporized across the sidewalk, brought many a pretty woman who had risked a spring bonnet. Not a few of the ladies who had been bidden to the Private View were in evening dress; and it was a brilliant throng which pressed down the broad corridor, past the dressing-rooms, and into the first gallery, where the President of the Society, surrounded by other artists of renown, stood ready to receive them.

Beyond the first gallery, and up half a dozen steps, was a smaller saloon, with a square room yet smaller to its right and to its left. Still farther beyond, and up a few more steps, was the main gallery, a splendid and stately hall, lofty and well proportioned, and worthy of the many

fine paintings which lined its walls two and
three deep. In the place of honor, facing the
entrance, was Mr. Frederick Olyphant's startling
picture, "The Question of the Sphinx," which
bore on its simple frame the bit of paper declaring that it had received a silver medal at the
Salon of the summer before. In a corner was
another painting by the same artist, a portrait of
his friend Mr. Laurence Laughton ; and balancing
this, on the other side of a landscape called "A
Sunset at Onteora," was a portrait of Mr. Rupert
de Ruyter, the poet, by a young artist named
Renwick Brashleigh, painted vigorously yet sym-
pathetically, and quite extinguishing the impres-
sionistic "Girl in a Hammock," which hung next
to it. Here and there throughout the spacious
room there were statuettes and busts ; one of the
latter represented Astroyd, the amusing comedian.
Landscapes drenched with sunshine hung by the
side of wintry marines ; and delicate studies of
still life set off purely decorative compositions
painted almost in monochrome.

The people who thronged the floor were wellnigh as various as the paintings which covered
the walls. There were artists in plenty, men of
letters and men about town, women who lived
for art and women who lived for society, visitors
of both sexes who came to see the exhibition, and
visitors of both sexes who came to be seen themselves. There were art-students and art-critics,
picture-buyers and picture-dealers, poets and nov-

elists, stock-brokers and clergymen. Among
them were Mr. Robert White, of the *Gotham
Gazette*, and Mr. Harry Brackett, formerly attached to that journal; Mr. Rupert de Ruyter,
who could not be kept away from his own portrait; Mr. Delancey Jones, the architect, with his
pretty wife; Mr. J. Warren Payn, the composer;
Mr. and Mrs. Martin, of Washington Square; and
Miss Marlenspuyk, an old maid, who seemed to
know everybody and to be liked by everybody.

Miss Marlenspuyk lingered before Olyphant's
portrait of Laurence Laughton, whom she had
known for years. She liked the picture until she
overheard two young art-students discussing it.

"It's a pity Olyphant hasn't any idea of color,
isn't it?" observed one.

"Yes," assented the other; "and the head is
hopelessly out of drawing."

"The man has a paintable face, too," the first
rejoined. "I'd like to do him myself."

"Olyphant's well enough for composition," the
second returned, "but when it comes to portraits,
he simply isn't in it with Brashleigh. Seen his
two yet?"

"Whose?" inquired the first speaker.

"Brashleigh's," was the answer. "Biggest
things here. And as different as they make 'em.
Best is a Wall Street man — Poole, I think, his
name is."

"I know," the first interrupted. "Cyrus Poole;
he's president of a big railroad somewhere out

West. Lots of money. I wonder how Brashleigh got the job?"

"Guess he did Rupert de Ruyter for nothing. You know De Ruyter wrote him up in one of the magazines."

The two young art-students stood before the portrait a few seconds longer, looking at it intently. Then they moved off, the first speaker saying, "That head's out of drawing too."

It gave Miss Marlenspuyk something of a shock to learn that the heads of two of her friends were out of drawing; she wondered how serious the deformity might be; she felt for a moment almost as though she were acquainted with two of the startlingly abnormal specimens of humanity who are to be seen in dime museums. As these suggestions came to her one after the other, she smiled gently.

"I don't wonder that you are laughing at that picture, Miss Marlenspuyk," said a voice at her right. "It's no better than the regulation 'Sunset on the Lake of Chromo,' that you can buy on Liberty Street for five dollars, with a frame worth twice the money."

Miss Marlenspuyk turned, and recognized Mr. Robert White. She held out her hand cordially.

"Is your wife here?" she asked.

"Harry Brackett is explaining the pictures to her," White answered. "He doesn't know anything about art, but he is just as amusing as if he did."

"I like Mr. Brackett," the old maid rejoined. "He's a little—well, a little common, I fear; but then he is so quaint and so individual in his views. And at my time of life I like to be amused."

"I know your fondness for a new sensation," White returned. "I believe you wouldn't object to having the devil take you in to dinner."

"Why should I object?" responded Miss Marlenspuyk, bravely. "The devil is a gentleman, they say; and besides, I should be so glad to get the latest news of lots of my friends."

"Speaking of the gentleman who is not as black as he is painted," said White, "have you seen the portrait of Cyrus Poole yet? It is the best thing here. I didn't know Brashleigh had it in him to do anything so good."

"Where is it?" asked Miss Marlenspuyk. "I've been looking at this Mr. Brashleigh's portrait of Mr. De Ruyter, and—"

"Pretty little thing, isn't it?" White interrupted. "Perhaps a trifle too sentimental and saccharine. But it hits off the poet to the life."

"And life is just what I don't find in so many of these portraits," the lady remarked. "Some of them look as though the artist had first made a wax model of his sitter and then painted that."

They moved slowly through the throng towards the other end of the gallery.

"Charley Vaughn, now, has another trick," said White, indicating a picture before them with a slight gesture. "Since he has been to Paris and

studied under Carolus he translates all his sit-
ters into French, and then puts the translation on
canvas."

The picture White had drawn attention to represented a lady dressed for a ball, and standing
before a mirror adjusting a feather in her hair.
It was a portrait of Mrs. Delancey Jones, the wife
of the architect.

Miss Marlenspuyk raised her glasses, and looked
at it for a moment critically. Then she smiled.
"It is the usual thing, now, I see," she said—"in-
timations of immorality."

White laughed, as they resumed their march
around the hall.

"If you say that of Charley Vaughn's picture,"
he commented, "I wonder what you will say of
Renwick Brashleigh's. Here it is."

And they came to a halt before the painting
which had the place of honor in the centre of the
wall on that side of the gallery.

"That is Cyrus Poole," White continued.
"President of the Niobrara Central, one of the
rising men of the Street, and now away in Europe
on his honeymoon."

The picture bore the number 13, and the cata-
logue declared it to be a "Portrait of a Gentleman." It was a large canvas, and the figure was
life size. It represented a man of barely forty
years of age, seated at his desk in his private
office. On the wall beyond him hung a map of
the Niobrara Central Railroad with its branches.

The light came from the window on the left, against which the desk was placed. The pose was that of a man who had been interrupted in his work, and who had swung around in his chair to talk to a visitor. He was a man to be picked out of a crowd as unlike other men, rather spare, rather below medium height, rather wiry than muscular. Beyond all question he was energetic, untiring, determined, and powerful. The way he sat indicated the consciousness of strength. So did his expression, although there was no trace of conceit to be detected on his features. His hair was dark and thick and straight, with scarce a touch of gray. He had a sharp nose and piercing eyes, while his lips were thin and his jaw massive.

Miss Marlenspuyk looked at the picture with interest. " Yes," she said, " I don't wonder this has made a hit. There is something striking about it — something novel. It's a new note ; that's what it is. And the man is interesting too. He has a masterful chin. Not a man to be henpecked, I take it. And he's a good provider, too, judging by the eyes and the mouth ; I don't believe that his wife will ever have to turn her best black silk. There's something fascinating about the face, but I don't see how—"

She interrupted herself, and gazed at the picture again.

" Is it a good likeness ?" she asked at last, with her eyes still fixed on the portrait.

" It's so like him that I wouldn't speak to it,"
White answered.

"I see what you mean," the old lady responded.
"Yes, if the man really looks like that, nobody
would want to speak to him. I wouldn't have
this artist—what's his name ?—Mr. Brashleigh ?—
I wouldn't have him paint my portrait for the
world. Why, if he did, and my friends once saw
it, there isn't one of them who would ever dare
to ask me to dinner again."

White smiled, and quickly responded, "As I
said before, you know, even the gentleman you
wanted to take you in to dinner is probably not
as black as he is painted."

"But I wouldn't want that man to take me in
to dinner," returned Miss Marlenspuyk, promptly,
indicating the portrait with a wave of her hand.
"Paint is all very well ; besides, it is only on the
outside, and women don't mind it ; but it is that
man's *heart* that is black. It is his inner man
that is so terrible. He fascinates me—yes—but
he frightens me too. Who is he ?"

"I told you," White answered. "He is Mr.
Cyrus Poole, the president of the Niobrara Central Railroad, and one of the coming men in the
Street. He turned up in Denver ten years ago,
and when he had learned all that Denver had to
teach him he went to Chicago. He graduated
from the Board of Trade there, and then came to
New York ; he has been here two years now, and
already he has made himself felt. He has engi-

neered two or three of the biggest things yet seen in the Street. As a result there are now two opinions about him."

"If this portrait is true," said the old maid, "I don't see how there can be more than one opinion about him."

"There were three at first," White rejoined. "At first they thought he was a lamb; now they know better. But they are still in doubt whether he is square or not. They say that the deal by which he captured the stock of the Niobrara Central and made himself president had this little peculiarity, that if it hadn't succeeded, instead of being in Europe on his honeymoon, Cyrus Poole would now be in Sing Sing. Why, if half they said about him at the time *is* true — instead of hanging here on the line, he ought to have been hanged at the end of a rope. But then I don't believe half that I hear."

"I could believe anything of a man who looks like that," Miss Marlenspuyk said. "I don't think I ever saw a face so evil, for all it appears frank and almost friendly."

"But I have told you only one side," White went on. "Poole has partisans who deny all the charges against him. They say that his only crime is his success. They declare that he has got into trouble more than once trying to help friends out. While his enemies call him unscrupulous and vindictive, his friends say that he is loyal and lucky."

3

Miss Marlenspuyk said nothing for a minute or more. She was studying the portrait with an interest which showed no sign of flagging. Suddenly she looked up at White and asked, "Do you suppose he knows how this picture affects us?"

"Poole?" queried White. "No, I imagine not. He is a better judge of values as they are understood in Wall Street than as they are interpreted at the Art Students' League. Besides, I've heard that he was married and went to Europe before the picture was quite finished. Brashleigh had to paint in the background afterwards."

"The poor girl!" said Miss Marlenspuyk. "Who was she?"

"What poor girl?" asked the man. "Oh, you mean the new Mrs. Cyrus Poole?"

"Yes," responded the old lady.

"She was a Miss Cameron," White answered; "Eunice Cameron, I think her name was. I believe that she is a cousin of Brashleigh's. By-the-way, I suppose that's how it happened he was asked to paint this portrait. He is one of the progressive painters a Wall Street man wouldn't be likely to appreciate off-hand. But it couldn't have been given to a better man, could it?"

Miss Marlenspuyk smiled.

"Well," said White, "Brashleigh has a marvellous insight into character; you can see that for yourself. Or at least he paints portraits as if he had; it's hard to tell about these artists, of course, and it's easy to credit them with more than they have. They see so much more than they understand; they have the gift, you know, but they can't explain; and half the time they don't know what it is they have done."

The old lady looked up and laughed a little.

"I think the man who painted that," she said, "knew what he was about."

"Yes," White admitted, "it seems as though no one could do a thing with the astounding vigor of this, unconsciously. But, as like as not, what Brashleigh thought about chiefly was his drawing and his brush-work and his values; probably the revelation of the sitter's soul was an accident. He did it because he couldn't help it."

"I don't agree with you, for once," Miss Marlenspuyk replied. "I find in this portrait such an appreciation of the possibilities of human villany. Oh, the man *must* have seen it before he painted it!"

"It's lucky I'm not a painter by trade," returned White, "or I should feel it my duty to annihilate you on the spot by the retort that laymen always look at painting from the literary side."

Miss Marlenspuyk did not respond for a minute. She was looking at the portrait with curious interest. She glanced aside, and then she gazed at it again.

"Poor girl!" she said at last, with a gentle sigh.

"Meaning Mrs. Poole?" White inquired.

"Yes," the old lady answered. "I'm sorry for her, but I think I understand how she had to give in. I can feel the sinister fascination of that face myself."

Above the babble of many tongues which filled the gallery there was to be heard a rumble of thunder, and then the sharp patter of rain on the huge skylight above them.

"Excuse me, Miss Marlenspuyk," said White, hastily, "but my wife is always a little nervous about thunder now. I must look her up. I'll send you Harry Brackett."

"You needn't mind about me," she answered, as he moved away. "I've taken care of myself for a good many years now, and I think I'm still equal to the task."

The hall was densely crowded by this time, and it was becoming more and more difficult to make one's way in any given direction. The rain fell heavily on the roof, and dominated the rising murmur of the throng, and even the shrill voices now and again heard above it.

Miss Marlenspuyk drifted aimlessly with the crowd, looking at the pictures occasionally, and listening with interest to the comments and the fragmentary criticisms she could not help hearing on all sides of her. She found herself standing before Mr. Charles Vaughn's "Judgment of Paris," when she was accosted by Harry Brackett.

"I've been looking for you everywhere, Miss

Marlenspuyk," he began. "White said you were here or hereabouts, and I haven't seen you for many moons."

They chatted for a few minutes about their last meeting, and the friends at whose house they had dined.

Then Harry Brackett, looking up, saw the huge painting before them.

"So Charley Vaughn's 'Judgment of Paris' is a Salon picture, is it?" he asked. "It looks to me better fitted for a saloon. It's one of those nudes that Renwick Brashleigh says are offensive alike to the artist, the moralist, and the voluptuary."

Miss Marlenspuyk smiled; and her smile was one of her greatest charms.

"Do you know Mr. Brashleigh?" she asked.

"I've known him ever since he came back from Paris," Brackett answered. "And he's a painter, he is. He isn't one of those young dudes who teach society girls how to foreshorten the moon. You don't catch him going round to afternoon teas and talking about the Spontaneity of Art."

"Have you seen his portrait of this Mr. Poole?" she inquired.

"Not yet," he replied, "but they tell me it's a dandy. I've never met Poole, but I used to know his wife. She was Eunice Cameron, and she's a cousin of Brashleigh's. Come to think of it, his first hit was a portrait of her at the Academy three years ago."

"What sort of a girl is she?" Miss Marlenspuyk asked.

"For one thing, she's a good-looker," he responded, "although they say she's gone off a little lately; I haven't seen her this year. But when Brashleigh introduced me to her she was a mighty pretty girl, I can tell you."

The pressure of the crowd had carried them along, and now Miss Marlenspuyk found herself once more in front of the "Portrait of a Gentleman," and once more she was seized by the power and by the evil which the artist had painted on the face of Cyrus Poole.

"They used to say," Harry Brackett went on, not looking at the picture, "that Brashleigh was in love with her. I think somebody or other once told me that they were engaged."

There was a sudden gleam of intelligence in Miss Marlenspuyk's eyes.

"But of course there wasn't any truth in it," he continued.

The smile came back to the old maid's mouth as she gazed steadily at the portrait before her and answered, "Of course not."

(1893.)

SPRING IN A SIDE STREET

ON the city the spring comes earlier than it does in the country, and the horse-chestnuts in the sheltered squares sometimes break into blossom a fortnight before their brethren in the open fields. That year the spring came earlier than usual, both in the country and in the city, for March, going out like a lion, made an April-fool of the following month, and the huge banks of snow heaped high by the sidewalks vanished in three or four days, leaving the gutters only a little thicker with mud than they are accustomed to be. Very trying to the convalescent was the uncertain weather, with its obvious inability to know its own mind, with its dark fog one morning and its brisk wind in the afternoon, with its mid-day as bright as June and its sudden chill descending before nightfall.

Yet when the last week of April came, and the grass in the little square around the corner was green again, and the shrubs were beginning to flower out, the sick man also felt his vigor returning. His strength came back with the spring, and restored health sent fresh blood coursing through his veins as the sap was rising in the

branches of the tree before his window. He had
had a hard struggle, he knew, although he did
not suspect that more than once he had wrestled
with death itself. Now his appetite had awakened again, and he had more force to withstand
the brooding sadness which sought to master
him.

The tree before his window was but a shabby
sycamore, and the window belonged to a hall bedroom in a shabby boarding - house down a side
street. The young man himself lay back in the
steamer chair lent him by one of the few friends
he had in town, and his overcoat was thrown over
his knees. His hands, shrunken yet sinewy, lay
crossed upon a book in his lap. His body was
wasted by sickness, but the frame was well knit
and solid. His face was still white and thin, although the yellow pallor of the sick-bed had gone
already. His scanty boyish beard that curled
about his chin had not been trimmed for two
months, and his uncut brown hair fell thickly on
the collar of his coat. His dark eyes bore the
mark of recent suffering, but they revealed also a
steadfast soul, strong to withstand misfortune.

His room was on the north side of the street, and
the morning sun was reflected into his window, as
he lay back in the chair, grateful for the warmth.
A heavy cart lumbered along slowly over the
worn and irregular pavement ; it came to a stand
at the corner, and a gang of workmen swiftly
emptied it of the steel rails it contained, drop-

ping them on the sidewalk one by one with a
loud clang which reverberated harshly far down
the street.   From the little knot of men who
were relaying the horse-car track came cries of
command, and then a rail would drop into position, and be spiked swiftly to its place.   Then
the laborers would draw aside while an arrested
horse - car urged forward again, with the regular
footfall of its one horse, as audible above the
mighty roar of the metropolis as the jingle of
the little bell on the horse's collar.   At last there
came from over the house-tops a loud whistle of
escaping steam, followed shortly by a dozen sim-
ilar signals, proclaiming the mid-day rest.   A rail
or two more clanged down on the others, and
then the cart rumbled away.   The workmen relaying the track had already seated themselves
on the curb to eat their dinner, while one of them
had gone to the saloon at the corner for a large
can of the new beer advertised in the window by
the gaudy lithograph of a frisky young goat bearing a plump young goddess on his back.

The invalid was glad of the respite from the
more violent noises of track - layers, for his head
was not yet as clear as it might be, and his nerves
were strained by pain.   He leaned forward and
looked down at the street below, catching the eye
of a young man who was bawling "Straw-b'rees!
straw-b'rees!" at the top of an unmelodious voice.
The invalid smiled, for he knew that the street
venders of strawberries were an infallible sign of

spring—an indication of its arrival as indisputa-
ble as the small square labels announcing that
three of the houses opposite to him were "To
Let." The first of May was at hand. He wondered whether the flower-market in Union Square
had already opened ; and he recalled the early
mornings of the preceding spring, when the girl
he loved, the girl who had promised to marry
him, had gone with him to Union Square to pick
out young roses and full-blown geraniums worthy
to bloom in the windows of her parlor looking
out on Central Park.

He thought of her often that morning, and
without bitterness, though their engagement had
been broken in the fall, three months or more before he was taken sick. He had not seen her since
Christmas, and he found himself wondering how
she would look that afternoon, and whether she
was happy. His revery was broken by the jan-
gling notes of an ill-tuned piano in the next house,
separated from his little room only by a thin
party - wall. Some one was trying to pick out
the simple tune of "Wait till the Clouds roll
by." Seemingly it was the practice hour for one
of the children next door, whose playful voices
he had often heard. Seemingly also the task was
unpleasant, for the piano and the tune and the
hearer suffered from the ill-will of the childish
performer.

A sudden hammering of a street rail in the
street below notified him the nooning was over,

and that the workmen had gone back to their labors. Somehow he had failed to hear the stroke of one from the steeple of the church at the corner of the Avenue, a short block away. Now he became conscious of a permeating odor, and he knew that the luncheon hour of the boarding-house had arrived. He had waked early, and his breakfast had been very light. He felt ready for food, and he was glad when the servant brought him up a plate of cold beef and a saucer of prunes. His appetite was excellent, and he ate with relish and enjoyment.

When he had made an end of his unpretending meal, he leaned back again in his chair. A turbulent wind blew the dust of the street high in the air and set swinging the budding branches of the sycamore before the window. As he looked at the tender green of the young leaves dancing before him in the sunlight he felt the spring-time stir his blood; he was strong again with the strength of youth; he was able to cope with all morbid fancies, and to cast away all repining. He wished himself in the country — somewhere where there were brooks and groves and grass— somewhere where there were quiet and rest and surcease of noise—somewhere where there were time and space to think out the past and to plan out the future resolutely—somewhere where there were not two hand-organs at opposite ends of the block vying which should be the more violent, one playing "Annie Laurie" and the other "An-

nie Rooney." He winced as the struggle between
the two organs attained its height, while the child
next door pounded the piano more viciously than
before. Then he smiled.

With returning health, why should he mind
petty annoyances? In a week or so he would be
able to go back to the store and to begin again to
earn his own living. No doubt the work would
be hard at first, but hard work was what he needed now. For the sake of its results in the future,
and for its own sake also, he needed severe labor.
Other young men there were a plenty in the thick
of the struggle, but he knew himself as stout of
heart as any in the whole city, and why might not
fortune favor him too? With money and power
and position he could hold his own in New York;
and perhaps some of those who thought little of
him now would then be glad to know him.

While he lay back in the steamer chair in his
hall room the shadows began to lengthen a little,
and the long day drew nearer to its end. When
next he roused himself the hand-organs had both
gone away, and the child next door had given over
her practising, and the street was quiet again, save
for the high notes of a soprano voice singing a
florid aria by an open window in the Conservatory
of Music in the next block, and save also for an
unusual rattle of vehicles drawing up almost in
front of the door of the boarding-house. With
an effort he raised himself, and saw a line of carriages on the other side of the way, moving slowly

towards the corner. A swirling sand-storm sprang up again in the street below, and a simoom of dust almost hid from him the faces of those who sat in the carriages—young girls dressed in light colors, and young men with buttoned frock-coats. They were chatting easily ; now and again a gay laugh rang out.

He wondered if it were time for the wedding. With difficulty he twisted himself in his chair and took from the bureau behind him an envelope containing the wedding-cards. The ceremony was fixed for three. He looked at his watch, and he saw that it lacked but a few minutes of that hour. His hand trembled a little as he put the watch back in his pocket ; and he gazed steadily into space until the bell in the steeple of the church at the corner of the Avenue struck three times. The hour appointed for the wedding had arrived. There were still carriages driving up swiftly to deposit belated guests.

The convalescent young man in the little hall bedroom of the shabby boarding-house in the side street was not yet strong enough to venture out in the spring sunshine and to be present at the ceremony. But as he lay there in the rickety steamer chair with the old overcoat across his knees, he had no difficulty in evoking the scene in the church. He saw the middle-aged groom standing at the rail awaiting the bride. He heard the solemn and yet joyous strains of the wedding-march. He saw the bride pass slowly up the aisle on the arm of her father, with the lace veil scarcely lighter or fairer than her own filmy hair. He wondered whether she would be pale, and whether her conscience would reproach her as she stood at the altar. He heard the clergyman ask the questions and pronounce the benediction. He saw the new-made wife go down the aisle again on the arm of her husband. He sighed wearily, and lay back in his chair with his eyes closed, as though to keep out the unwelcome vision. He did not move when the carriages again crowded past his door, and went up to the church porch one after another in answer to hoarse calls from conflicting voices.

He lay there for a long while motionless and silent. He was thinking about himself, about his hopes, which had been as bright as the sunshine of spring, about his bitter disappointment. He was pondering on the mysteries of the universe, and asking himself whether he could be of any use to the world—for he still had high ambitions. He was wondering what might be the value of any one man's labor for his fellow-men, and he thought harshly of the order of things. He said to himself that we all slip out of sight when we die, and the waters close over us, for the best of us are soon forgotten, and so are the worst, since it makes little difference whether the coin you throw into the pool is gold or copper—the rarer metal does not make the more ripples. Then, as he saw the long shafts of almost level sunshine sifting through the tiny leaves of the tree before his window, he took heart again as he recalled the great things accomplished by one man. He gave over his mood of self-pity; and he even smiled at the unconscious conceit of his attitude towards himself.

He was recalled from his long revery by the thundering of a heavy fire-engine, which crashed its way down the street, with its rattling hose-reel tearing along after it. In the stillness that followed, broken only by the warning whistles of the engine as it crossed avenue after avenue farther and farther east, he found time to re-member that every man's struggle forward helps along the advance of mankind at large; the hum-ble fireman who does his duty and dies serves the cause of humanity.

The swift twilight of New York was almost upon him when he was next distracted from his thoughts by the crossing shouts of loud-voiced men bawling forth a catchpenny extra of a third-rate evening paper. The cries arose from both sides of the street at once, and they ceased while the fellows sold a paper here and there to the householders whose curiosity called them to the door-step.

The sky was clear, and a single star shone out sharply. The air was fresh, and yet balmy. The clanging of rails had ceased an hour before, and the gang of men who were spiking the iron into place had dispersed each to his own home. The

4

day was drawing to an end.   Again there was an
odor of cooking diffused through the house, herald-
ing the dinner-hour.

But the young man who lay back in the steamer
chair in the hall bedroom of the boarding-house
was unconscious of all except his own thoughts.
Before him was a picture of a train of cars speeding along moonlit valleys, and casting a hurrying
shadow.   In this train, as he saw it, was the bride
of that afternoon, borne away by the side of her
husband.   But it was the bride he saw, and not
the husband.   He saw her pale face and her lu-
minous eyes and her ashen-gold hair; and he
wondered whether in the years to come she would
be as happy as if she had kept her promise to
marry him.

   (1893.)

A DECORATION-DAY REVERY

THERE had been a late spring, set off by frequent rain; and when Decoration Day dawned there was a fresh fairness of foliage, as though Nature were making ready her garlands for our honored dead. When at length the march began, the sunshine sifted through the timid verdure of the trees in the square, and fell softly on the swaying ranks that passed beneath. The golden beams glinted from the slanting bayonets, and seemed to keep time with the valiant old war-tunes as they swelled up from the frequent bands. There was a contagion of military ardor in the air, and even the small boy who had climbed up into the safe eyry of a dismantled lamp-post had within him inarticulate stirrings of warlike ambition. In the pauses of the music fifes shrilled out, and the roll and rattle of drums covered the rhythmic tramping of the soldiers. I lingered for a while near the noble statue of the great admiral, who stood there firm on his feet, with the sea-breeze blowing back the skirt of his coat, and so presented by the art of the sculptor that the motionless bronze seemed more alive than most of the ordinary men and women

who clustered about its base. Here, I thought,
was the fit memorial of the man who had done
his duty in the long struggle, to the heroes of
which the day was sacred; and I was glad that
the marching thousands should pass in review
before that mute image of the best and bravest
our country can bring forth. At that moment
a detachment of sailors swung into view, and
cheers of hearty greeting broke forth on all
sides.

As I loitered, musing, a battalion of our little
army strode by us in turn, with soldierly bearing,
clad in no gaudy garb, but ready for their bloody
work; ready with cold steel to give a cold welcome to the invading foreigner, ready with a
prompt volley to put an end to lawless strife at
home. After an interval came the first ranks
of the citizen soldiery, trim in their workmanlike
uniforms, with stretchers, with ambulances, with
Gatling-guns. One after another advanced the
regiments of the city militia, and no man need
doubt that they would be as swift now to go forward to battle as were their former fellow-mem-
bers whose deeds gave them the right to bear
flags emblazoned with more than one battle as
hard fought as Marathon or Philippi, Fontenoy
or Waterloo. As they swept on down the Avenue
in the morning sunlight, with the strident music
veiled now and again by ringing cheers, my
thoughts went back to the many other thousands
I had seen go down that Avenue, now more than

a quarter of a century ago, coming from the pine forests and the granite hills of New England, and going to the silent swamps and the dark bayous of the South. In those drear days of doubt I had watched the ceaseless tramp of the troops down that Avenue, a thousand at a time—young, earnest, ardent; and I remembered that I had seen them return but a scant hundred or two, it may be, worn and ragged, foot-sore and heart-sick, but resolute yet and full of grit. Death, like the maddened peasants in the strife of the Jacquerie, fights with a scythe; and for four long years Time held a slow glass and Death mowed a broad swath. There is many a house now where an old woman cannot hear the trivial notes of "Tramp, tramp, tramp, the boys are marching," without a sharp pain in the throat and a sudden vision of the prison-pen at Andersonville. No doubt there is many another woman south of that Mason and Dixon's line which was washed out in the blood of the war where the sentimental strains of "My Maryland" have an equal poignancy and an equal tenderness. Shiloh and Malvern Hill and Gettysburg are names made sacred forever by the deeds done there, and by the dead who lie there side by side in a common grave, where the gray cloth and the blue have faded into dust alike, and there is now naught to tell them apart. It is well that a spring day, fresh after rain and fair with blossoms, should help to keep their memory sweet.

Down the Avenue regiment after regiment went
on briskly, with the easy pace of health and enjoyment. After the young men of the militia
came the veterans, with flowers for their fallen
comrades. Some of the older men were in carriages, with here and there a crutch across the
seat; but for the most part they walked, keeping
time, no doubt, though with a shorter stride. As
a handful of brave men filed before us, bearing
aloft the tattered remnant of a battle-flag, I raised
my hat with instinctive reverence. For a moment
the gesture shielded my eyes from the rays of the
sun, and I caught sight of a group in the window
of a house opposite. A lady, tall and stately,
wearing a widow's cap above her gray hair as
though it were a crown, stood in the centre with
her hands on the shoulders of two young men—
her sons, beyond all question—stalwart young
fellows, with features at once fine and strong,
bearing themselves with manly grace. I looked,
and I recognized. When I lowered my eyes again
to the procession I saw another set of faces that I
knew by sight. In a carriage sat a man of some
fifty years, stout, vulgar, with a cigar alight in
the coarse hand which rested on the door of the
vehicle. He had a shock of hair, once reddish
and now grizzling to an unclean white. He wore
in his button-hole the button of the Grand Army
of the Republic. In the open barouche with him
were three youngish men, noisy in laughter—apparently professional politicians of the baser sort.

"DISTRACTED BY THE CROSSING SHOUTS OF LOUD-VOICED MEN"

The man bowed effusively, with a broad and
unctuous smile, when he saw a friend on the sidewalk; and the crowd about me recognized him,
and called him by name one to another; and a
little knot of young fellows on the corner raised
a cheer.

I knew both groups, the unclean creature in the
carriage and the noble lady in the window above
him. I knew that both were survivals of the war.

As the procession passed on, I could hear an
occasional cheer run along the line of spectators
when one or another recognized the politician. I
was not surprised, for the man's popularity with
a portion of the people is patent to all of us. He
was a soldier who had never fired a shot, a colonel who had never seen the enemy. His tactical
skill had been shown in the securing of a detail
for himself where there was chance of profit with
no risk of danger. His strategy had been to secure the good word of those who dispensed the
good things of life.

While others were battling for the country he
was looking out for himself. When the war was
over he presented his claims for recognition, and
he was sent as consul to the Orient. In due time
there came across the ocean rumors of scandals,
and an investigation was ordered; whereupon he
resigned, and the matter was never probed. Then
he went into politics : he was ready of speech and
loud-mouthed ; he flattered the mob, believing
that in politics the blarney-stone is the stepping-

stone to success. He never paused to weigh his
words when he assailed an opponent, believing
that in politics billingsgate is the gate of success.
He was prompt to set people by the ears that he
might lead them by the nose the more readily.
As though to make up for his delinquencies during the struggle, he was now untiring in his abuse
of the Southern people, and his denunciation of
them was always violent and virulent. In every
election he besought his fellow-citizens to vote as
they had shot. He was unfailingly bitter in his
abuse of those who had fought for the cause of
the South. He was, in short, a specimen of the
scum which may float on the surface whenever
there is an upheaval of the deep.

Brutal in political debate and brazen in political chicanery, he was a fit leader for the band of
hirelings he had organized with no small skill.
His position was not unlike that of the *condottieri*
of the foreign mercenaries in the mediæval quar-
rels of the Italian republics. Like them, he led a
compact body, prompt to obey orders so long as
it received the pay and had hopes of the plunder
for which it was organized. Although he belonged nominally to one of the two great parties
which contended for the control of the nation, he
was always ready to turn his forces against it if
his pay and his proportion of the spoils of office
failed to satisfy himself and his men-at-arms ; or
even in revenge for a slight, and in hope of higher
remuneration from the other side.

For me, as I stood on the corner under Farragut's statue and watched the veterans file past, the knowledge of this man's career, and the sight of his presence among those who had fought a good fight for a high motive, seemed to tarnish the sacred occasion and to stain the glory of the morning. Again I looked up at the window where I had seen the lady with her two sons. She was still there, leaning forward a little, as though in involuntary excitement, and one hand clinched the arm of the soldierly young fellow at her right. The sight of those three refreshed me, for I knew who they were, and what they stood for in the history of our country—a shining example in the past and a beacon of hope for the future. The widow's cap which crowns the brow of that mother brought up before me the memory of a deed as noble as it was simple.

A fife-and-drum corps of boys dressed as sailors preceded a model of a monitor mounted on wheels and artfully adorned with flowers and wreaths. Behind this came the scanty score of old sailors who had formed themselves into Post Rodman R. Hardy. When they came abreast of the window where the lady stood with her two sons, they looked up and cheered. The eyes of Captain Hardy's widow had filled with tears when she caught sight of his old comrades; and when they cheered her and her boys her face flushed and the arm which rested on her son's trembled. She bowed, the two young men raised their hats, and the Post passed on down the Avenue to perform their sad office; though they might not deck with flowers the grave of their old commander, for he lies buried at the bottom of the sea, and great guns were firing many a salute with shot and shell when his body was lowered into its everlasting resting-place.

I have heard it said that a soldier's trade is learning how to kill and how to die, and that how he lives is little matter. Captain Hardy lived like a man, like a gentleman, like a Christian; and he died like a hero. He came of a generation of sailors. His great-grandfather had sailed with the fleet under Amherst when Louisburg was taken in 1758. His grandfather had been a midshipman with Paul Jones in the *Bonhomme Richard*. His father served on "Old Ironsides" when the *Constitution* captured the *Guerrière*. He himself had gone to sea in time to take part in the siege of Vera Cruz. When the war broke out he had been married but three years. He was on the *Cumberland* when the *Merrimac* sank her. While the new monitors were building he had a few brief weeks with his wife and his two baby boys. When the *Onteora* was finished he was a captain, and he was appointed to take command.

And there was no monitor which did better service or had more hard work than the *Onteora*. Just before the grand attack on Fort Davis he ran under the guns of a Confederate battery to shell a cruiser which had retreated up the river behind the strip of land on which the earthworks stood. Regardless of the fire from the battery, which bade fair to hammer his ship till it might become unmanageable, he trained his guns on the cruiser. He had no more than got the range when a fog settled down and hid the combatants from each other. The battery ceased firing or aimed wildly a few chance shots. The monitor, relying on the accuracy of its gunners, continued to send shell after shell through the thick wall of fog to the invisible place where the enemy's ship lay. When the fog lifted, the cruiser was on fire ; and then the monitor fell back out of the range of the guns of the battery, having done the work Captain Hardy had set it to do.

The next day came the grand assault on Fort Davis. The admiral ordered the *Onteora* to follow the flag-ship in the attack. The channel was defended not only by the cannon of the fort itself and of its supporting earthworks and by a flotilla of gunboats, but also by hidden torpedoes, the position of which was wholly unknown even to the pilots, Union men of the port who had volunteered to guide our vessels through the tortuous windings of the entrance. The iron ship was made ready for battle ; its deck was sunk level with the surface of the sea ; and nothing projected but the revolving turret, with its two huge guns. In the little box of a pilot-house Captain Hardy took his place with the pilot. The admiral gave the signal to advance, and the *Onteora* followed in the wake of the flag-ship.

The first turning of the channel was made safely, and the monitor was at last full under the fire of the fort. The turret revolved slowly, and both guns were discharged against a pert gunboat which had ventured out beyond the protection of the fort. The second shot struck the steam-chest of the gunboat, and it blew up and drifted at the mercy of the current. Still the admiral advanced, and the *Onteora* followed. Then a sudden shock was felt, there was a dull roar, the monitor shivered from stem to stern, and began to settle. A torpedo had blown a hole in the bottom of the boat, and the *Onteora* was sinking. Almost at the same time a shot from Fort Davis struck the turret, and a fragment smote Captain Hardy and tore off his right arm. In the scant seconds after the explosion of the torpedo, before the shuddering ship lurched down, half a score of men escaped from the turret and flung themselves into the river. The captain had barely time to climb into the open air when his ship went down beneath him. When he arose from the vortex of whirling waters his unwounded hand grasped a chance fragment of wood, which served to sustain him despite the weakness from his open wound. He found himself by the side of the pilot, who was struggling vainly with the waves, his strength almost spent.

"Can't you swim?" asked Captain Hardy.

"Only a little," answered the pilot; "and I am almost gone now, I fear."

"Take this bit of wood," said the sailor.

The pilot reached out his arm and with despairing fingers gripped the broken plank. It was too small to support two men, and Captain Hardy released his hold. He sought to sustain himself with one hand, and for a little he succeeded. Then his strength failed him, and at last he went under almost where the *Onteora* had sunk beneath him. The battle raged above; shell from ship after ship answered shell from the fort and the batteries; another ironclad took up the work of the *Onteora;* brave hearts and quick heads were at work on sea and on shore; but Rodman Hardy was dead at the bottom of the river, leaving to his widow and his sons the heritage of a manly death.

The widow's cap which the young wife took that night she has never discarded to this day. His sons she has brought up to follow in their father's footsteps. One has already begun to make his mark in the navy, having been graduated from Annapolis, high up in his class. The other is a lawyer, who is solving for himself the problem of the scholar in politics. Although not yet thirty, he has spent two terms in the Legislature of the State, where he has done yeoman service for the city.

The parade was over at last—for the Rodman R. Hardy Post had been one of the latest in

line — and I turned away across the square.
The sight of the widow with her two sons had
cleansed the atmosphere from the miasma that
trailed behind the politician as he rode by me in
his vulgar barouche. The memory of a great
deed is an oasis in the vista of life, and the recollection of Captain Hardy's death made the day
seem fairer. The sunshine flooded the streets
with molten gold. A pair of young sparrows
flitted across the park before me and alighted on
a bough above my head. From over the house-
tops came floating echoes of "John Brown's
Body" and "Marching through Georgia."

(1890.)

IN SEARCH OF LOCAL COLOR

THE novelist stood at the corner of Rivington Street and the Bowery, trying to find fit words to formulate his impression of the most characteristic of New York streets as it appeared on a humid morning in June. The elevated trains clattered past over his head and he gave no heed to them, so intent was he in making a mental record of the types which passed before him. Suddenly he was almost thrown off his feet. A young man, slipping on the peel of a banana cast away carelessly upon the sidewalk, had stumbled heavily against him.

"I beg your pardon," cried the young man as he recovered himself. "I—why, Mr. De Ruyter!" he exclaimed, recognizing the author.

"John Suydam!" returned Rupert de Ruyter, holding out his hand cordially. "Well, this is good-fortune! Do you know, I was on my way to the University Settlement to look you up."

"You would have found me there in ten minutes," Suydam answered. "This is my week to be in residence; in fact, I think I shall be here for the summer now. You see, I passed my A.M. examination at Columbia last week—"

"So they examine you for it now, eh?" the novelist queried. "In my time we got it almost for the asking—at least, I did—and that was only twenty years ago. What are you going to do with it, now you've got it? I heard you were to study for the ministry."

"I had thought of the Church," answered Suydam. He was a tall, spare young fellow, with straight brown hair and a resolute chin. "But I don't know now what I shall do. I have a little money, you know—enough to live on, if I choose. So I may stay here at the Settlement; the work is very interesting."

"No doubt," the novelist responded, readily; "you must see many curious cases. I wish I could cut loose for a while, and spend a month with you here."

"Why don't you?" suggested Suydam, eagerly.

"Oh, I have too much on hand," De Ruyter replied. "I've got to read the Phi Beta Kappa poem at Harvard next week; and besides, I've promised to finish a series of New York stories for the *Metropolis*. That is why I was on my way to find you this morning. I want you to help me."

"But I never wrote a story in my life," said the young man, promptly.

"I don't want you to write the stories," De Ruyter retorted. "Of course I can do that for myself. But I thought that you could help me to a little local color."

"Local color?" echoed Suydam, doubtfully.

"Yes," the novelist went on, "local color— that's what I want—fresh impressions."

"I don't quite see—" the young man began, hesitatingly.

"Oh, I can explain what I want," Rupert de Ruyter interrupted. "You see, I'm a New-Yorker born, as you are, and I've lived here all my life, and I know the city pretty well—that is, I know certain aspects of it thoroughly. I can do the Patriarchs, or a Claremont tea, or any other function of the smart set; I know the way men talk in clubs; I've studied the painters and the literary men and the journalists; I can describe a first night at the theatre or a panic in the Street; but I've pretty nearly exhausted the people I know, and I thought I would come down here and get introduced to a set I didn't know."

"I shall be glad to take you to the Settlement," Suydam responded, "and—"

"It isn't the Settlement I want, thank you," De Ruyter interrupted. "The people in the Settlement are variants of types I know already. The people I want to meet are people I don't know anything about—the very poor people, the tenement-house people, the people who work for the sweaters. Do you know any of those?"

"Yes," Suydam answered, "I know many of them. But they are not half so picturesque and so pathetic as the sensational newspapers make them out.   Wouldn't you rather go and see the Chinese quarter?"

"That isn't what I want," the novelist made answer.   "The Chinese quarter is barbarous ; it is exotic ; it is extraneous ; it is a mere accidental excrescence on New York.   But the tenement-house people have come to stay ; they are an integral and a vital part of the city.   I don't care about Chinatown, and I do care about Mulberry Bend.   Now, Suydam, you know Mulberry Bend, don't you?"

"Yes," Suydam returned.   "I know Mulberry Bend."

"Do you know any tenement - house in the Bend, or near it, which is characteristic—which is typical of the worst that the Bend has to show?" De Ruyter asked.

"Yes," Suydam responded again.   "I think I could find a tenement of that kind."

"Then take me there now, if you can spare me an hour or two," said the novelist.

"I can put off my errand till this afternoon," the young man answered.   "I think I can show you what you want.   Come with me."

They had been standing where they had met, at the corner of the Bowery and Rivington Street. Now, under John Suydam's guidance, they walked a little way up the Bowery, beneath the single track of the elevated railroad.   Then they turned into a side street, and pushed their way westward.

Whenever they came to a crossing De Ruyter remarked that three of the corners always, and four of them sometimes, were saloons. The broad gilt signs over the open doors of these bar-rooms bore names either German or Irish, until they came to a corner where one of the saloons called itself the Caffè Cristoforo Colombo. A wooden stand, down the side street, and taking up a third of the width of the walk, had a sign announcing ice-cold soda-water at two cents a glass with fruit syrups ; with chocolate and cream, the price was three cents. Right on the corner of the curb stood a large wash-tub half filled with water, in which soaked doubtful young cabbages and sprouts ; its guardian was a thin slip of a girl with a red handkerchief knotted over her head.

At this corner Suydam turned out of the side street, and went down a street no wider perhaps, but extending north and south in a devious and hesitating way not common in the streets of New York. The sidewalks of this sinuous street were inconveniently narrow for its crowded population, and they were made still narrower by tolerated encroachments of one kind or another. Here, for instance, from the side of a small shop projected a stand on which unshelled pease wilted under the strong rays of the young June sun. There, for example, were steps down to the low basement, and in a corner of the hollow at the foot of these stairs there might be a pail with dingy ice packed about a can of alleged ice-cream, or else a board bore half a dozen tough brown loaves, also proffered for sale to the chance customer. Here and there, again, the dwellers in the tall tenements had brought chairs to the common door, and were seated, comfortably conversing with their neighbors, regardless of the fact that they thus blocked the sidewalk, and compelled the passer-by to go out into the street itself.

And the street was as densely packed as the sidewalk. In front of Suydam and De Ruyter as they picked their way along was a swarthy young fellow with his flannel shirt open at the throat and rolled up on his tawny arms; he was pushing before him a hand-cart heaped with gayly colored calicoes. Other hand-carts there were, from which other men, young and old, were vending other wares—fruit more often than not; fruit of a most untempting frowziness. Now and then a huge wagon came lumbering through the street, heaped high with lofty cases of furniture from a rumbling and clattering factory near the corner. And before the heavy horses of this wagon the children scattered, waiting till the last moment of possible escape. There were countless children, and they were forever swarming out of the houses and up from the cellars and over the sidewalks and up and down the street. They were of all ages, from the babe in the arms of its dumpy, thick-set mother to the sweet-faced and dark-eyed girl of ten or twelve really, though she might seem a precocious fourteen. They ran wild in the street; they played about the knees of their mothers, who sat gossiping in the doorways; they hung over the railing of the fire-escapes, which gridironed the front of every tall house.

Everywhere had the Italians treated the balcony of the fire-escape as an out-door room added to their scant accommodation. They adorned it with flowers growing in broken wooden boxes; they used its railings to dry their parti-colored flannel shirts; they sat out on it as though it were the loggia of a villa in their native land.

Everywhere, also, were noises and smells. The roar of the metropolis was here sharpened by the rattle of near machinery heard through open windows, and by the incessant clatter and shrill cries of the multitude in the street. The rancid odor of ill-kept kitchens mingled with the mitigated effluvium of decaying fruits and vegetables.

But over and beyond the noises and the smells and the bustling business of the throng, Rupert de Ruyter felt as though he were receiving an impression of life itself. It was as if he had caught a glimpse of the mighty movement of existence, incessant and inevitable. What he saw did not strike him as pitiful; it did not weigh him down with despondency. The spectacle before him was not beautiful; it was not even picturesque; but never for a moment, even, did it strike him as pathetic. Interesting it was, of a certainty—unfailingly interesting.

"I haven't found anything so Italian as this for years," he said to his guide, as they picked their way through a tangle of babies sprawling out of a doorway. "I remember seeing nothing more Italian in my first walk in Italy—up the hill-side at Menaggio, after we landed from the boat to Como. Some of the faces here are of a purer Greek type than any you meet in northern Italy. Did you see that young mother we passed just now?"

"The one nursing the infant?" Suydam returned.

"Yes," De Ruyter went on. "She had the oval face and the olive complexion the Greeks left behind them in Sicily. She was not pretty, if you like, but she had the calm beauty of a race of sculptors. Her profile might have come off a Syracusan coin. And to see such a face here, in the city that was New Amsterdam and is New York!"

"We haven't time down here to think of Syracuse and New Amsterdam," said Suydam; "we are too busy thinking about New York. And if we ever do think of Sicily it is only to remember that the Sicilians we have here are the hottest tempered of all the Italians, the most revengeful and vindictive."

"If I didn't know," the novelist remarked, "that the Italians had developed their mercantile faculty at the expense of all their artistic impulses, I should wonder how it was that scions of the race of Michael Angelo and Leonardo da Vinci and Raffael of Urbino could now be willing to live in a house as hideous as that!" and with a sweep of his hand he indicated a lofty double tenement, made uglier by much misplaced ornament. "It isn't even picturesque by decay. In fact, this whole region is in better repair than I had expected."

"Look at the house behind you," answered his companion.

The house behind them was one of the oldest tenements in the street. The balconies of its fire-escape were as cluttered as those of the neighboring dwellings; and every window gave signs that the room behind was inhabited. Yet the building, as a whole, seemed neglected.

"This house does seem out at elbows and dishevelled," De Ruyter admitted. "It looks like a tramp, doesn't it?"

"It does not look very clean," said Suydam. "And the back building is dirtier yet. That's where we are going, if you like."

"Well," De Ruyter answered, "if there is local color to be found anywhere round here, I guess we shall find a fair share of it in this place."

"This way, then," Suydam said, plunging into a covered alleyway, which extended under the house, and led into a small yard paved with uneven flag-stones, and shut in on all four sides by the surrounding buildings. Even on that sunny pure morning there was a dank chill in the air, and there were patches of moisture here and there on the pavement.

"The new building laws don't allow back buildings of this sort," Suydam explained. "But there are thousands of them in the city, put up before the new laws went into effect. Perhaps we had better try the basement first."

In one corner of the yard half a dozen steps led down into the basement of the back building. Followed by the novelist, the young man from the University Settlement went down these steps and into the cellarlike room, which occupied about half the space under the back building.

The air in this room was so foul that De Ruyter held his breath for a moment. The room was not more than twelve feet square ; its walls were unplastered, showing the coarse foundation-stones ; its floor was of earth, trodden to hardness, except where the drippings from the beer-cans had moistened it ; the beams of the floor above seemed rotten. In the damp heat of this room ten or a dozen men and boys were seated on old chairs and on broken boxes, smoking, playing cards by the light of a single foul and flaring kerosene-lamp, and drinking the dregs of beer-kegs collected in old cans.

The inhabitants of the cellar looked up as Suydam and De Ruyter entered, and then they resumed their previous occupations, with no further attention to the intruders.

The man nearest to the door was a powerfully

built fellow of fifty, with gray hair cropped close to his head. He was playing cards. He had a knife thrust in his leathern belt.

"Good-morning, Giacomo," said Suydam to this grizzled brute. "I haven't heard of you for a long while now. When did you get off the Island?"

"Las' week," was the gruff answer.

"And where is your wife now?" the young man asked.

"She work," answered Giacomo.

Suydam did not pursue the conversation further. Judging that the novelist had seen enough, he turned and went up the rickety steps again, followed by his friend.

"Ouf!" said De Ruyter, drawing a long breath, as they stood again in the cramped yard. "I don't see how they can breathe that air and live."

"They don't live," answered Suydam — "at least, the weaker are soon pushed to the wall and die, leaving only the tougher specimens you saw. Now we will go up-stairs, if you like."

"I'm ready," De Ruyter responded. "This is exactly what I came to see."

In the centre of the back building there was an entry. The door was off its hinges. Just inside the passage were the stairs, with the railing broken, and many of the steps dangerously decayed. There was little light as they went up, and a rank odor of decaying fish accompanied them.

At the head of the stairs there was a door on either hand. Suydam knocked at them in turn, and then tried to open them; but they were locked, and there was no response to the repeated hammerings.

"I say," remarked the novelist, as they went up to the floor above, "do these people like to have us intrude on them in this way?"

"Some don't," Suydam answered, promptly, "and of course I try never to intrude. But most of them don't mind. Most of them have no sense of home. Most of them don't know what privacy means. How could they?"

"True," echoed the novelist. "How could they?"

"Here is an exemplification of what I mean," said the young man from the Settlement as they came to the next landing.

The door leading into the room on the right was open. The room was perhaps ten feet square; it contained two beds. On one of the beds a man sat cross-legged sewing; he glanced up for a moment only as the two visitors darkened the doorway, and then he went on with his work. On the other bed were two little children, half naked and asleep; one was a boy of three, the other a girl of nearly two. On the edge of this bed sat a tall boy of seventeen, also sewing. In the narrow alley between the two beds were two sewing-machines, one tended by a girl of fifteen or sixteen perhaps, a thin, stunted child, with bent shoulders. The other machine was operated by the mother of these children, a large-framed woman of forty, with the noble head so often seen among the Trasteverines.

She knew Suydam, and she smiled.

"Good-mornin'," she said.

"Good-morning," responded Suydam. "I am showing a friend over the building. You seem a little crowded here."

"Not crowd' now," she answered. "Only one boarder now," and she indicated the man seated cross-legged on the bed. "Last week two."

"Where is your husband?" asked the young man.

"Oh, he got another girl," she replied, with a vague gesture, apparently of disapproval.

Suydam and De Ruyter went a floor higher, glancing into the rooms which were open. Suydam knew most of the inhabitants, and they seemed glad to see him. Evidently they looked on him as a friend.

On the top floor, under the steps which led to the roof, was a den scarce six feet by eight. Small as it was, this room had better furniture than most of those De Ruyter had seen; it contained evidences of a desire to make a home. There were violent chromos pinned to the wall. The bed had a parti-colored coverlet. The sole inhabitant was a tall, dark Italian with fiery eyes. He was cooking macaroni with ropy cheese over an oil-lamp. His door was ajar only.

"Good-morning, Pietro," said Suydam, cheerfully.

Pietro obeyed his first impulse, and shut the door swiftly. Then he changed his mind, for he opened the door and peered out suspiciously. Recognizing Suydam, he was about to throw it wide, when he caught sight of De Ruyter. There was a moment of hesitancy, and then he took his hand from the knob of the door and went on with his cooking.

"I am showing my friend over the building," explained Suydam.

The Italian said nothing. Apparently his cooking absorbed all his attention. But he gave De Ruyter a searching glance.

Suydam turned to the novelist. "This is Pietro Barretti," he said; "he is one of the most expert layers of mosaic in America. He is from Naples; that's the reason he cooks macaroni so well, I suppose."

"Certainly I haven't seen macaroni cooked that way since I was in Naples last," the novelist remarked, for the sake of talk, not knowing just what to make of the Italian's manner.

"Your wife not here?" asked Suydam.

"No," the Italian answered, abruptly.

"Where is she?" persisted the young man.

"She mort," responded Barretti.

"Dead?" Suydam cried. "That is very sad. When did she die?"

" Ten days," the Italian replied.

When Suydam and De Ruyter had made an end of their visit, and were going down the stairs cautiously, the young man from the University Settlement asked the novelist if he had seen anything interesting.

" Oh yes," was the answer.   " I've got lots of color ; just what I wanted.   And that Italian whose wife was mort—he's copy, I'm sure."

" Copy ?" queried Suydam.

"I mean I can use him in one of my sketches for the *Metropolis*," the novelist explained.   "I wish I knew what his wife was like."

" She was a pretty girl—dark-haired, dark-eyed, with a lively smile," Suydam said.   " He was very jealous of her.   I've been told they used to quarrel bitterly."

" I shouldn't like to have that fellow for an enemy," De Ruyter declared, as they passed through the alleyway and came out in the open air.   " He has an eye like a glass stiletto."

The novelist and the young man from the University Settlement walked up the street together. As they drew near to a police-station, jealously guarded by its green lamps, three officers came out and turned down the street.

When the policemen were abreast of the two friends, one of them stepped aside and accosted the young man from the Settlement.

"Mr. Suydam," he said, " you gentlemen from the Settlement sometimes know what's going on

better than we do.   Have you seen Pietro Barretti
lately—the one they call Italian Pete?"

"I saw him not ten minutes ago—in his own
room," Suydam answered.

"He's all right, boys," cried the policeman.
"He's there."

"Do you want him?" asked Suydam.

"Don't we?" the policeman replied, promptly.
"We've got to bring him in."

"What has he done?" De Ruyter inquired.

"Oh, he's done enough!" responded the officer.
"He murdered his wife last week, that's what
he's done."

Suydam looked at De Ruyter.

"Yes," said De Ruyter, "that completes the
picture.   I can get a good *mot de la fin* now."

(1893.)

BEFORE THE BREAK OF DAY

HE lived in a little wooden house on the corner of the street huddled in the shadow of two towering tenements. There are a few frail buildings of this sort still left in that part of the city, half a mile east of the Bowery and half a mile south of Tompkins Square, where the architecture is as irregular, as crowded, and as little cared for as the population. Amid the old private houses erected for a single family, and now violently altered to accommodate eight or ten—amid the tall new tenements, stark and ugly — here and there one can still find wooden houses built before the city expanded, half a century old now, worn and shabby and needlessly ashamed in the presence of every new edifice no better than they. With the peak of their shingled roofs they are pathetic survivals of a time when New York still remembered that it had been New Amsterdam, and when it did not build its dwellings in imitation of the polyglot loftiness of the Tower of Babel. It was in one of these little houses with white clapboarded walls, ashen gray in the paling moonlight, that Maggie O'Donnell lay fast asleep, when the bell in a far-off steeple tolled three in the morning of the day that was to be the Fourth of July.

73

She was asleep in the larger of the two little
rooms over the saloon. In that part of the city
there are saloons on every corner almost, and
sometimes two and three in a block. The signs
over the doors of most of these saloons and over
the doors of the groceries and of the bakeries and
of the other shops bear strangely foreign names.
The German quarter of the city is not far off, nor
is the Italian, nor the Chinese; but hereabouts the
houses are packed with Poles chiefly, and chiefly
Jews—industrious, docile, and saving. Not until
midnight had the whir of the sewing-machines
ceased in the tenements which occupied the three
other corners. The sign over the door of the saloon above which Maggie lay fast asleep bore an
Irish name, the name of her husband, Terence
O'Donnell. But the modest boards which displayed his name were overawed by the huge
signs that flanked them, filling a goodly share
of the wall on either street and proclaiming the
" McGown's Pass Brewery, Kelly & Company."

These brewer's signs were so large that they
made the little house seem even smaller than it
was — and it was not more than twenty feet
square. The doors of the saloon were right at the
corner, of course, to catch trade. On one street
there were two windows, and on the other one
window and a door over which was the sign "Family Entrance." This door opened into a little passage, from which access could be had to the saloon, and from which also arose the narrow stairs

leading to the home of Terence O'Donnell and
Maggie, his wife, on the floor above. The saloon
filled the whole ground - floor except the space
taken up by this entry and the stairs. A single
jet of gas had burned dimly over the bar ever
since Terry had locked up a little after midnight.
The bar curved across the saloon, and behind it
the sideboard with its bevelled·- edge mirrors
lined the two inner walls. The sideboard glit-
tered with glasses built up in tiers, and a lemon
lay yellow at the top of every pyramid. The
beer-pumps were in the centre under the bar; at
one end was the small iron safe where Terence
kept his money; and at the other end, against the
wall, just behind the door which opened into the
Family Entrance, was a telephone.

Up-stairs there were two little rooms and a
closet or two. The smaller of the rooms Maggie
had turned into a kitchen and dining-room. The
larger — the one on the corner — was their bedroom, and here Maggie lay asleep. The night
was close and warm, and though the windows were
open, the little white curtains hung limp and motionless. The day before had been hot and cloudless, so the brick buildings on the three other corners had stored up heat for fifteen hours, and had
been giving it out ever since the sun had set. Stifling as it was, Maggie O'Donnell slept heavily.
It was after midnight when Terry had kissed her
at the door, and she had been asleep for three
hours. Already there were faint hints of the com-

ing day, for here in New York the sun rises early
on the Fourth of July—at half-past four. A breeze
began to blow lazily up from the East River and
fluttered the curtains feebly. Maggie tossed uneasily, reached out her hand, and said "Terry."

Suddenly she was wide awake. For a moment
she looked stupidly at the empty place beside her,
and then she remembered that Terry would be
gone all night, working hard on the boat and the
barges making ready for the picnic. She turned
again, but sleep had left her. She lay quietly in
bed listening; she could catch nothing but the
heavy rumble of a brewery wagon in the next
street and the hesitating toot of a Sound steamer.
Then she heard afar off three or four shots of a
revolver, and she knew that some young fellow
was up early, and had already begun to celebrate
the Fourth on the roof of the tenement where he
lived.

She tried to go to sleep, but the effort was
hopeless. She was awakened fully, and she knew
that there was small chance of her dropping off
into slumber again. More than once she had
wakened like this in the middle of the night, an
hour or so before daybreak, and then she had to
lie there in bed quietly listening to Terry's regular breathing. She lay there now alone, thinking of Terry, grateful for his goodness to her,
and happy in his love. She lay there alone, wondering where she would be now if Terry had not
taken pity on her.

Then all at once she raised herself in bed, and held her breath and listened. For a second she thought she heard a noise in the saloon below her. She was not nervous in the least, but she wished Terry had not left so much money in the safe; and this was the first night he had been away from her since they had been married— nearly two years ago. She strained her ears, but the sound was not repeated. She sank back on the pillow again, making sure that it was a rat dropping down from the bar, where he had been picking up the crumbs of cheese. There were many rats in the cellar, and sometimes they ventured up even to the bedroom and the kitchen next door.

Time was when it would have taken a loud noise to wake the girl who was now Terence O'Donnell's wife out of a sound sleep. After her mother died, when Maggie was not five years old, her father had moved into one of the worst tenements in the city, a ram-shackle old barrack just at the edge of Hell's Kitchen; and there was never any quiet there, day or night, in the house or in the street. There was always a row of some sort going on, whatever the hour of the day; if profanity and riot could keep a girl awake she would never have had any sleep there. But Maggie did not recall that she had been a wakeful child; indeed, she remembered that she could sleep at any time and anywhere. On the hot summer nights, when her father came home in-

toxicated, she would steal away and climb up
to the roof and lie down there, slumbering as
healthily as though she were in their only room.

Even then her father used to get drunk often,
on Saturday night always, and frequently once or
twice in the middle of the week. And when he
had taken too much he was mad always. If he
found her at home he beat her. She could recall
distinctly the first time her father had knocked
her down, but the oaths that had accompanied
the blow she had forgotten. He had not knocked
her down often, but he had sworn at her every
day of her life. The vocabulary of profanity
was the first that her infant ears had learned to
distinguish.

Her father quit drinking for a month after he
married again. They moved away from Hell's
Kitchen to a better house near the East River.
All went well for a little while, and her step-
mother was good to her. But her father went
back to his old ways again, and soon his new
wife turned out to be no better. When the fit
was on they quarrelled with each other, and they
took turns in beating Maggie, if she were not
quick to make her escape. It was when aiming
a blow at Maggie one Saturday night that her
father pitched forward and fell down a flight of
the tenement-house stairs, and was picked up dead.
The neighbors carried him up to the room where
his wife lay in a liquorish stupor.

Maggie was nearly fourteen then. She **went**

on living with her step-mother, who got her a
place in a box-factory. The first days of work
were the happiest of Maggie's girlhood. She remembered the joy which she felt at her ability
to earn money ; it gave her a sense of being her
own mistress, of being able to hold her own in
the world. And she made friends among the
other girls. One of them, Sadie McDermott, had
a brother Jim, who used to come around on Saturday night and tease his sister for money. Jim
belonged to a gang, and he never worked if he
could help it. He had no trade. Maggie remembered the Saturday night when she and Sadie
had walked home together, and when Jim got
mad because his sister would not divide her
wages with him. He snatched her pocket-book
and started to run. When Maggie reproved him
with an oath and caught him by one arm, he
threw her off so roughly that she fell and struck
her head on a lamp-post so hard that she fainted.

As Maggie lay in her bed that Fourth of July
morning, while her past life unrolled itself before
her like a panorama, she knew that the scar on the
side of her head was not the worst wound Jim
McDermott had dealt her. As she looked back,
she wondered how she had ever been friendly
with him; how she had let him follow her about;
how she had allowed him to make love to her.
It was on Jim McDermott's account that she had
had the quarrel with her step-mother. Having
robbed a drunken man of five dollars, Jim had in-

vited Maggie to a picnic; and the step-mother, a little drunker than usual that evening, had said that if Maggie went with him she would not be received again. Maggie was not one to take a dare, and she told Jim she would go with him in the morning. The step-mother cursed her for an ungrateful girl; and when Maggie returned with him from the picnic late the next night, and came to the door of the room where she and her step-mother lived, they found it locked against her, and all Maggie's possessions tied in a bundle, and scornfully left outside on the landing.

It had not taken Jim long that night to persuade Maggie to go away with him; and she had not seen her step-mother since. A week later, but not before he and Maggie had quarrelled, Jim was arrested for robbing the drunken man; he was sent up to the Island. Since the picnic Maggie had not been back to the factory. Jim had taken her with him one night to a dance-hall, and there she went without him when she was left alone in the world. There she had met Terry a month later. When she first saw Terry the thing plainest before her was the Morgue; she was on the way there, and she was going fast, and she knew it. Although winter had not yet come, she had already a cough that racked her day and night.

And as she lay there in her comfortable bed, and thought of the chill of the Morgue from which Terry had saved her, she closed her eyes to keep out the dreadful picture, and she clinched her fists across her forehead. Then she smiled as she remembered the way Terry had thrashed Jim, who had got off the Island somehow before his time was up. Jim said he had a pull with the police, and he came to her for money, and he threatened to have her taken up. It was then Terry had the scrap with him, and did him up. Terry had had a day off, for his boss kept closed on Sundays; at that time Terry was keeping bar at a high-toned café near Gramercy Park.

When he thrashed Jim that was not the first time Terry had been good to her. Nor was it the last. A fortnight later he took her away from the dance-hall, and as soon as he could get a day off he married her. They went down to the Tombs, and the judge married them. The judge knew Terry, and when he had kissed the bride he congratulated Terry, and said that the new-made husband was a lucky man, and that he had got a good wife.

A good wife Maggie knew she had been, and she was sure she brought Terry luck. When the man who had been running the house which now bore the name of Terence O'Donnell over its door got into trouble and had to skip the country, the boss had put Terry in charge, and had let Maggie go to house-keeping in the little rooms over the saloon; and when the boss died suddenly, his widow knew Terry was honest, and sold out the place to him, cheap, on the instalment plan. That was a year and a half ago, and all the instal-

ments had been paid except the last, which was
not due for a week yet, though the money for it
lay all ready in the safe down-stairs. And Terry
was doing well; he was popular; his friends would
come two blocks out of the way to get a drink at
his place; and he had just had a chance to go into
a picnic speculation. He was sure to make money;
and perhaps in two or three years they might be
able to pay off the mortgage on the fixtures. Then
they would be rich; and perhaps Terry would
get into politics.

Suddenly the current of Maggie's thoughts
was arrested. From the floor below there came
sounds, confused and muffled, and yet unmistak-
able. Maggie listened, motionless, and then she
got out of bed quickly. She knew that there
was some one in the saloon down-stairs; and at
that hour no one could be there for a good purpose. Whoever was there was a thief. Perhaps
it was some one of the toughs of the neighbor-
hood, who knew that Terry was away.

She had no weapon of any kind, but she was
not in the least afraid. She stepped cautiously
to the head of the stairs, and crept stealthily
down, not delaying to put on her stockings. The
sounds in the saloon continued; they were few
and slight, but Maggie could interpret them plainly enough; they told her that a man having got
into the house somehow, had now gone behind the
bar. Probably he was trying to steal the change
in the cash-drawer; she was glad that Terry had

locked all his money in the safe just before he went off.

When Maggie had slipped down the stairs gently, and stood in the little passageway with the door into the saloon ajar before her, she felt a slight draught, and she knew that the thief had entered through a window, and had left it open. Yet there was no use in her calling for assistance. The only people within reach of her voice were the poor Poles, who were too poor - spirited to protest even if they saw her robbed in broad daylight ; they were cowardly creatures all of them; and she could not hope for help from them as she would if they were only white men. The policeman might be within reach of her cry; but he had a long beat, and there was only a slim chance that he was near.

Her head was clear, and she thought swiftly. The thing to do, the only thing, was to make use of the telephone to summon assistance. The instrument was within two feet of her as she stood in the passage, but it was on the other side of the door at the end of the bar, and therefore in full view of any one who might be in the saloon. And it would not be possible to ring up the central office and call for help without being heard by the robber.

Having made up her mind what it was best for her to do, Maggie did not hesitate a moment; she pushed the door gently before her and stepped silently into the saloon. As the faint light from the single dim jet of gas burning over the bar fell upon her, she looked almost pretty, with the aureole of her reddish hair, and with her firm young figure draped in the coarse white gown. She glanced around her, and for a second she saw no one. The window before her was open, but the man who had broken in was not in sight.

As she peered about she heard a scratching, grating noise, and then she saw the top of a man's head just appearing above the edge of the bar behind which his body was concealed. She knew then that the thief was trying to get into the safe where Terry's money was locked up.

Leaving the door wide open behind her, Maggie took the two steps that brought her to the telephone, and rapidly turned the handle. Then she faced about swiftly to see what the man would do.

The first thing he did was to bob his head suddenly under the bar, disappearing wholly. Then he slowly raised his face above the edge of the bar, and Maggie found herself staring into the shifty eyes of Jim McDermott.

"Hello, Maggie !" he said, as he stood up. "Is that you ?"

She saw that he had a revolver in his right hand. But she put up her hand again and repeated the telephone call.

"Drop that !" he cried, as he raised the revolver. "You try to squeal and I'll shoot— see ?"

"Where did you steal that pistol, Jim McDermott?" was all she answered.

"None o' your business where I got it," he retorted. "I got it good and ready for you now. I kin use it too, and don't you forget it! You quit that telephone or you'll see how quick I can shoot. You hear me?"

She did not reply. She was waiting for the central office to acknowledge her call. She looked Jim McDermott square in the eyes, and it was he who was uncomfortable and not she.

Then the bell of the telephone rang, and she turned and spoke into the instrument clearly and rapidly and yet without flurry. "This is 31 Chatham. There's a burglar here. It's Jim McDermott. Send the police quick."

This was her message; and then she faced about sharply and cried to him, "Now shoot, and be damned!"

He took her at her word, and fired. The bullet bored a hole in the wooden box of the telephone.

Maggie laughed tauntingly, and slipped swiftly out of the door, but not swiftly enough to avoid the second bullet.

Five minutes later when the police arrived, just as the day was beginning to break, they found Jim McDermott fled, the window open, the safe uninjured, and Maggie O'Donnell lying in the passageway at the foot of the stairs, her night-gown stained with blood from a flesh wound in her arm.

(1893.)

7

A MIDSUMMER MIDNIGHT

FTER three years' service at sea on the flag-ship of the White Squadron, Lieutenant John Stone had a long leave of absence. It was late in the afternoon of one of the hottest days of August when he left the navy-yard and took the ferry to New York. The street-car in which he rode across town crawled along, the horses seeming to be exhausted by the wearing weather of the preceding fortnight, and the driver had no energy to keep them up to their work.

It mattered little to John Stone how slowly they went ; he was in no hurry ; he had nothing to do ; he had nobody waiting for him. At forty he was alone in the world, without a blood-relation anywhere or any nearer than a second cousin, without a home, without an address, except " Care of the Navy Department, Washington, D.C." He was almost without ambition even in the service now, for he had not yet had a command, and he would not get his step for three or four years more. He was fond of his profession, and of late he had been working lovingly at its early history. He had come to New York now to look up in the libraries a few missing links in an account of the

rise and fall of Carthage as a sea power. To be
near the books he had to consult, he was going to
stay at a hotel within two or three blocks of
Washington Square.

When he had registered at the hotel, the clerk,
reading his name upsidedown, said, courteously:
"I'm sorry we can't do better for you, Mr. Stone,
but I shall have to put you on the sixth floor.
You see, we are overrun with our Southern and
Western trade now; they have found out that
New York is the finest summer resort in the
country. The best I can do for you is to give
you a room on the Avenue, with a bath-room
attached."

"That will do very well," Stone answered.

"Front!" called the clerk. "Show Mr. Stone
up to 313."

When the naval officer reached room 313 it
was nearly six o'clock. He threw open the window and looked down at the street below. Even
at that height the heat welled up from the stone
sidewalks and from the brick walls opposite. To
his ear it seemed almost as though the mighty
roar of the metropolis rose to him muffled and
made more remote by the heat. He lighted a
cigar and leaned out of the window, and wondered how many people there were in all the city
whom he knew by sight, and how very few there
were who could call him by name.

A sweltering wind from the west swayed the
thick and dusty branches of the trees which lined

the curb far down below him. He threw his cigar away half smoked. Then he took a cold bath, and went down to the dining-room somewhat refreshed.

At the table to which the head waiter waved him there was already one man sitting, a tall, handsome young fellow of twenty-five, perhaps. Stone liked the man's face, and he liked the way the flannel shirt was cut so as to leave the full throat free. The manner in which the simple scarf was knotted and its ends tucked into the shirt he noticed also; and he saw that the young fellow had insisted on bringing his black slouch hat with him into the dining-room, having hung it on the back of the next chair. When this seat was given to Stone, the hat was promptly transferred to the chair on the other side of the owner. Stone made up his mind that his neighbor was a ranchman of some sort, who had come East on business.

It does not take long for two lonely men to get acquainted; and before he had eaten his green corn, Stone knew all about his neighbor at table, and the neighbor knew something about him.

"I sized you up when you come in," the young fellow said, "an' I took stock in you from the start. Somehow I kind o' thought you was one of Uncle Sam's boys, though o' course I didn't 'low you was a sailor. I never see a sailor till this mornin', when I went down on the dock to

get news of this *Touraine* steamer, an' the sailor
down there was a Frenchman, an' not like you,
not by a jugful. I suppose, now, Uncle Sam's
sailors are like his other boys I've seen at home
often. There's Dutchmen that ain't bad men, an'
I've seen Dagoes you could tie to, and sometimes
a greaser, now and then — not but what they's
powerful skase, greasers you can trust—but Uncle Sam's boys are white men every time."

The young fellow was Clay Magruder. He
was a cowboy, as Stone had supposed, and he was
in New York on a mission of the highest importance to himself. He was waiting for the girl he
wanted to marry, and she was expected to arrive
the next morning on the French steamer.

"The grub here ain't so bad, is it?" Magruder
said, as the repast drew to an end. "O' course
it ain't like what we get at home. I don't find
nowhere no beef that's equal to the beef we've
been gettin' right along now for two years, ever
since I've been with Old Man Pettigrew. The
Hash-knife Outfit always has the best cookin' on
the trail. It's jest notorious for it. Things here
in New York is good enough, but the flavor don't
take hold of you like it does at home ; an' their
coffee East is poor stuff, ain't it? It don't bite
you like coffee should."

After dinner they went into the smoking-room
of the hotel, and Stone offered a cigar to his new
friend.

"No, thank you," he responded, taking a small

brier-wood pipe out of his trousers-pocket. "I don't go much on cigars; I can git more solid comfort out of a pipe, I reckon." After he had filled his pipe and pulled at it half a dozen times, he said to Stone, suddenly: "Say! is there any show in town to-night? I've got a night off, you know, and I've allus heerd that for shows New York could lay over everything in sight. You've been to this town before, haven't you?"

Stone admitted that this was not his first visit to New York.

"I reckoned so," was Clay Magruder's comment. "An' so you know your way here, an' I don't; there's too many trails crossin' for me to keep to the road. Suppose we go to the show together—ef there is a show in town?"

Stone bought an evening paper, and looked over the list of amusements. He wondered what would best suit the tastes of his new friend.

"There's Deadwood Dick's Wild Western Exhibition at Niblo's—" he began.

"Deadwood Dick?" interrupted the cowboy, in great contempt; "he's a holy show, he is. He's a fraud; that's what he is. An' is he the only thing we can take in to-night?"

"Oh no," the sailor replied. "There are half a dozen other things to see. There's a comic opera at the Garden Theatre, with a variety show up in the roof garden afterwards."

"A comic opera—singing, and funny business, and pretty girls, I suppose?" said the Westerner.

"I reckon we'd might as well go there—unless you'd rather go somewhere else."

"The comic opera and the roof garden will just suit me," Stone responded.

They were fortunate in getting good seats at the theatre, where they arrived as the curtain was rising on the first act of "Patience." Even in midsummer the attire of Stone's new friend attracted some attention, and a group of pretty girls in the row behind them nudged each other as he came in and giggled. In their hearts they were glad to look at so handsome a man.

During the first act Magruder's face was a study for Stone. It was evident that the cowboy failed wholly to understand the narrow and insular satire of "Patience." When the curtain fell at last, he could contain himself no longer.

"I never see such a fool play," he said. "There ain't no sense in makin' believe that one fellow could round up a bunch of girls that way. It's the plumb-stupidest show I've seen for years and years. It's bad as Deadwood Dick 'most. 'Patience' they call it? Well, I 'ain't got none to see no more of it. What's this roof garden you told me about?"

So Stone took him up to the roof garden, and they were glad to get again into the open air, baked as the atmosphere was even at the top of the building. They had a drink and a smoke while they listened to the music.

When the variety show began on the little

stage, Stone went forward in time to secure advantageous positions for Magruder and himself. Early on the programme was a French song by a highly-colored young lady wearing an enormous hat.

"That's a good enough song," the cowboy declared, "but what sort of a lingo is it she's singin' it in? Why isn't plain United States good enough for songs? Not but what she's a pretty girl, too, and lively on her feet."

The part of the performance which excited Clay Magruder's warmest appreciation was the serpentine dance of Mademoiselle Éloise. When he beheld the coiling draperies of that graceful young woman curving about in picturesque and unexpected convolutions, and heightened in effect by the changing colors of the lime-lights directed upon the stage, his enthusiasm rose to a height.

"That's *some!*" he cried. "It reminds me of an Eyetalian gal I saw dance once in Cheyenne. She was a daisy, too; but this is bigger. They's no doubt about it, this is a heap bigger."

Magruder joined in accomplishing the inevitable recall and the repetition of a part of the dance. Perhaps this was the reason why the next two or three numbers of the programme seemed to him to be less interesting. At all events, both the cowboy and the sailor tired of the entertainment. So they made their way through the crowd and down to the street.

As they walked back to the hotel Magruder

told Stone what had brought him to New York. It was to meet the *Touraine* on her expected arrival in the morning, and to persuade one of the passengers to marry him.

"She's jest got to marry me," he said, earnestly. "I can't get along without her any longer. She's a sort of governess to Old Man Pettigrew's sister's kids — learns them to read and play the pianner. They was all in Miles City last winter, and that was when I first see her. I made up my mind right off on the spot that there was Mrs. Clay Magruder if I could get her. And I'm here now to get her if I can. She's as pretty as a picture—better'n that, too, for I never see no chromo half as good - lookin' as her. Once last winter they was 'most a blizzard ; leastways the wind set back on its hind - legs and howled. You ought to have seen her then, with the color in her cheeks ! An' everything was froze stiff, and she was skeered of fallin'. Why, she teetered along jest like a chicken with a jag." And he laughed out loud at the recollection. "She'll be here in the mornin', and you shall see her. I'm goin' to be down on that dock good an' early to-morrow, and no French sailor ain't goin' to stand me off."

As they drew near to the hotel, Magruder remarked : "Say ! ain't they a jag-factory somewheres round here ? Come in and have one with me."

Stone went with him, and they drank the young lady's health, Magruder expatiating on her charms and on the happiness that awaited him when he should marry her. Then they crossed the street to the hotel and went up to their rooms.

As it happened, the room of Clay Magruder was exactly opposite John Stone's, so it was at their own doors that they parted for the night with a hearty grasp of the hand.

The sailor found the air of his room stifling. He threw wide the window and stood for a while looking out over the heated city as it lay around him in the darkness. He wondered what the girl was like whom Magruder had come East to meet, and he caught himself almost envying the cowboy. Then he sighed unconsciously and made ready for bed. As he wound up his watch he saw that it was nearly half - past eleven. Five minutes afterwards he was asleep.

He had been asleep but five minutes, as it seemed to him, when he was waked slowly with a slight difficulty in breathing, and with the feeling that all was not well. While he was still drowsy, he was conscious of a crackling sound like the snapping of dry twigs. When he opened his eyes he found that they smarted. The first long breath that he drew filled his lungs with thin smoke. In an instant he was wide awake. The meaning of the crackling and the snapping was not doubtful. The hotel was on fire.

He sprang out of bed and opened the door of his room. The corridor was full of smoke, and the sound of the flames was louder. At the bend in the hall where the stairs were, sharp tongues of flame were licking around the corner. Stone saw that his retreat that way was cut off, and that he must rely on the windows for escape. He crossed to the door opposite, pounded at it heavily, and cried "Fire! Fire! Get up at once!" till Clay Magruder answered. The floor of the corridor was hot beneath his feet as he went back to his own room, closed the door, and dressed himself as swiftly as he could, the murmur of the fire growing nearer and nearer.

When he was still in his shirt-sleeves he stepped again to the corridor and called across to Magruder.

The door opposite opened, and the cowboy appeared in it, half-dressed.

"The stairs are on fire," cried Stone; "we can't get out that way. We must try the windows. Take your sheets and your blankets and come in here."

"I wish I'd a couple of lariats here," said Magruder, as he went back for the bed-linen.

The air in the hall was now thick and suffocating, and the stairs at the corner were a furnace of fierce flames. Here and there thin threads of smoke were rising from the floor of the corridor.

The cowboy reappeared in his doorway, with his arms full of bedclothes.

"Come in here quick, so that I can get this door shut and keep out the smoke," said the sailor, standing back to leave the doorway open.

As Magruder stepped out of his room, the floor of the corridor gave way with a crash, and a red-hot gulf yawned between the two rooms. Stone leaned far forward to try and save his new friend. But the falling of the floor was too sudden, and Magruder went down into the roaring furnace below, from which the flames sprang up fiercely. In a moment he was lost to sight in the seething fire. Stone stood stock-still for a second, bent over the blazing opening, with his arm outstretched until the heat scorched it. Then he rose to his feet swiftly and shut the door behind him.

His own room was now full of smoke, and he knew that the door would be on fire in less than a minute. He threw open the window and looked down, seeing at once that his bedding alone would be useless, as it would take him down two stories at the most, while the fire had already broken out at the front of the building. He discovered that there was a ledge or narrow cornice running around the house just on the end of his floor. He stepped out upon this, and closed the window behind him. As he did so, the flames burst through from the corridor into his room.

Standing outside of his window on the narrow ledge, which gave him a scant foothold, he saw in front of him on his right what he had not before observed—a tall tower with an illuminated clock face. The hands pointed to four minutes past midnight. From the street below there arose a confused murmur of noises—shouts and cries of command, the rattle of heavy wheels as the engines rushed up, the regular rhythmic beat of the pumps as they got into play, the hissing of steam as a dozen streams of water curved upward and smote the burning building. The foliage of the trees which lined the curb was so thick that Stone could not see the sidewalk just below him, and apparently those in charge of operations had not seen him.

The sailor had faced death before — he had weathered many a fierce gale at sea; he had been at Samoa during the hurricane; he had been overboard for an hour once in the Bay of Biscay—and he was not afraid to die. He recalled his sensations when he believed himself to be drowning, and he remembered that his dominant thought had been that such a death then and there was needless and served no purpose. On that occasion he was more or less passive, being spent with the struggle against the waves; at present he was strong and ready to make a fight for his life. Then he had to contend with water, and now he knew that water was his chief hope.

At that moment there came a louder roar from far down in the street below : the water-tower had arrived. It was speedily erected and in service, and from its long trunk a thick stream of water was forced into the blazing hotel perhaps fifty feet from where Stone was standing. He watched it at work, and then he raised his eyes and again caught sight of the illuminated dial, whereon the hands now pointed to seven minutes after midnight.

Stone wondered whether the firemen would be able to get the better of the flames. He doubted it, but he wished that he could take part in the fight. It was rather the helplessness of his position than its fearfulness that he felt most keenly. He was in danger, and the danger was deepening with every minute of delay, but he could do nothing. The ledge on which he was standing was barely a foot wide, and it was perhaps ten feet long. Its length measured the width of his room, which projected a yard or more beyond the main line of the building. Stone moved cautiously to the right till he came to the end of the ledge, in the hope that it continued around the side, and that by following it he might pass along the whole front of the hotel, and perhaps find some way to escape to the roof of the house next door.

But the hope was futile, for the slight cornice shrank away as it turned back till it was barely an inch wide. The sailor was used to an insecure footing at a great height, and his nerves were steady; but he knew that it was certain destruction for him to try to advance in that direction. With his back pressed tight to the wall, he glided along to the window, now lighted up by the flames which filled his room. He pushed past it to the left until he came to the end of the ledge on that side, finding that the projection ceased on the one

8

hand as it had on the other. He felt himself a prisoner, held fast, with little hope of rescue; neither to the right nor to the left could he move; behind him was the wall of the blazing hotel, and before him was a sheer drop of sixty feet to the street below. He glanced down for an instant, and then raised his head again. To the right, in the distance, was the clock-tower, and it was now nine minutes past twelve. He wondered if the clock had stopped suddenly, for it seemed to him nearly an hour since he had awaked to find himself in peril of his life.

He thought of Magruder, and he wondered why the man who had hopes and joys before him should be cut off, while the man who had little to live for should be given a chance for his life. That the cowboy had perished in the flames he had no doubt; and in a flash his imagination bore him outside of the exigencies of the moment, and he had a vision of the *Touraine* making her way past Sandy Hook, and drawing near to Staten Island and anchoring there, too far from the city for its passengers to see the glare of the conflagration. Yet the fire was one to be seen from afar, for there was a sullen roar, and the roof of a wing of the hotel fell in. A myriad of sparks was blasted upward, and the crowd in the street raised a loud shout of warning. Stone looked down, and he saw a woman at a window of the floor below him; she was shrieking with terror, and at last she gave a wild spring forward. He beheld her crash through the branches of the trees, and he heard her body strike the sidewalk. There was a yell of horror from the crowd, and then silence. A few seconds later Stone caught the quick clang of an ambulance bell in the side street. He counted the strokes automatically until they died away in the distance. His ear was so strained to catch this sound that he heard the rattle of a train stopping at the station of the elevated railroad only a block away, and he seized even the shrill squeak of the brakes as they grated against the wheels. Then he aroused himself, and wondered why he had noted such trifles. Turning his head, he found the single eye of the clocktower still beaming at him. He blinked stupidly before he saw that it was now thirteen minutes after twelve.

More engines had arrived in the street below, and another hook-and-ladder truck. Several small ladders had been put up to the lower windows, and women and children had been carried down in safety. Stone watched while the firemen tried to raise one of the taller ladders which might reach to the third or fourth floor. The branches of the trees were so close that the men found it impossible to get this longer ladder into position. A man was sent up into the tree, and he was cutting away the branches, when flames burst out of the nearest window. A torrent of water was at once directed into the window, while a second stream splashed down upon the tree and made a watery

shield for the fireman, who went on lopping off
the limbs. He labored swiftly, but the fire was
swifter still. At almost the same time the flames
burst forth from three or four other of the lower
windows.

Stone had been noting every effort of the men
below. At first he had not been seen. But after
the man had cut away a few of the branches of
the tree, two or three of the firemen caught sight
of the sailor. They shouted to him, but in the
roar of the fire behind him and below him he
could not make out their words. A captain gave
a sudden command, and two men sprang forward
with short scaling-ladders, which they succeeded
in hooking to the second-story window immediately below the ledge on which he was standing.
Looking down, he could see the heads of these
men as they climbed the ladders, their bodies
being foreshortened into invisibility. The men
could not get above the second story, for the fire
was gushing forth as though the window were the
mouth of hell. The smoke rose black and dense,
enshrouding Stone.

He saw that it was useless to hope that they
could now get a ladder up to him; the flames
would not give them time. The wall behind him
was becoming hotter, and the heat had broken
the glass of the window of his room. The fire
was creeping along the roof above his head, and
every now and again it peered over the edge at
him, as though seeing how far it had still to go

before it could grasp him. The smoke from below was thickening, and threatened to choke him. Through its haze he could see the cyclops eye of the clock-tower gloating over his inevitable fate. The hands on the illuminated dial had slowly crept forward, and it was now nearly twenty minutes past twelve.

Stone knew that his position was untenable for many seconds longer. At any moment the wall might fall back and bury him in the blazing ruins. To remain was impossible ; and there seemed no way of escape. A crash shook the building, and then another ; and he guessed that two of the floors had fallen in. He slid along again to the end of the narrow ledge and tried to peer around the corner, in the vague hope that there might be some possible means of escape. He found that he could not twist his head far enough to see anything while his back was flat against the wall. To turn was to risk a fall to the pavement below. He looked down fearlessly, and calculated his chances if he missed his footing. Immediately beneath him the tree was taller than its fellows, and its foliage was thicker ; it was barely possible that the branches might break his fall ; but the chance was slim. The smoke poured heavily from the window three feet from him. He hesitated no longer, but turned slowly and steadily. His nerves were unshaken, and he executed the manœuvre in safety. Standing with his face to the wall—which rose sheer above him, and which gave him no hold for his hands—he was able to thrust out his head sideways and to look around the corner. What he saw gave him a thrill of hope.

His room projected perhaps a yard beyond the main line of the building, forming what might be termed a square bay-window. From his position on the narrow shelf of marble, which ran around the front of the hotel on every floor, he thought he could reach forward and touch the main wall of the building. And here was his one possible chance of escape. In the corner formed by the junction of the projection and the main line there was the leader which conducted the rain-water from the roof. It was of tin only, and in the eyes of the sailor gazing at it with upspringing hope it seemed frail, insecurely fastened, perhaps rotten. But it offered a chance, and the only chance, of life, and therefore it was welcome. Stone prepared to make the best of it.

He gave a final glance around before he made the irrevocable move. He caught sight of the clock, and he saw that it was twenty-two minutes after midnight. He reached forward, and he found that the space was wider than he had thought. It was with the tips of his fingers only that he could touch the tin pipe; it was beyond the reach of his grasp. Yet to seize it was the one way to the street below. He did not hesitate. He stood on his left foot on the very end of the ledge, with his right foot dangling in space. He made a carefully measured plunge forward, and he griped the leader with his left hand and then instantly with his right. It yielded under the sudden strain, but it did not part. With the habit of a sailor, he clasped his legs about it, and so eased the pressure. Then he began slowly to slide down, gaining velocity as he descended.

At every floor there was a shelf of stone like that on which he had stood outside his window, and through which the tin tube passed. Stone had therefore to release his feet, and by his hands alone to cling to the pipe, which spread from the wall with the weight of his body. Then he clasped his legs again below the ledge and let go one hand after the other. The tin was broken and jagged here and there, and Stone's flesh was cut to the bone. But he did not notice this in the tension of his swift descent.

When he came to the first floor and tried to take a fresh grip with his legs, he found nothing to clasp with his knees. From there to its connection with the gutter the pipe went inside the building. Stone hung from the ledge by his hands, not knowing how far he was above the sidewalk. The smoke was pouring up from the cellar grating beneath him, and in a minute he would have suffocated. So he let go.

The drop was ten feet or more, and he came down on a trunk which had been thrown out of a window. From this he pitched to the sidewalk with a broken leg and a dislocated shoulder. He was dimly conscious of being lifted gently, and of a brief but painful ride. The sharp clang of the ambulance bell he felt as though it were a physical blow.

When he came to himself again it was morning, and he was in bed in a long room with a row of cots on both sides of it, under the slanting sunbeams.

He lay still, wondering.

The occupant of the next bed was unfolding a newspaper, and Stone heard him say to the nurse, with an Alsacian accent: " Ve're goin' have nodder hot day ; I vonder how dhose people yust back from Paris on dhe *Douraine* vill like dot ?"

(1892.)

A VISTA IN CENTRAL PARK

IT was the last Sunday in September, and the blue sky arched above the Park, clear, cloudless, unfathomable. The afternoon sun was hot, and high overhead. Now and then a wandering breeze came without warning and lingered only for a moment, fluttering the broad leaves of the aquatic plants in the fountain below the Terrace. At the Casino, on the hill above the Mall, men and women were eating and drinking, some of them inside the dingy and sprawling building, and some of them out-doors at little tables set in curving lines under the gayly colored awnings, which covered the broad walk bending away from the door of the restaurant. From the bandstand in the thick of the throng below came the brassy staccato of a cornet, rendering "The Last Rose of Summer." Even the Ramble was full of people; and the young couples, seeking sequestered nooks under the russet trees, were often forced to share their benches with strangers. Beneath the reddening maples lonely men lounged on the grass by themselves, or sat solitary and silent in the midst of chattering family groups.

The crowd was cosmopolitan and unhurried.

For the most part it was good-natured and well-
to-do. There was not a beggar to be seen ; there
was no appealing poverty. Fathers of families
there were in abundance, well-fed and well-clad,
with their wives and with their sons' wives and
with their sons' children. Maids in black dresses
and white aprons pushed baby-carriages. Young
girls in groups of three and four giggled and gos-
siped. Young men in couples leaned over the
bridge of the Lake, smoking and exchanging opinions. There was a general air of prosperity gladly displaying itself in the sunshine ; the misery
and the want and the despair of the great city
were left behind and thrust out of mind.

Two or three yards after a portly German with
a little boy holding each of his hands while a
third son still younger rode ahead astride of his
father's solid cane, there came two slim Japanese
gentlemen, small and sallow, in their neatly cut
coats and trousers. A knot of laughing mulatto-
girls followed, arm in arm ; they, too, seemed ill-
dressed in the accepted costume of civilization,
especially when contrasted with half a dozen Italians who passed slowly, looking about them with
curious glances ; the men in worn olive velveteens
and with gold rings in their ears, the women with
bright colors in their skirts and with embroidery
on their neckerchiefs. Where the foot - path
touched the carriage-drive there stood a plain but
comfortably plump Irishwoman, perhaps thirty
years of age ; she had a baby in her arms, and a

"TWO SLIM JAPANESE GENTLEMEN"

little girl of scant three held fast to her patched
calico dress; with her left hand she was proffering a basket containing apples, bananas, and
grapes; two other children, both under six, played
about her skirts; and two more, a boy and a girl,
kept within sight of her—the girl, about ten years
old, having a basket of her own filled with thin
round brown cakes; and the boy, certainly not
yet thirteen, holding out a wooden box packed
with rolls of lozenges, put up in red and yellow
and green papers. Now and again the mother or
one of the children made a sale to a pedestrian
on his way to the music. The younger children
watched, with noisy glee, the light leaps of a gray
squirrel bounding along over the grass behind the
path and balancing himself with his horizontal
tail.

The broad carriage-drive was as crowded as
any of the foot-paths. Bicyclists in white sweaters and black stockings toiled along in groups of
three and four, bent forward over the bars of their
machines. Politicians with cigars in the corners
of their mouths held in impatient trotters. Park
omnibuses heavily laden with women and children drew up for an instant before the Terrace, and
then went on again to skirt the Lake. Old-fashioned and shabby landaus lumbered along with
strangers from the hotels. Now and then there
came in sight a hansom cab with a young couple
framed in the front of it, or a jolting dog-cart, on
the high seat of which a British-looking young

man was driving tandem. Here and there were other private carriages—coupés and phaetons, for the most part, with once and again a four-in-hand coach rumbling heavily on the firmly packed road.

A stylish victoria sped along, spick and span, with its glistening harness and its jingling steel chains, with its stalwart pair of iron-gray steppers and with two men on the box, correct and impassive. Suddenly, as it passed close to the walk at the end of the Terrace, the coachman drew up sharply, pulling his horses back on their haunches and swearing inaudibly at the plump Irishwoman who had dropped her basket of fruit just in time to rescue one of her children from being run over.

"It's more careful ye ought to be!" cried the mother, as she stood again on the walk with her daughter clasped to her waist.

"We are very sorry, indeed," said the lady in the victoria, leaning forward. "It was an accident."

"An accident, was it?" returned the Irishwoman. "An' it's an accident, then, ye wouldn't like if it was yer own children ye were runnin' over like that."

The childless couple in the carriage looked at each other for a moment only; and then the husband said, swiftly, "Drive on, John!"

He was a man of fifty, spare in frame and round-shouldered; he had a keen glance, and a weary smile came and went on his lips, not hidden by his sparse gray moustache. His wife was a woman of perhaps thirty, tall, dark, with passionate eyes and a full figure.

She was still leaning forward, clinching the side of the carriage as it turned northward and rolled along by the side of the Lake. Her voice showed that her excitement had not subsided, as she faced her husband again and said : "John is getting very careless. That is the third time this week he has nearly run over a child!"

"He has not quite run over one yet. It will be time enough to discharge him when he does," her husband answered, calmly. "That little girl there is none the worse for her fright. She seemed a pretty little thing, and she has been saved to grow up in a tenement-house and to go to the devil ten years from now. So her mother has cause to be thankful."

His wife looked at him indignantly. "I suppose," she said, "you mean that it is a pity that John didn't run over the child and kill her."

"I didn't mean that exactly," he responded. "But perhaps it is true enough. Death is not the worst thing in this world, you know."

"You are always talking of dying," returned his young wife, impatiently. "I wonder you don't commit suicide."

"I have thought of it," he answered, looking at her with a tolerant smile. "But life amuses

me still—I have so much curiosity, you know.
But I might do it, if I were sure I could have the
privilege of coming back to see what you will be
up to when I'm gone."

She looked straight before her and made no
answer, keeping her lips firmly compressed.

There was a touch of tenderness in his tone as
he went on, a curious cynical tenderness, quite
characteristic of him. "Don't let some rascal
marry you for my money. That would annoy
me, I confess. And yet, I don't know why I
should suggest the possibility of such a thing, for
you will be a most fascinating widow."

She gazed ahead steadily and said nothing, but
she had joined her hands together, and her fingers
kept moving.

"Still," he continued, "I'm afraid I'm good for
ten years more. We're a hardy stock, you know.
My father lived to be eighty, and he was fifty
when I was born. Besides, you take such good
care of me always."

He held out his hand to her, and she took it
and clasped it tight in both of hers, while the
tears brimmed her eyes.

"But perhaps you are letting me stay out too
long this afternoon," he said. "It is balmy, I
know, but I'm getting tired already."

"John," she cried, hastily, "you may turn now,
and go home."

"I don't want you to lose this lovely September
afternoon," her husband declared. "Take me

home, and come back to the Park here for an hour, while I have a nap, if I can."

Just then there was a break in the stream of vehicles, and the coachman took advantage of it and turned the horses' heads southward. In five minutes the victoria swerved to the westward, leaving the Lake behind, and making for the Riverside Drive.

The Lake was gay with boats. Black gondolas with white canopies and brilliant American flags were propelled adroitly by their standing boatmen. Light canoes were paddled briskly in and out of the bays and channels, where the ducks and swans swam lazily about. Young fellows in their shirt-sleeves tugged inexpertly at the oars of row-boats laden down with young women. By regular and easy strokes the Park watermen rowed the capacious barges, with their striped awnings, in the prescribed course around the Lake. The oars flashed in the flickering sunlight, and the sunshine gilded the prows of the distant canoes as they shot across the vista. The yellow leaves of the maples high on the bank over the opposite shore fluttered loosely away on the doubtful breeze, and at last fell languidly into the water. To the west a towering apartment-house lifted itself aloft over the edge of the Park, and seemed to shorten the space between. To the east the gilded dome of a new synagogue rose over the tree-tops. Above all was the blue concave of the calm and illimitable sky.

9

When the victoria, with its two men on the box and with its pair of high-stepping horses, returned to the Park, and skirted the Lake again, and approached the Terrace, the lady sat in it alone. As she came in sight of the Mall she bent forward, eagerly looking for the little girl whom they had almost run over half an hour earlier.

Near the Terrace she saw the pleasant-faced Irishwoman, with her basket of fruit in one hand and the baby in the other arm; the three little children were playing about their mother's feet, while the elder boy and girl were only a few yards away.

The lonely woman in the victoria bade the coachman draw up.

Seeing the carriage stop at the side of the road the Irishwoman came forward, proffering her fruit. Then she recognized the lady and checked her approach, hesitating.

The handsome woman in the carriage smiled, and said, "Which is the little girl we almost ran over?"

"That's the one," answered the mother, indicating the slip of a child who was now clasping the edge of the fruit-basket while staring at the strange lady with wide-open eyes.

"What a pretty child she is!" said the lady. "I hope she is none the worse for her fright?"

"Ye didn't break any bones, if that's what ye mean," the mother responded.

"And how old is she?" was the next question.

"She'll be three years old come Christmas," was the answer.

The lady in the carriage felt in her pocket, and brought out her purse and looked through it.

"Here," she said at last, as she took out a five-dollar gold-piece ; "here is something I wish you would give her on Christmas morning as a present from me.   Will you?"

"I will that," the mother replied, taking the money, "and gladly too.   It's richer than her sisters she'll be now."

"How many children have you?" the lady inquired.

"Six ; thank ye, ma'am, for askin'," was the response, "an' all well and hearty."

"Six?" echoed the woman in the victoria, with a hungry gleam in her eyes.   "You have six children?"

"It's six I have," the mother answered ; "and it's a fine lot they are altogether, though I say it that shouldn't."

The lady put her hand in her purse again.

"Buy something with this for the others," she said, placing a bank-note in the Irishwoman's hands.   Then she raised her voice and added, "You may drive on, John!"

As the victoria rolled away to the westward the fruit-vender courtesied, and the children all looked after the carriage with interest.

"That lady must be very rich," said the eldest boy, the one who had the lozenges for sale.   "I shouldn't wonder if she had two millions of dollars!"

"She must be very happy," the eldest girl added. "I suppose she can have ice-cream every day, and go to the Seaside Home for two weeks whenever she wants."

"It's a kind heart she has anyway, for all her money," was the mother's comment, as she unfolded the bank-note and saw the X in the corner of it.

Meanwhile the lady in the victoria was eaten with bitter thoughts as the carriage rattled along in the brilliant sunshine beneath the unclouded sky.

"Six children!" she was saying to herself. "That Irishwoman has six children! Why is it that some women have so much luck?"

(1893.)

THE SPEECH OF THE EVENING

THE more immaterial part of the banquet was about to begin. The guests had made an end of eating, and the waiters were filling the small cups with black coffee, and passing boxes of cigars and cigarettes. At the five long tables which gridironed the great room the hum of conversation rose higher and higher ; while at the shorter table, raised on the platform at the western end of the hall, there was almost silence, as the men who were to make speeches saw the oratorical moment approaching. The musicians, hidden behind a screen of greenery, were playing a medley of the latest popular airs ; and here and there, at the tables below, a little group of the diners now and again took up a chorus, with intermittent energy, to the amusement of the ladies who were arriving and filling rapidly the broad boxes in the galleries.

The organizers of the dinner had felt that it was a great occasion, and they had sought to make it memorable artistically. The severe white of the beautifully proportioned concert-hall was relieved by foliage plants, massed and scattered with a delicate understanding of decorative ef-

fect; against the absolutely colorless walls, with
their carved caryatides, were palms in pots ;
gayly colored silken banners floated down from
the ceiling ; and everywhere, on the ceiling and
the walls and the balconies and the platforms, the
electric lights glowed and twinkled, illuminating
the lofty hall with steady brilliancy.

Near the eastern end of one of the long tables
there sat a young man—at least, he was barely
thirty.   He was so placed that he had before him
the whole scene.   He had an uninterrupted view
of the raised table, where the speakers were absorbed in self-communion.   He commanded the
entrance to the gallery opposite, and he could see
the ladies as they arrived in little groups, eager
for the unwonted pleasure of attendance at a
great public dinner.   He could hear the feminine
chatter rising shrill above the masculine babble
below.   He gazed at the boxes curiously, as
though he did not know any of the ladies in
them ; and he remained quiet while the diners
about him at that end of the table exchanged
salutations with the occupants of one box or another.   Apparently he had few if any acquaintances even on the floor of the hall, the men on
each side of him being generally engaged in conversation with their neighbors.

Seemingly his solitude was lightly borne, and
he found solace for it in amused observation of
the gathering.   He lighted his own cigar, and
was soon helping to make the blue haze which

hung over the tables, rising in time almost to the level of the boxes in the long balconies.

Yet he was not averse to conversation, and when his right-hand neighbor turned back to pick up a fresh cigarette, he took occasion to say, "It isn't usual to let ladies in at dinners here in New York, is it?"

"No," his right-hand neighbor responded, with a slight but obvious German accent, "I don't think it is. I've been lifing in New York for a long vile now—'most eleven years—and I never saw it before."

Then the right-hand neighbor, having lighted his cigarette, sat back in his chair again and resumed his interrupted talk with the man on the other side of him.

The young man who was apparently a stranger was allowed to keep silence only for a minute or two, however, as his left-hand neighbor, to whom he had hardly spoken during the dinner, now engaged him in conversation.

"I thought it was about time they did that," said the neighbor, indicating the waiters who were removing the potted orange-trees and the sugar-trophies from the upper table. "Now we can see who's who."

"I suppose those are the more distinguished guests?" the young man suggested.

"Most of the men who are going to make speeches are up there," the neighbor responded. "Hello, hello! there's Alexander Macgregor down

at that end there, the one with the full red beard.
He's the President of the St. Andrew's Society.
He's a first-rate American, too, for all he was born
in Edinburgh. You know, he's the man they
call the 'Star-spangled Scotchman.'"

"And who is that clean-shaved, clean-looking,
fair-haired man next to him?" asked the young
man.

"That?" the neighbor replied, "that's—oh, I
forget his name—but he's the President of the St.
George's Society, I think. He's an Englishman—
that is, he was; I suppose he's been naturalized—
but then you can never tell about Englishmen,
can you? They will live in a place for years,
and they will be Britons to the backbone all the
time."

"Who is the presiding officer?" was the next
question.

"Don't you know *him?*" the neighbor retorted. "Why, that's Crowninshield Eliot, the lawyer. He used to be President of the New England Society. He's a clever man and he makes
a rattling good speech sometimes, but then he's
mighty uncertain. He may speak well or he
may make a bad break. A speech from him is a
regular grab-bag—you never know what you are
going to have. But things don't get rusty when
he is around, I tell you. You can rely on him to
wake all the other speakers up. And I guess we
shall have some fun before we get through; it
isn't often you see so many representative New-

Yorkers together; it's really a typical gathering."

The young man made no response to this, being for the moment busy with his own ironic thoughts.

"Now there's a man who will make the fur fly if he gets a chance," continued the loquacious neighbor, "that tall, thin, dignified-looking man, with the black goatee and mustache; that's Colonel Fairfax. He's Secretary of the Southern Society—all rebels, you know, but reconstructed by this time, most of them. He's District Attorney for the second term now, and you ought to hear him talk to a jury. He could get a verdict against the angel Gabriel for stealing the silver trumpet. When I was on the grand jury last year he—"

Here the young man's neighbor interrupted himself to say, "Hello, hello! that is odd, isn't it? Right next to Colonel Fairfax is the man who was foreman of our grand jury; I didn't catch sight of him till that waiter took away that candy Statue of Liberty. See him? The bald one with the scar on his jaw; it's a bullet wound he got at Shiloh. That's S. Colfax Morrison; he was major of the 200th Ohio, but he's been living in New York for ten years now at least. That's 'the Ohio idea' they talk about: to come to New York to live as soon as they can. I was born in Ohio myself."

And the talker let his loquacity taper off into a laugh, in which the young man joined courteously.

There was a sudden diminution of the roar of talk as the gentleman sitting in the middle of the raised table rose to his feet and rapped for silence. Even in the boxes, now filled to over-flowing with ladies, the chatter ceased as the man who had been selected to preside over the dinner began his remarks by recalling the event they had met to commemorate. In felicitous phrases and with neatly turned strokes of humor he declared the reason why they were assembled together. And when he had made an end of this, he an-nounced that the first toast of the evening would be "New York, the Empire City, sitting at the gates of commerce, and holding the highways of trade."

There was a burst of applause and a pushing back of chairs as all the guests rose with their glasses in their hands.

Then the presiding officer prepared to intro-duce the speaker who was to make the response to this important toast.

"I saw only this morning," he began again, "the report of some remarks made by a Senator from Nevada, in which New York was called a 'city of kites and crows.' There are Congress-men who cannot open their mouths without disseminating miscellaneous misinformation; and the only appropriate retort would be with the plain-spoken bowie of the mining-camp or with the unambiguous derringer of Nevada. No ad-equate answer is possible in the sterilized vocabulary permitted to us by the conventions of modern society. And yet it is well that once in a while New York should assert herself—that she should celebrate herself — that she should rest from her mighty labors, if only for a moment, to contemplate her own great work. We are fortunate in having with us here to-night a man who can do justice to this imposing theme, a man who loves New York as we all love her, who is proud of New York as we are all proud of her—a man whom there is no need for me to introduce to an assembly of New-Yorkers. Works of supererogation are discountenanced, and who is there here who does not know Horace Chauncy?"

As the chairman ceased the gentleman who had been sitting at his right rose, and immediately there was great applause from all parts of the hall. Men clapped their hands and rapped upon the table with the handles of their fruit-knives. Even the ladies in the boxes waved their handkerchiefs.

Then, as the chairman, having done his duty, took his seat, there was the customary hum of anticipated enjoyment, dying away swiftly as Mr. Chauncy prepared to speak.

The left-hand neighbor of the young man down at the far end of the long table turned to him again, and said, "Now you keep your eyes open. I shouldn't wonder if this was the speech of the evening."

The young man looked at the new speaker and

liked his face, at once masterful and intelligent.
Mr. Chauncy's attitude was one of conscious
strength and of perfect ease. He was a man of
fifty, perhaps, with gray hair and a curling gray
mustache.

"Upon a mellow October night like this," the
speaker began, and his voice was rich and firm,
while his delivery was as clear as a line en-
graving — "upon a mellow October night like
this, possible in no other city in this country or
in Europe, I think, and illustrative of the fact that
here in New York we have really a climate, while
most of the other great towns of the world have
only weather—upon a night like this, and under
this graceful tower, uplifting its loveliness into
the azure air and topped by a Diana fairer than that
of the Ephesians smiling down upon gardens more
beautiful than any ever hanging in Babylon, there
is no need for me to present any defence of the
Empire City, or to proffer any apology for her.
If you seek for proof of her superiority, look
about you here to-night, and remember that nowhere else in the United States could any such
company as this be gathered together; nowhere
else in the United States is there a banquet-hall
so beautiful; nowhere else in the United States
would a feast like this be graced by the presence
of so many lovely women. Yet I feel that I
should be derelict to my duty—that I should let
slip a precious occasion—if I did not dwell for a
while upon a few of the many things in the his-

tory of this city which give her proud pre-emi-
nence; which make her what she is—the mighty
and magnificent metropolis of a great people."

Again the applause broke forth. After a pause
the speaker continued, having the attention of
every man and woman in the hall. Even as he
warmed to his subject he preserved the perfection of his delivery, and he poured forth facts,
figures, illustrations, one after the other, with never a broken accent or a blurred syllable.

"I will not detain you by detailing the many
natural advantages of New York—the noble river
which sweeps by on one side and the arm of the
ocean which embraces the other, and the spacious
and beautiful bay, with its harborage ample for
all the fleets of all the nations of the earth. It
is not my purpose to-night to linger long over
the works of art which make this island of ours
distinguished as the works of nature have made
possible her prosperity; and therefore I shall say
nothing of the Statue of Liberty, of the Brooklyn
Bridge, of the Riverside Drive, of the libraries
and the museums and the colleges and the churches; I shall even say nothing of Central Park, truly
the finest single work of art yet produced by any
American, and, simply as a work of art, unequalled
by any pleasure-ground of Europe."

There was another burst of applause, but the
speaker scarcely waited for it to die down before
he began again.

"Passing by these works of God and man, ever

present before our eyes, I am going to call your attention to things less material—to things which do not cling to our remembrance as they ought. Secure in our material prosperity, we New-Yorkers do not always recall those incidents in the history of the city which deserve to be forever memorable. We are not often accused of modesty—but we are over-modest, are we not?—when we allow our children to be taught that the first bloodshed of the Revolution was in the Boston Massacre, forgetting that the Liberty Pole fight took place in New York six weeks earlier. It was here in New York that the Stamp Act Congress met, the forerunner of the federation of the American colonies which cast off the British yoke. And in the long and weary war of the Revolution only one of the thirteen colonies furnished its full quota of men, money, and supplies—and that colony was the colony of New York!"

Once more was the speaker interrupted by a tumult of approval; and once more he went on again as soon as he could make himself heard.

"When the critical period in the history of this country came—that is, when the need of a new constitution was felt by all—no men had a larger share in the making of that constitution than two New-Yorkers, Alexander Hamilton and John Jay, while the nervous English of that great instrument was due to a third New-Yorker, Gouverneur Morris. It was in New York that the foundations of American literature were laid, by the pub-

lication of *Knickerbocker's History*, the earliest
book to be printed in America which keeps its
popularity to-day — and more than fourscore
years have not yet tarnished its humor.   To the
author of this immortal book, to Washington Irving, was due the first work of American authorship which won acceptance outside of the boun-
daries of the United States.   And as it was the
Sketch-Book of Washington Irving which was
the first American book to win its way in England, so it was the *Spy* of another citizen of
New York, Fenimore Cooper, which was the first
American book to achieve fame outside of the
English language.   It was here in New York that
our American literature was first fostered, as it is
here in New York that our American authors are
most abundant, most highly honored, and most
richly rewarded."

The speaker paused again, but only for a moment.

"As in letters, so in the arts.   Here in New
York the National Academy of Design was
founded, and later the Society of American Artists; and to two painters of New York, to Robert
Fulton and to Samuel F. B. Morse, we owe the
steamboat and the telegraph.   Here in New York
was founded the Children's Aid Society—than
which no city in the world has a nobler charity—
the first of the kind and the most successful.
Here in New York, also, Peter Cooper established
the first institution intended to provide instruc-
10

tion to all ambitious youth—an institution that
has been imitated in almost every city of the
Union, although no city of the Union has ever
had a citizen more esteemed or better beloved
than was Peter Cooper here in New York. It is
not in 'a city of kites and crows' that men of
Peter Cooper's character choose to dwell; it is
not in 'a city of kites and crows' that men of
Peter Cooper's character are cherished and re-
vered."

Here the speech was again broken into by prolonged applause. Men rose to their feet and
cheered, waving their napkins over their heads.

When there was quiet once more the speaker
went on:

"After years of peace and of prosperity, the
people of the United States suddenly found themselves face to face with armed rebellion, and war
loomed before us inevitable. New York was
ready then as always. The first regiment to
reach the capital of the country—to secure it
against traitors—was a regiment of New York
City militia. Nor was there ever after any lack
of men here in this city who despised the snares
of death and defied the pains of hell, and who
went into battle bravely, and gayly, and glad that
—in the words of one of them—glad that 'there
is lots of good fighting along the whole line.'
I have been told—I confess I have not been able
to verify the figures—but I have been told, that
the number of men who enlisted into the army

and the navy of the United States from this city of ours during those four long years of doubt and anxiety exceeded the number of the male inhabitants of fighting age in the year when the rebellion broke out. And not content with furnishing men to fight, the city of New York saw to it that the wounded were duly attended to and their anguish lightened as far as might be—for it was here that the United States Sanitary Commission was organized."

There where cheers once more and yet again, and it was not for a full minute that the speaker was enabled to continue.

"Your applause tells me that I need say no more," he began. "A successful city is the spoiled child of fortune, and perhaps, like other spoiled children, it is all the better for a sound thrashing now and then. But what has New York done amiss now, that she should be scourged with scorpions? In the welter of politics it may be considered adroit to suggest that your opponent is either a wolf in sheep's clothing or an ass in a lion's skin; but it is more adroit still, it seems to me, to avoid personality altogether. The louder the report of the gun, the more violent the kick is. When a New-Yorker hears his beloved town called 'a city of kites and crows' his first impulse is to laugh; his second is to inquire as to the man who said it; and his third is to laugh again and louder when he discovers that the author of this assertion is from Nevada, a state where even

Santa Claus on Christmas Eve does not dare go his rounds for fear of being held up by road-agents!"

This time a burst of hearty laughter mingled with the abundant applause as the speaker sat down.

"That's a very good speech," the young man who seemed to be a stranger said to his left-hand neighbor.

"Good speech?" echoed the other enthusiastically; "I should think so. It's the speech of the evening, sure! There's not one of them can beat that."

"I've been in Japan for the past five years, and I seem to have lost track of people here in the city," said the young man. "What is the name of the gentleman who made the speech?"

"Horace Chauncy," was the answer. "I thought everybody knew him. His father was United States Senator from West Virginia, and his mother was a famous Kentucky belle in her day. He himself used to be the leader of the California bar before he moved here a few years ago. He caught on at once in New York; he's one of the most popular speakers we have now; some fellows call him 'Our Horace.' Haven't you ever heard about him, really?"

"Well," the young man retorted, "you mustn't expect me to know all these people. You see, I was born in New York."

(1894.)

A THANKSGIVING–DAY DINNER

THANKSGIVING DAY had dawned clear and cold, an ideal day for the foot-ball game. Soon after breakfast the side-streets had been made hideous by small bands of boys, strangely disguised as girls some of them, or as Indians and as negroes, with improvised costumes and with staring masks; they blew fish-horns, and besought coppers. A little later in the day groups of fantasticals paraded on horseback or in carriages; and straggling target companies — some of them in the uniforms worn during the political campaign which had culminated in the election three weeks earlier—marched irregularly up the avenues under the elevated railroads, preceded by thin lines of pioneers, and by slim bands of music that played spasmodically before the many adjacent saloons, at the doors of which the companies came to a halt willingly.

The sun shone out and warmed one side of the street as people came from church; and the wind blew gently down the avenues, and fluttered the petals of the yellow chrysanthemums which expanded themselves in many button-holes. Little groups of young people passed, the girls with knots of blue at their throats or with mufflers of orange and black, the young men with college-buttons or with protruding handkerchiefs of the college colors. The fashionable dealers in men's goods had arranged their windows with impartial regard for future custom—one with blue flannels and scarfs, shirts and socks, and the other all orange and black. Coaches began to go by, draped with one set of colors or the other, and filled with young men who split the air with explosive cheers, while waving blue pennants with white letters, or yellow pennants with black. The sun shone brightly, and the brisk breeze shivered the bare branches of the trees. It rippled the flags which projected from the vehicles gathering at Madison Square and streaming up the avenue in thick succession — coaches, private carriages, omnibuses, road-wagons of one kind or another.

Towards nightfall the tide turned and the coaches began to come back, the young men hoarse with incessant shouting of their staccato college cries. Some of them, wild with joy at the victory of their own team, had voice still for exulting yells. Others were saddened into silence by the defeat of their side. Most of those who had gone out to see the game belonged neither to the college of the blue nor to the college of the black and orange, but they were all stimulated by the struggle they had just seen—a struggle of strength and of skill, of gumption and of grit. The sun had gone down at last, and the

bracing breeze of noon had now a touch of damp-
ness which chilled the flesh. But the hearty young
fellows paid no heed to it ; they cheered and they
sang and they cried aloud one to the other as
though the season were spring, and they were
alone on the sea-shore.

Robert White caught the fever like the rest,
and as he walked down the avenue to the College
Club he was conscious of an excitement he had
not felt for years. He was alone in the city for
a week, as it happened, his wife having taken the
children into the country for a long-promised visit;
and he had been spending his evenings at the College Club. So it was that he had joined in char-
tering a coach, and for the first time in a dozen
years he had seen the foot-ball game. He had
been made happy by the success of his own college, and by meeting classmates whom he had not
laid eyes on since their Commencement in the heat
of the Centennial summer. One of them was now
the young governor of a new Western State, and
another was likely to be a member of the new
President's cabinet.

On the way out to the game White had sat beside a third classmate, now a professor in the old
college, and they had talked over their four years
and their fellow - students. They recalled the
young men of promise who had failed to sustain
the hopes of the class ; the steady, hard-working
fellows, who were steady and hard-working still;
the quiet, shy man who had known little Latin

and less Greek, but was fond of science, and who was now developing into one of the foremost novelists of the country; the best base-ball player of the class, now the pastor of one of the leading churches of Chicago; and others who had done well for themselves in the different walks of life. They talked over the black sheep of the class—some dead, some worse than dead, some dropped out of sight.

"What has become of Johnny Carroll?" asked the professor.

"I have not seen him since class-day. There was some wretched scandal before Commencement, you know, and I doubt if Johnny ever got his degree," White answered.

"I know he didn't," the professor returned. "He never dared to apply for it."

"They managed to keep the trouble very quiet, whatever it was," White went on. "I never knew just what the facts were."

"I didn't know then," responded the professor; "I have been told since. But there is no need to go into that now. The girl is dead long ago, and Johnny too, for all I have heard."

"Poor Johnny Carroll," White said; "I can remember how handsome he looked that last night, the night of class-day. But he was always handsome and always well dressed. He was not very clever or very anything, was he? Yet we all liked him."

"I remember that he tried to get on the Fresh-

COMING FROM CHURCH

man crew," the professor remarked, after a pause, "but the temptations of high living were too much for him. He wouldn't train."

"Training was just what he needed most," White added; "moral and mental as well as physical. Fact is, he always had more money than was good for him. His father was in Wall Street then, and making money hand over fist."

"It wasn't till the year after we were graduated that old Carroll committed suicide, was it?" the professor inquired. "Blew out his brains in the bath-tub, didn't he?"

"And didn't leave enough money to pay for his funeral," White answered. "Johnny was in hard luck always: he had too much money at first, and none at all when he needed it most."

"His great misfortune," said the professor, "was that his father was 'one of the boys.'"

"Yes," White agreed, "that is pretty rough on a fellow. I wonder where Johnny is, if he is alive? Out West, perhaps, prospecting on a grub stake, or else stoker on an ocean steamer, or perhaps he's a member of the Broadway squad, earning a living by elbowing ladies over the crossing."

"I hope he has as good a berth as that," the professor answered; "but I don't believe that Johnny Carroll would stay on the force long, even if he got the appointment. Do you remember how well he sang 'The Son of a Gamboleer'?"

It was this question of the professor's which Robert White remembered after he had got off

the coach and was walking towards Madison
Square. Three young fellows, mere boys two
of them, were staggering on just in front of him.
They were arm in arm, in hope of a triplicate sta-
bility quite unattainable without more ballast than
they carried, and they were singing the song Johnny Carroll had made his own in college. The wind
was still sharpening, and the wooden signs which
projected across the sidewalk here and there swung
heavily as they felt its force. There were knots of
eager young men and boys going to and fro before
the brilliantly lighted porticos of the hotels.

As White stepped aside to get out of the way
of one of these groups, rather more hilarious than
the others, he knocked into a man who was standing up against the glaring window of a restaurant.
The man was thin and pinched ; his face was clean-
shaven and blue ; his clothes were threadbare ; his
attitude was as though he were pressing close to
the glass in the hope of a reflected warmth.

"I beg your pardon," cried White.

The man turned stiffly. "It's of no con—" he
began, then he saw White's face in the bright
light which streamed across the sidewalk. He
stopped, hesitated for a moment, and then turned
away.

The moment had been enough for White to recognize him. "Johnny Carroll !" he called.

The man continued to move away.

White overtook him in two strides, and laid a
hand on his shoulder. "Johnny !" he said again.

The man faced about and answered doubtfully, "Well, what do you want?"

"Is this really you, Johnny Carroll?" asked White, as he held out his hand.

"Oh yes," said the other, "it's Johnny Carroll —and you are Bob White."

White's hand was still extended. After a long pause his classmate took it. White was shocked at the chill of Carroll's fingers. "Why, man," he cried, "you are cold."

"Well," the other answered, simply, "why not? It isn't the first time." Then, after a swift glance at White's face, he turned his own away and said, "I'm hungry, too, if you want to know."

"So am I," said White, cordially. "I was going to have my Thanksgiving dinner alone. Will you join me, Johnny?"

"Do you mean it?" asked the other.

"Why shouldn't we dine together?" White responded, setting off briskly and putting his arm through his classmate's. "Our team has won to-day, you know—eighteen to nothing; we'll celebrate the victory."

"Where are you taking me?" inquired Johnny, uneasily.

"To the College Club, of course," answered White. "We'll—"

"I mustn't go there," said Johnny, stopping short. "I couldn't face them now. I — oh, I couldn't!"

"Very well, then," White agreed. "Where

shall we go? What do you say to Delmonico's?"

Again Johnny asked: "Do you mean it? Honest?"

"Of course I mean it, Johnny," he replied.

"I haven't been in Delmonico's for ten years and more," said the other. "I'd like to have just another dinner there. But you can't take me there. Look at me!"

White looked at him. The thin coat was buttoned tight; it was very worn, and yet it was not ragged; it was in better condition than the hat or the boots.

As the two men stood there facing each other on the corner of the street there was a foretaste of winter in the wind which smote them and ate into their marrow.

White linked his arm again in his classmate's. "I've seen you look sweller, Johnny, I confess," he said; "but I haven't dressed for dinner myself to-night."

"So it's Delmonico's?" Johnny asked.

"It's Delmonico's," White responded.

"Then take me into the café," said the other. "I can stand the men, I think, but I'm not in shape to go into the restaurant where the women are."

"Very well," agreed White. "We'll try the café."

When they entered the café it was crowded with young men. There was already a blue haze

of smoke over the heads of the noisy throng.
Boys drinking champagne at adjacent tables
were calling across to each other with boisterous
merriment.

White was able to secure a small table near
the corner on the Broadway side. As he walked
over to it he nodded to half a score of acquaintances, some of whom looked askant at his companion, and exchanged whispered comments after he
had passed.

Apparently Johnny neither saw the looks nor
heard the whispers. He followed White as if in
a dream ; and White had noticed that when they
had entered the heated room Carroll had drawn a
long breath as though to warm himself.

"I don't need an overcoat in here," he said, as
he took the chair opposite White's with the little
marble-topped table between them.

When the waiter had deftly laid the cloth,
Johnny fingered its fair softness, as with a cat-
like enjoyment of its cleanness.

"Now, what shall we have?" asked White, as
the waiter handed him the bill of fare in its narrow frame. "What would you like?"

"I?" the guest responded ; "oh, anything—
whatever you want—some roast beef."

"Then your taste has changed since you left
college," White declared. "I asked you what
you would *like*."

"What *I'd* like?" echoed Johnny. "Do you
mean it? Honest?"

White smiled as the old college phrase dropped again from the lips of his classmate.

"Of course I mean it," he said ; "honest. There's the bill of fare. Order what you please. And remember that it is Thanksgiving, and that I'm hungry, and that I want a good dinner."

"Very well, then," said Johnny, as he took the bill of fare. He was already warmer, and now he seemed to expand a little with the unwonted luxury of the occasion.

He looked over the bill of fare carefully.

"Blue Points on the half-shell, of course," he began, adding to the waiter, "be sure that they are on the deep shell. Green turtle soup — the green turtle here used to be very good fifteen years ago. *Filet de sole, à la Mornay*—the sole is flounder, I suppose, but *à la Mornay* a man could eat a Hebrew manuscript. Then a canvas-back apiece — two canvas-back, you understand, real canvas-back, not red-head or mallard—with samp, of course, and a mayonnaise of celery. Then a bit of Chedder cheese and a cup of coffee. How will that suit you, White ?"

"That will suit me," White responded. "And now what wine ?"

"Wine, too ?" Johnny queried.

White smiled and nodded.

"Well, I'll go you," the guest went on. "I might as well see the thing through, if you are bound to do it in style." He turned over the bill of fare and scanned the wine list on the under side. "Yquem '74 with the oysters; and they tell me there is a Silver Seal Special '84 *brut* that is better than anything one has tasted before. Give us a quart of that with the duck. And let us have it as soon as you can."

He handed the bill of fare to the waiter, and then, for the first time, he ventured to glance about the room.

The oysters were brought very soon, and when Johnny had eaten them and part of a roll, and when he had drunk two glasses of the Yquem, White said to him: "Tell me something about yourself. What have you been doing all these years?"

Johnny's face fell a little. "I've done pretty nearly everything," he answered, "from driving a Fifth Avenue stage to keeping books for a Third Avenue pawnbroker. I've been a waiter at a Coney Island chowder saloon. Two summers ago I waited on the man who has just taken our order—I waited on him more than once. I've dealt faro, too."

The waiter brought the soup and served them. When he left them alone again, White asked: "Can't some of your old friends help you out of this—give you a start and set you up again?"

"It's no good trying," Johnny replied. "You can't pull me up now. It's too late. I guess it was too late from the start."

"Why don't you drop this place?" White queried, "and go out West, and—"

11

"What's the use of talking about that?" Johnny interrupted. "I can't live away from New York. If I got out of sight of that tower over there I'd die."

"You will die here soon enough at this rate," White answered.

"That's so, too," admitted Johnny; "but it can't be helped now." He was eating steadily, sturdily, but not ravenously.

After the waiter had served the fish, White asked again, "What can we do for you?"

"Nothing," Johnny answered—"nothing at all. Yes, you can give me a five, if you like, or a ten; but don't give me your address, or the first time I'm down again I'd look you up and strike you for ten more."

A band of undergraduates, twenty of them or more, four abreast, arm in arm, went tramping down Broadway, yelling forth the chorus of a college song.

"You used to sing that song, Johnny," said White.

"I used to do lots of things," he answered, as the waiter opened the champagne.

"I never heard anybody get as much out of 'The Son of a Gamboleer' as you did," White continued.

"I joined a negro-minstrel troupe as second tenor twelve years ago, but we got stranded in Hartford, and I had to walk home. I've tried to do a song and dance in the Bowery dime museums since then, more than once. But it's no use."

When they had made an end of the canvas-backs and the *brut* '84, Johnny sat back in his chair and smiled, and said, "Well, this was worth while."

Then the coffee came, and White said, "You forgot to order the liqueur, Johnny."

"You see what it is to be out of practice," he replied. "I'd like some orange curaçoa."

"And I will take a little green mint," said White to the waiter. "And bring some cigars—Henry Clays."

"That's right," Johnny declared. "My father was always a Henry Clay man, and I suppose that's why I like those cigars."

After the cigars were lighted White looked his companion square in the face. "Are you sure," he asked, "that we can do nothing for you?"

"Dead sure," was the answer.

"Nothing?"

"You have given me a good dinner," said Johnny. "That's enough. That's more than most of my old friends would give me. And there's nothing more to be done."

White held his peace for the moment.

Johnny took a long sip of his coffee, and drew three or four times at his cigar. "That's a first-rate cigar," he said. "I haven't smoked a Henry Clay for nearly two years, and then I picked up one a man had lighted, between the acts, outside of Daly's."

He puffed at it again with voluptuous appreciation, and then leaned across the table to White and remarked, confidentially, "Do you know, Bob, 'most everything I've cared for in this world has been immoral, or expensive, or indigestible."

"Yes," White admitted ; "I suppose that's the cause of your bad luck."

"I've had lots of luck in my life," was the response, "good and bad—better than I deserved, most of it—this dinner, for example ; I should remember it even without to-morrow's dyspepsia. But what's the use of anticipating evil ? I'll let the next day take care of itself, and make the best of this one. There are several hours of it left— where shall we go now ?"

(1892.)

IN THE MIDST OF LIFE

IT was late in the afternoon when John Suydam turned into Twenty-third Street, and he remarked the absence of the gleam of color generally visible far away to the westward beyond the end of the street and across the river. There was no red vista that Christmas Eve, for the sky was overcast and lowering, and there was a damp chill in the air, a premonition of approaching snow. It was about the edge of dusk as he skirted Madison Square and saw the electric-lights twinkle out suddenly up and down Fifth Avenue, and in the square here and there.

The young man crossed Broadway, skilfully avoiding a huge express wagon, and springing lightly out of the path of a clanging cable-car. He crossed Fifth Avenue, threading his way through the carriages and the carts piled high with paper-covered packages. The white walls of the hotel on the opposite side of Twenty-third Street were dingy under the leaden sky as the haze of the swift twilight settled down. The wind died away altogether, and yet the atmosphere was raw and dank. Suydam bought an evening paper from the crippled newsboy who sat in his rolling-chair, warmly wrapped against the weather, and seemingly cheerful and contented with his takings.

A few steps farther the young man passed an old French sailor standing on the curb-stone, and using his single hand to wind the machinery of a glazed box, wherein a ship was to be seen tossing on the regular waves while a train of cars kept crossing a bridge which spanned an estuary. Almost under the sailor's feet there was an old woman huddled in a dirty heap over a tiny hand-organ, from which she was slowly grinding a doubtful and dolorous tune. By her side, but a little beyond, two boys were offering for sale green wreaths and stars and ropes of greenery, to be used in festooning. Close to the broad windows of a dry-goods store, whence a yellow light streamed forth, a tall, thin man had a board on a trestle, and on this portable table he was showing off the antics of a toy clown who tumbled artlessly down a steep flight of steps. The people who hurried past, with parcels under their arms, rarely stopped to look at the ship tossing on the waves, or to listen to the hesitating tune of the wheezy organ, or to buy a bit of green or a performing clown. Yet the open-air bazaar, as it might plainly be called, the out-door fair, extended all the way along the street, and on both edges of the sidewalk the fakirs were trying to gather in their scanty Christmas harvest.

Before John Suydam came to the corner of

Sixth Avenue the snow began at last to fall ; the first flakes descended hesitatingly, scurried by a brief wind that sprang up for a minute or two, and then died away absolutely. After a while the snow thickened and fell faster, sifting down softly and silently, but filling the air under the electric-lights which were clustered at the corner, and reddening under the glare of the engines on the elevated railroad overhead, as the cars rushed along girt with swirling clouds of steam. The snow clustered upon the boughs of the unsold Christmas-trees which stood irregularly along the sidewalk before a florist's a few doors down Sixth Avenue, and by the time Suydam had turned the corner, they looked like the shrouded ghosts of balsam pines.

All along the avenue he had to make his way through the same crowds of belated Christmas shoppers, hurrying in and out of the overgrown stores, availing themselves of their last chance to buy gifts for the morrow ; but as he advanced, the throng thinned a little, driven home perhaps by the snow-storm. Yet though the purchasers were fewer, the peddlers persisted. Suydam noted one old man, bent and shrivelled, and with a long gray beard, who had a tray before him hung on a strap over his shoulders, and on the narrow board were plaster figures of Santa Claus carrying aloft a branching Christmas - tree besprinkled with glittering crystalline flakes. Under the hood of the staircase of the station of the

elevated railroad he saw a little blind woman
wrapped in a scant shawl, silently proffering half
a dozen lead-pencils. And high over the centre
of the roadway the snow-clad trains thundered
up and down, with white plumes of steam trailing
from the engines.

As Suydam neared Fourteenth Street he found
the crowds compacting again; and at the corner
there was a chaos of carriages, carts, and street-
cars. The flights of stairs leading to the elevated
railroad station were packed with people bearing
bundles and boxes, most of them, ascending and
descending with difficulty, jostling one another
good-naturedly. Long lines of children of all
ages spread along the wide plate-glass windows
at the corner of one huge store, gazing wonder-
ingly at a caravan of toy animals in gorgeous
trappings, with chariots and palanquins, which
kept circling around in front of painted palm-
trees and gayly-decorated tents. The snow was
now falling fast, but still the young ones looked
admiringly and waited willingly, though their
hats were whitened, and though the soft flakes
melted on their capes and on their coats.

The mass of humanity clustering about these
windows forced Suydam almost to the edge of the
sidewalk; but this was the last crowd he had to
make his way through. Lower down there were
no solid groups, although the avenue was still
thronged. He was able to quicken his pace. So
he sped along, passing the butchers', where car-

casses of sheep and of beeves hung in line gar-
landed with ropes of evergreen ; passing the gro-
cers', where the shelves were battlemented with
cans of food ; passing the bakers', where bread
and cakes, pies and crullers, were displayed in
trays and in baskets. He glanced into the yellow
windows of candy-stores, and saw the parti-colored
sweetmeats temptingly spread out. He caught
a glimpse of more than one dealer in *delicatessen*
whose display of silver-clad sausage and heavy
pasty and wicker-work flask was enough to stim-
ulate the appetite of a jaded epicure. He saw
the signs of a time of plenty, but no one knew
better than John Suydam that just then there
was truly a season of want.

Night had fallen before he reached the court-
house, with its high roof and its lofty turret, before he came to the market, with its yawning
baskets of vegetables and its long rows of pendent turkeys beneath the flaring jets of gas. He
crossed the avenue and turned into a small street
—not here at right angles to the thoroughfare, as
are the most of the side streets of New York. At
last he stopped before a little house, an old two-
story building, worn with long use, and yet dignified in its decay. The tiny dwelling had a Dutch
roof, with two dormer-windows ; and it had been
built when the Dutch traditions of New Amsterdam were stronger than they are to-day.

The young man mounted the high stoop, on
which the snow was now nearly half an inch

thick. He rang the bell twice with a measured
interval between. The flying step of a girl was
heard, and then the door was thrown open, and
Suydam disappeared within the little old house.

As the door closed, the young man took the
young woman in his arms and kissed her.

"Oh, John," she said, "it is so good of you to
come on Christmas Eve. How did you manage to
get away?"

"I've only two hours," he answered, "and I
had to get something to eat, so I thought that
perhaps you—"

"Of course we can," the girl interrupted. "And
mother will be delighted. She has made one of
her old-fashioned chicken pies, and it's ever so
much too much for us two. It will be ready
at six."

"Then I know where I'm going to get my dinner," her lover returned, as he followed her into
the little parlor. "But I shall have to go back
as soon as I've had it. I've told them that I think
the office ought to be kept open till midnight, and
I said I'd stay. It would be a sorrowful thing,
wouldn't it, if any one who wants help couldn't
get it on Christmas Eve?"

"And there must be many who want help this
hard winter," said the girl. "I went as far as
Broadway this afternoon, on an errand for mother, and I passed six beggars—"

"Oh, beggars—" he began.

"Yes, I know," she interrupted again. "I did

not give them anything, though it seemed so cruel
not to. I knew what you thought about indis-
criminate charity, and so I steeled my heart. And
I suffered for it, too. I know I should have felt
happier if I had given something to one or two
of them."

"I suppose you did deprive yourself of the virtuous glow of self-satisfaction," Suydam admitted. "But that virtuous glow is too cheap to
be valuable. If we want to help our neighbor
really, we must practise self-sacrifice, and not pur-
chase an inexpensive self-gratification at the cost
of his self-respect."

"I should feel as though I wasn't spending
Christmas if I didn't give away something," she
protested.

"Exactly," he returned. "You haven't yet
freed yourself from the pestilent influence of
Dickens, though you have much more sense, too,
than nine women out of ten. You have blindly
followed the belief that you ought to give for
your own sake, without thinking whether it was
best for the beggar to receive. Dickens's Christmas stories are now breeding their third generation of paupers ; and I doubt if we can convince
the broad public of the absurdity of his sociology
in another half-century. It takes science to solve
problems ; hysteric emotionalism won't do it."

"You don't think all the beggars I saw to-day
were humbugs, do you ?" she asked.

"There isn't one chance in ten that any one of

the half-dozen is really in need," he answered; "and probably five out of the six have taken to begging partly out of laziness, and partly because they can beg larger wages than they can earn honestly."

"But there was one old man; he must have been forty, at least," urged the girl, "who was positively starving. Why, just as I turned out of Broadway, I saw him spring down to the gutter and pick up a crust of bread and begin to eat it greedily. I felt in my pocket for my purse, of course, but a gentleman had seen it, too, and he went up to the man and talked to him and gave him a five-dollar bill. Now, there was a real case of distress, wasn't it?"

Suydam smiled, sadly. "The starving man was about forty, you say? Tall and thin, wasn't he, with a thin, pointed beard, and a mark on his right cheek?"

The girl looked at him in wonder. "Why, how did you know?" she cried.

"That's Scar-faced Charley," he answered.

"And is he a humbug, too?" she asked.

"I followed him for two hours one afternoon last week," he explained, "and I saw him pick up that bit of bread and pretend to eat it at least twenty times. When I had him arrested he had more than ten dollars in his pockets."

"Well," the young woman declared, "I shall never believe in anybody again."

"But I don't see how it is Scar-faced Charley

is out to-day," Suydam went on. "We had him sent up for a month only, for the judge was easy with him. If he's out again so soon, I suppose he must have a pull of some sort. Those fellows often have more influence than you would think."

"He took me in completely," the girl admitted. "If Scar-faced Charley, as you call him, can act so well, why doesn't he go on the stage and earn an honest living?"

"That's the first thing that astonished me when I went to live in the University Settlement last spring, and began to study out these things for myself. I found beggars who were fond of their profession, and who prided themselves on their skill. What are you to do with them? And if you let them ply their trade, how are you going to distinguish them from those who are really in need?"

"It is all very puzzling to me," the girl confessed. "Since I've heard you talk, charity doesn't seem half as simple as it used to."

"No," said Suydam, "it isn't simple. In fact, it is about as complicated and complex a problem as the twentieth century will have to solve. But I'm coming to one conclusion fast, and that is that the way to tell those who need help from those who don't need it is, that the latter ask for it, and the former won't. New York is rich and generous, and there's never any difficulty about getting money enough to relieve every case of distress in the city limits—none whatever. The real difficulty is in getting the money to the people who really need it, and in keeping it from the people who ought not to have it. You see that those who ask for assistance don't deserve it—not once in fifty times; and those who deserve it won't ask for it. There are men and women—women especially—who will starve before they will face the pity of their fellows. Every day I hear of cases of suffering borne silently, and discovered only by accident."

"I've been wondering for a week if we haven't one of those cases in this house now," said the girl.

"In this house?" the young man repeated.

"I've been meaning to tell you all about it every day," she went on, "but I've seen so little of you, and when you do come we have so many things to talk about, you know."

"I know," Suydam repeated. He was seated by her side on the sofa, and his arm was around her waist. He drew her closer to him and kissed her. "Now tell me about your case of distress," he said.

"Well," the girl began, "this house is too big for mother and me alone, so we let one room on the top floor to two old ladies. They have been here since before Thanksgiving. They are foreigners—Cubans, I think. The mother must be seventy, and I can see she has been very handsome. The daughter is nearly fifty, I'm sure; and a more devoted daughter you never saw. She waits on her mother hand and foot. They didn't bring any baggage to speak of—no trunk, only just a little bag—and we saw at once that they

were very, very poor. They paid two weeks'
rent in advance, and since then they've paid two
weeks' more. A fortnight ago the daughter told
mother that they would be obliged if she would
let them defer paying the rent for a little while,
as a letter they were expecting had not come.
And I suppose that was so, for the postman never
whistled but the daughter came running down
stairs to see if there wasn't something for them.
But it hasn't come yet, and I don't believe they've
got enough money to get things to eat, hardly.
The daughter used to go out every morning, and
come back with a tiny little parcel. You see,
there's a gas-stove in their room, and they do
their own cooking. But she hasn't been out of
the house for two days, and we haven't seen either
of them since the day before yesterday, when the
daughter came to the head of the stairs and asked
if there was a letter for her mother. We can
hear them moving about overhead gently, but we
haven't seen them. And now we don't really know
what to do. I'm so glad you've come, for I told
mother I was going to ask you about them."

"Do you think they have no money ?" Suydam
asked.

"I'm afraid it's all gone," she answered. "And
they have no friends at all so far as we know."

"You say they are Cubans ?"

"I think they are. Their name is De los Rios—
Señora de los Rios, I heard the daughter call her
mother when she asked the postman about a letter."

12

"If it wasn't so late," said the young man, looking at his watch, "I would go to the Spanish Consulate. But it's nearly six now, and the consulate
is certain to be closed. If there is any reason to
think that they are actually suffering for want of
food, can't you find some feminine reason for in-
truding on them."

"I'm afraid we can't," she answered. "We
did try yesterday morning. When we found that
the daughter didn't go out for something to cook,
we misdoubted they might be hungry, and so we
talked it over and over, and did our best to hit on
some way of helping them. At last mother had
an idea, and she made a sort of Spanish stew —
what they call an *olla podrida*, you know. She
got the receipt out of the cook-book, and she took
it up and knocked at the door. They asked who
it was, and they didn't open the door but a little.
Mother told the daughter that she had been trying to make a Spanish dish, and she didn't know
as she'd got it right, and so she'd come up to ask
them as a favor if they wouldn't taste it, and tell
her if it was all right. You see that was mother's
idea. She thought she might get them to eat it
that way, and save their pride. But it wouldn't
do. The daughter said that she was sorry, but she
couldn't taste it then, she couldn't, nor her mother
either. They had no appetite then, and so they
couldn't judge of the *olla podrida*. She said they
had just been cooking some chops and steaks."

"Chops and steaks?" echoed Suydam.

"That's what she said," the girl continued.
"But of course that was only her excuse for refus-
ing. That was her way of impressing on mother
that they didn't need anything. So mother had
to give it up, and bring the stew down-stairs
again. Mother doesn't feel so badly about them,
however, because they had been cooking something yesterday. She smelt fish—yesterday was
Friday, you know."

"I know," repeated the young man; "but still
I—"

Just then the shrill whistle of the postman was
heard, and a sharp ring at the bell.

The girl jumped up, and went to the door. As
she opened it there came in the faint melody of
distant sleigh-bells, and the roar of the street already muffled by the snow.

She returned to the parlor with a long blue
envelope in her hand.

"Here is the letter at last," she said.

"What letter?" asked Suydam.

"The letter the old ladies are waiting for," she
answered, handing it to him.

He held it up nearer the single gas-jet of the
parlor and read the address aloud, "'Marquisa de
los Rios,' and it's registered."

"Yes," the girl returned, "and the postman is
waiting to have the receipt signed. He said he
guessed it was money or a Christmas present of
some sort, since it had so many seals on it. I
wanted you to know about it; but I'll take it
right up now."

She tripped lightly up-stairs, and John Suydam heard her knocking at the door of the room the two old ladies occupied. After an interval she rapped again, apparently without response. Then he heard her try the door gently.

Two seconds later her voice rang out in a cry of alarm : "Mother! mother! Oh, John!"

Suydam sprang up - stairs, and found her just outside of the door of the old ladies' room. She was trembling, and she gripped his hand.

"Oh, John," she said, "something terrible has happened ! It was even worse than I thought ! They really were starving !"

Then she led him silently into the room, where her mother joined them almost immediately.

After waiting five minutes the postman at the front door below became impatient. He rang the bell sharply and whistled again. He was kicking the snow off his boots and swinging his arms to keep warm, when at last the door opened and John Suydam appeared, with the long blue envelope in his hand.

"I'm afraid that you will have to take this letter away again," Suydam said to the postman. "There is no one here now to sign for it. The Marquisa de los Rios is dead !"

OUTLINES IN LOCAL COLOR

AN INTERVIEW WITH
MISS MARLENSPUYK

T was a chill day early in January, and at four in the afternoon a gray sky shut in the city, like the cylindrical background of a cyclorama. Now and then a wreath of steam chalked itself on the slate-colored horizon; and across the river, far over to the westward, there was a splash of pink, sole evidence of the existence of the sun, which no one had seen for twenty-four hours.

As Miss Marlenspuyk turned the corner of the side street she stood still for a moment, looking down on the long Riverside Drive and on the mighty Hudson below, flowing sluggishly beneath its shield of ice. She had long passed the limit of threescore years and ten, and she had been an indefatigable traveller; and as she gazed, absorbing the noble beauty of the splendid scene, unsurpassable in any other city she had ever visited, she was glad that she was a New-Yorker born and bred, and that it was her privilege to dwell where a vision like this was to be had for the asking. But while she looked lovingly up and down the solemn stream the wind sprang up again, and fluttered her gray curls and blew her wrappings about her.

161

Two doors above the corner where Miss Marlenspuyk was standing a striped awning stretched
its convolutions across the sidewalk and up the
irregular stone steps, and thrust itself into the
door-way at the top of the stoop. A pretty young
girl, with a pleasantly plump figure and with a
dash of gold in her fair hair, passed through
this twisting canvas tunnel just ahead of Miss
Marlenspuyk; and when the door of the house
was opened to admit them they entered together,
the old maid and the young girl.

The house was illuminated as though it were
already night ; the curtains were drawn, and the
lamps, with their fantastically extravagant shades
of fringed silk, were all alight. The atmosphere
was heavy with the perfume of flowers, which
were banked up high on the mantel-pieces and
the tables, while thick festoons of smilax were
pendent from all the gas-fixtures and over all
the mirrors. Palms stood in the corners and in
the fireplaces ; and at one end of the hall they
were massed as a screen, through which glimpses
could be caught of the bright uniforms of the
Hungarian band.

In the front parlor, before a broad table on
which there were a dozen or more beautiful bou-
quets tied with bows of ribbon, and under a bow-
er of solid ropes of smilax, stood the lady of the
house with the daughter she was that afternoon
introducing to society. The hostess was a handsome, kindly woman, with scarce a gray hair in

her thick dark braids. The daughter was, like her mother, kindly also, and also handsome ; she was better looking, really, than any of the six or seven pretty girls she had asked to aid her in receiving her mother's friends and acquaintances.

The young woman who had preceded Miss Marlenspuyk into the house happened also to precede her in entering the parlor. The hostess, holding her bunch of orchids in the left hand, greeted the girl pleasantly, but perhaps with a vague hint of condescension.

"Miss Peters, isn't it ?" said the lady of the house, pitching her voice low, but with an effort, as though the habit had been acquired late in life. "So good of you to come on such a nasty day. Mildred, you know Miss Peters ?"

Then the daughter stepped forward and smiled and shook hands with Miss Peters, thus leaving the mother at liberty to greet Miss Marlenspuyk ; and this time there was no trace of condescension in her manner, but rather a faint suggestion of satisfaction.

"Oh, Miss Marlenspuyk," she said, cordially, "this is a pleasure. So good of you to come on such a nasty day."

"It did blow as I came to the top of your hill here," Miss Marlenspuyk returned, "and I'm not as strong as I was once upon a time. I suppose that few of us are as frisky at seventy-five as we were at seventeen."

"I protest," said the hostess; "you don't

look a day older now than when I first met
you."

"That's not so very long ago," the old maid
answered. "I don't think I've known you more
than five or ten years, have I? And five or ten
years are nothing to me now. I don't feel any
older than I did half a century ago; but as for my
looks—well, the least said about them is soonest
mended. I never was a good-looker, you know."

"How can you say so?" responded the hostess, absently noting a group of new-comers gathering in the door-way. "Mildred, you know
Miss Marlenspuyk?"

"Oh yes, indeed I do," the girl said, heartily,
shaking hands with the vivacious old maid.

The young woman with the touch of gold in
her light hair was still standing by Mildred's
side. Noting this, and seeing the group of new-
comers breaking from the door-way and coming
towards her, the hostess spoke hastily again.

"Do you know Miss Peters, Miss Marlenspuyk?" she asked. "Well, at all events, Miss
Peters ought to know you."

Then she had just time to greet the group of
new-comers and to lower her voice again, and to
tell them it was so good of them to come on such
a nasty day.

The daughter was left talking to Miss Marlenspuyk and Miss Peters, but within a minute her
mother called her — "Mildred, you know Mrs.
Hitchcock?"

As the group of new-comers pressed forward the old maid with the bright blue eyes, and the young woman with the pleasantly plump figure, fell back a little.

"I've heard so much of you, Miss Marlenspuyk, from my grandfather," began the younger woman.

"Your grandfather!" echoed the elder lady. "Then your father must be a son of Bishop Peters?"

Little Miss Peters nodded.

"Then your grandfather was a great friend of my younger brother's," Miss Marlenspuyk continued. "They went to school together. I remember the first time I saw the Bishop—it must be sixty years ago — it was the day he was put into trousers for the first time! And wasn't he proud of them!"

Miss Peters joined Miss Marlenspuyk in laughing at this amusing memory.

Then the old maid asked, "Your father married in the South after the war, didn't he? Wasn't your mother from Atlanta?"

"He lived there till mother died; I was bo'n there," said the girl. "I've been No'th only two years now this Christmas."

"I don't suppose you found many of your grandfather's friends left. Nowadays people die so absurdly young," the old maid remarked. "Is your father here this afternoon?"

"Oh dear no," responded Miss Peters; "he

has to live in Southe'n Califo'nia for his health.
I'm in New Yo'k all alone."

"I'm sorry for you, my child," said the elder
woman, taking the girl's hand. "I've been alone
myself a great deal, and I know what it means.
But you must do as I did — make friends with
yourself, and cultivate a liking for your own society."

The younger woman laughed lightly, and answered, "But I haven't as cha'ming a companion
as you had."

Miss Marlenspuyk smiled back. "Yes, you
have, my child. I'm not an ill-looking old woman now, I know, but I was a very plain girl; and
I know it isn't good for any one's character to be
conscious that she's almost ugly. But I set out
to make the best of it, and I did. I thought it
likely I should have a good deal of my own society, and so I made friends with this forced ac-
quaintance. Now, I'm very good company for
myself. I'm rarely dull, for I find myself an
amusing companion, and we have lots of inter-
ests in common. And if you choose you can
also cultivate a friendship for yourself. But it
won't be as necessary for you as for me, because
you are a pretty girl, you see. That glint of
gold in your fair hair is really very fetching. And what are you doing here in New York
all alone?"

"I'm writing," Miss Peters replied.

"Writing?" echoed Miss Marlenspuyk.

"My father's in ve'y bad health, as I told you," the younger woman explained, "and I have to suppo't myself. So I write."

"But I don't think I've seen anything signed Peters in the magazines, have I?" asked the old maid.

"Oh, the magazines!" Miss Peters returned— "the magazines! I'm not old enough to have anything in the magazines yet. You have to wait so long for them to publish an article, even if they do accept it. But I get things into the weeklies sometimes. The first time I have a piece printed that I think you'd like, I'll send it to you, if I may."

"I will read it at once and with pleasure," Miss Marlenspuyk declared, cordially.

"I don't sign my own name yet," continued Miss Peters; "I use a pen-name. So perhaps you have read something of mine without knowing it."

"Perhaps I have, my child," said Miss Marlenspuyk. "I shall be on the lookout for you now. It must be delightful to be able to put your thoughts down in black and white, and send them forth to help make the world brighter and better."

Little Miss Peters laughed again, disclosing a fascinating dimple.

"I don't believe I shall ever write anything that will make the world better," she said; "and if I did, I don't believe the editor would take it.

I don't think that is just what editors are after nowadays—do you ? They're on the lookout for stuff that 'll sell the paper."

"Sad stuff it is, too, most of it," the old maid declared. "When I was a girl the newspapers were violent enough, and the editors abused each other like pickpockets, and sometimes they called each other out, and sometimes somebody else horsewhipped them. But the papers then weren't as silly and as cheap and as trivial as the papers are now. It seems as though the editors to-day had a profound contempt for their readers, and thought anything was good enough for them. Why, I had a letter from a newspaper last week —a printed form it was, too — stating that they were 'desirous of obtaining full and correct information on Society Matters, and would appreciate the kindness if Miss Marlenspuyk would forward to the Society Editor any information regarding entertainments she may purpose giving during the coming winter, and the Society Editor will also be happy to arrange for a full report when desired.' Was there ever such impudence ? To ask me to describe my own dinners, and to give a list of my guests ! As though any lady would do a thing like that !"

"There are ladies who do," ventured Miss Peters.

"Then they are not what you and I would call ladies, my child," returned Miss Marlenspuyk.

The face of the Southern girl flushed suddenly,

and she bit her lip in embarrassment. Then she mustered up courage to ask, "I suppose you do not read the *Daily Dial*, Miss Marlenspuyk?"

"I tried it for a fortnight once," the old maid answered. "They told me it had the most news, and all that. But I had to give it up. Nobody that I knew ever died in the *Dial*. My friends all died in the *Gotham Gazette*."

"The *Gazette* has a larger family circulation," admitted the younger woman.

"Besides," Miss Marlenspuyk continued, "I could not stand the vulgarity of the *Dial*. I'm an old woman now, and I've seen a great deal of the world, but the *Dial* was too much for me. It seemed to be written down to the taste of the half-naked inhabitants of an African kraal."

"Oh," protested the other, "do you really think it is as bad as that?"

"Indeed I do," the old maid affirmed. "It's worse than that, because the poor negroes wouldn't know better. And what was most offensive, perhaps, in the *Dial* was the unwholesome knowingness of it."

"I see what you mean," said Miss Peters, and again the color rose in her cheeks.

"There was that Lightfoot divorce case," Miss Marlenspuyk went on. "The way the *Dial* dwelt on that was unspeakable. I'm willing to allow that Mrs. Lightfoot was not exactly a nice person; I'll admit that she may have been divorced more times than she had been married—"

"That's admitting a good deal!" said the young woman, as the elder paused.

"But it is going altogether too far to say that, like Cleopatra, she had the manners of a kitten and the morals of a cat—isn't it?"

Miss Peters made no response. Her eyes were fixed on the carpet, and her face was redder than ever.

"Of course it isn't likely you saw the article I mean," the old maid continued.

"Yes," the younger responded, "I saw it."

"I'm sorry for that," said Miss Marlenspuyk. "I may be old-fashioned—I suppose I must be at my age—but I don't think that is the kind of thing a nice girl like you should read."

Again Miss Peters made no response.

"I happen to remember that phrase," Miss Marlenspuyk continued, "because the article was signed 'Polly Perkins.' Very likely it was a man who wrote it, after all, but it may have been a woman. And if it was I felt ashamed for her as I read it. How could one woman write of another in that way?"

"Perhaps the writer was very poor," pleaded Miss Peters.

"That would not be a good reason, and it is a bad excuse," the old maid declared. "Of course I don't know what I should do if I were desperately poor—one never knows. But I think I'd live on cold water and a dry crust sooner than earn my bread and butter that way—wouldn't you?"

Miss Peters did not answer this direct question. For a moment she said nothing. Then she raised her head, and there was a hint of high resolve in the emphasis with which she said, "It is a mean way to make a living."

Before Miss Marlenspuyk could continue the conversation she was greeted by two ladies who had just arrived. Miss Peters drew back and stood by herself in a corner for a few minutes as the throng in front of her thickened. She was gazing straight before her, but she was not conscious of the people who encompassed her about. Then she aroused herself, and went into the dining-room and had a cup of tea and a thin slice of buttered bread, rolled up and tied with a tiny ribbon. And perhaps fifteen minutes later she found herself in front of the hostess.

She told the hostess that she had had such a very good time, that she didn't know when she had met such very agreeable people, and that she was specially delighted with an old friend of her grandfather's, Miss Marlenspuyk. "Such a very delightful old maid, with none of the flavor of desiccated spinsterhood. She does her own thinking, too. She gave me some of her ideas about modern journalism."

"She is a brilliant conversationalist," said the hostess. "You might have interviewed her."

"Oh, she talked freely enough," Miss Peters responded. "But I could never write her up properly. Besides, I'm thinking of giving up newspaper wo'k."

Three ladies here came towards the hostess, who stepped forward with extended hand, saying, "So good of you to come on such a nasty day." Miss Peters availed herself of the opportunity, and made her escape.

It might be half an hour afterwards when Miss Marlenspuyk, having had her cup of tea and her roll of bread-and-butter, returned to the front parlor in time to overhear a bashful young man take leave of the hostess, and wish the hostess's daughter "many happy returns of the day."

As it happened, there was a momentary stagnation of the flood of guests when Miss Marlenspuyk went up to say farewell, and she had a chance to congratulate the daughter of the house on the success of her coming-out tea.

"Then I must tell you, Miss Marlenspuyk," said the hostess, "that you completely fascinated little Miss Peters."

"She's a pretty little thing," the old maid returned, "with excellent manners. That comes with the blood, I suppose ; she told me she was a granddaughter of the Bishop, you know. She isn't like so many of the girls here, who take what manners they have out of a book. They get them up overnight, but she was born with them. And she has the final sign of breeding, which is so rare nowadays—she listens when her elders are talking."

"Yes," the hostess replied, "Pauline Peters has pleasant manners, for all she is working on a newspaper now."

"On a newspaper?" repeated Miss Marlenspuyk. "She told me she was writing for her living, but she didn't say she was on a newspaper."

"She said something about giving it up as she went out," the hostess remarked; "but I shouldn't think she would, for she has been doing very well. Some of her articles have made quite a hit. You know she is the 'Polly Perkins' of the *Daily Dial*?"

"No," said Miss Marlenspuyk—"no, I didn't know that."

(1895)

A LETTER OF FAREWELL

THERE had been a hesitating fall of snow in the morning, but before noon it had turned to a mild and fitful rain that had finally modified itself into a clinging mist as evening drew near. The heavy snow-storm of the last week in January had left the streets high on both sides with banks that thawed swiftly whenever the sun came out again, the water running from them into the broad gutters, and then freezing hard at night, when the cold wind swept across the city. Now, at nightfall, after a muggy day, a sickening slush had spread itself treacherously over all the crossings. The shop-girls going home had to pick their way cautiously from corner to corner under the iron pillars supporting the station of the elevated railroad. Train followed train overhead, each close on the other's heels; and clouds of steam swirled down as the engines came to a full stop with a shrill grinding of the brakes. From the skeleton spans of the elevated road moisture dripped on the cable-cars below, as they rumbled along with their bells clanging sharply when they neared the crossings. The atmosphere was thick with a damp haze; and there was a halo about every

175

yellow globe in the windows of the bar-rooms at the four corners of the avenue. More frequent, as the dismal day wore to an end, was the hoarse and lugubrious tooting of the ferryboats in the East River.

Under the steps of the stairs leading up to the aërial station of the railroad overhead, an Italian street vender had wheeled the barrow whereon he proffered for sale bananas and apples and nuts. At one end of this stand was the cylinder in which he was roasting peanuts, and which he ground as conscientiously as though he were turning a hand-organ. A scant quarter past six o'clock it might have been, when he opened his fire-box to throw in a stick or two more of fuel and to warm his stiffened fingers in the flame. The sudden red glare, glowing through the drizzle, caught the eye of a middle-aged man who was crossing the avenue. So insecure was his footing that this momentary relaxation of his attention was sufficient cause for a false step. His feet slipped from under him and he fell flat on his back, striking just below the right shoulder-blade upon a compact mass of snow, hardened by the chilly breeze, and yet softer than the stone pavement.

The concussion knocked the breath out of him; and he lay there for a minute almost, gasping again and again, wholly unable to raise himself. As he struggled to get to his feet and to refill his lungs with air, he heard a shop-girl cry, "Oh, Liz, did you see him fall ? Wasn't it awful ?" And then he heard her companion respond, " I say, Mame, you ask him if he's hurt bad." Then two men stepped from the sidewalk and lifted him to his feet, while a boy picked up his hat and handed it to him.

" That's all right," said one of the men; " there ain't no bones broke, is there ?"

The man who had fallen was getting his breath back slowly. " No," he panted, " there's nothing broke "—and he cautiously moved his limbs to make sure.

" Ye've knocked the wind out of ye," the other man returned, " but ye'll get it again in a jiffy. Come into Pat M'Cann's here and have a drink ; that 'll put the life into ye again."

" That's it," agreed the man who had been helped to his feet—" that's it; get me into Pat M'Cann's—they know me there—I can rest a bit —then I'll be all right again in a little." He broke his sentences short, but even thus he was able to speak only with effort.

Taking him each by one arm, the two men helped him into the saloon almost at the door of which he had slipped. They led him straight up to the bar.

" Good-evenin', Mr. Malone," was the barkeeper's greeting. " The boss was after askin' for ye." Then seeing the ashen face of the newcomer, he added, " It's not well ye're lookin'. What can I give ye ?"

The man addressed as Malone was plainly attired; his clothes were tidy but shiny; his overcoat was thin, and it was now thickly stained down the back by the slush into which he had fallen. The bronze button of the Grand Army was in the buttonhole of his threadbare coat.

He steadied himself by the railing before the bar. "Ye may give me—a little whiskey, Tom," he said, still gasping, "and ask these gentlemen —what they'll take."

These gentlemen joined him in taking whiskey. Then they again assured him he would be all right in a jiffy; and with that they left him standing before the bar, and went their several ways.

There was nobody else in the saloon, for the moment, as it chanced; and Tom, the barkeeper, was able to give undivided attention to Mr. Malone.

"It's sorry the boss 'll be to hear of yer fallin' here at his door, an' he not there to pick ye up," he remarked. "But ye'd better bide till he comes in again. Ye'll not get your breath back so easy either — I've been knocked out myself, an' I know—though it wa'n't no ice that downed me."

"So Pat M'Cann wanted to see me, did he?" asked Malone, trying to draw a long breath and finding it impossible, as the bruised muscles of his back refused to yield. "Oh—well, then I'll sit me down here and wait."

"There's yer old place in the corner," Tom responded.

"I'll smoke a pipe," said Malone, moving away, "if I haven't broke it in my fall. No; I've got it right enough," he added, taking the brier-wood from the breast-pocket of his coat.

As Malone was shuffling slowly forward towards a table in a corner of the saloon, the street-door was pushed open and the owner of the bar-room entered—a tall man, with a high hat and a fur-trimmed overcoat. M'Cann went straight to the bar.

"Tom," he asked, "how many of those labor-tickets have I now in the glass there?"

Tom looked in a tumbler on the top shelf of a rack against the wall behind him. "There's five of 'em left," he answered.

"Barry M'Cormack will be in before we close and he'll ask ye for them, and ye'll give him three of them," said the owner of the saloon. "Tell him it's all I have. An' if Jerry O'Connor is here again wantin' me to go bail for his brother in the Tombs, ye must stand him off. I don't want to do it, ye see, an' I don't want neither to tell him I don't want to."

"An' what will I tell him, then?" asked the barkeeper. "Hadn't I better say ye've gone to Washington to see the Sinator?"

"Tell him what you please," responded M'Cann, "but be easy with him."

"I'll do what I can," Tom promised. "Ye

was askin' for Danny Malone before ye went out.
That's him now in the corner. It's a bad fall he
had out there on the ice. The drop knocked
him out—but there's no bones broken."

"What I've got to tell him won't make him
feel easier," returned M'Cann. "But I'll get it
over as soon as I can." And with that he crossed
the saloon to the farther corner, where Malone
had taken his seat before a little table.

Looking up as M'Cann came towards him,
Malone recognized the owner of the saloon and
tried to rise to his feet; but the suddenness of his
movement was swiftly resented by the strained
muscles of his back, and he dropped sharply on
the seat, his face wincing with the pain, which
also took his breath away again.

"Well, Dan, old man," said M'Cann, "so ye've
had a bad fall, sure. I'm sorry for that. Don't
get up !—rest yerself there, and brace up."

The tall frame of the saloon-keeper towered
stiffly beside the bent figure of the man who had
had the fall, and who now looked up in the face
of the other in the hope of seeing good news
written there.

"Well, Pat," he began, getting his breath
again, "I've had a fall—but it's nothin'—I'll be
over it—in an hour or two. I'm strong enough
yet—for any place ye can get me—"

He had fixed his gaze hungrily on the eyes of
the other, and he was waiting eagerly for a word
of hope.

The saloon-keeper lowered his glance and then cleared his throat. He had unbuttoned his overcoat and the large diamond in his shirt-front was now exposed.

Before he made answer to this appeal the elder man spoke again, overmastered by anxiety.

"Did ye see him?" he asked.

"Yes," was the response, "I saw him."

"An' will he do it for ye?" was the next passing question.

"He'd do it for me if he could, but he can't," returned M'Cann.

"He can't?" asked Malone. "An' why not?"

"Because the appointment isn't his, he says," the saloon-keeper explained. "He'd be glad to give the place to a friend of mine if he could, he told me—but there's the civil-service. He's got to follow that, he says, more by token that they raised such a row the last time he tried to beat the law."

"But I'm a veteran," pleaded the other, "I served my three years. The civil-service has got to count that, hasn't it?"

"Ye might be on the list this very minute, and it wouldn't do any good," the saloon-keeper responded; "there's veterans to burn on the list now!"

"My post will recommend me, if I ask 'em—won't that help?"

"Nothing will help, he says," M'Cann explained. "It isn't a pull that 'll do ye any good, or I could get ye the job myself, couldn't I ?"

"There ain't no influence that 'll help me, then ?" was the elder man's next question.

"As I'm tellin' ye, I done what I could, and I don't believe any man in the district couldn't do more," the saloon-keeper answered. "He says he'd rather give ye the job than not, but he can't. He's got to take the civil-service man."

"Then there ain't nothin' else you can do ?" asked Malone, hopelessly.

"I'd do anythin' I could," M'Cann replied. "But I don't see nothin' more to be done. That dog won't fight, that's all. The jig's up, there ain't no two ways about it. Of course, if I hear of anythin' else I'll tell ye—and I'll get it for ye, if I can. But it's been a pretty cold winter for the boys, so far; you know that well enough."

The other said nothing ; his head had fallen, and his eyes were staring vacantly at a box of sand across the saloon.

The saloon-keeper drew a breath of relief that the interview was over.

"Well," he said, turning away, "I must be goin' now. I've got to see the new man who's got that contract for fillin' in up on the Harlem."

"Don't think I ain't beholden to you, Pat," Malone declared, raising his head again. "Ye know I am that, and I know ye've done yer best for me."

"I did that," M'Cann admitted, taking the hand the other held out; "an' it's better I hope I can do some other time, maybe."

With that he shook Malone's hand gently and left the saloon, calling to the barkeeper as he passed, "I'll be back in an hour, if there's anybody wants me. An' make Danny Malone as comfortable as ye can. It's a bad shock he's had."

As the owner of the saloon left it three customers came in, and were served, and tossed off their drinks standing, and went out again; and the dank night-air was blown in as they swung open the outer door.

Then the barkeeper went down to the corner where Malone was sitting, with his pipe in his fingers, unlighted and unfilled, gazing fixedly at vacancy.

"Mr. Malone," he said, "is it better ye're feelin' now? Have ye got yer breath again?"

"Yes, yes," answered Malone, rousing himself, "I'm better now." And he tried to rise again; and again he sat down suddenly, seized with muscular pangs. "I'm better—but I'd best —stay here a while yet—I'm thinking."

"That's it," responded Tom, cheerfully, "get a rest here. Let me fill yer pipe for ye. There ain't nothin' so soothin' as a pipe, I don't think. An' I don't believe a drop of old ale would hurt ye, would it now?"

Five minutes later Dan Malone had his pipe alight in his mouth and a glass of ale before him

on the table. He drank the liquid slowly, barely
a mouthful at a time ; and he smoked irregularly
also, scarcely keeping the pipe alight. He sat
there by himself, limp on the seat, with his last
hope washed out of him.

Half an hour afterwards the saloon happened
again to be empty, and seeing the barkeeper at
liberty, Malone asked for the loan of an inkstand
and a pen, and for a sheet of paper and an envelope. When the table had been wiped off, and
these things were placed on it before him, he ordered another glass of ale, and he filled his pipe
again.

After he had taken a sip or two of the ale and
pulled four or five times at the pipe, he squared
himself painfully to the task of writing.

First, he addressed the envelope to " Hon.
Terence O'Donnell, Assembly, Albany"; then he
thrust this on one side to dry, and began on the
letter itself. His handwriting was more irregular than usual ; it had always been cramped and
straggling, but now it was shaky also.

" FRIEND TERRY,—Ime writing you this at Pat M'Canns,
and its the last letter you will ever have from me. I slipped
at the corner here and I fell flat on my shoulders and I
knocked all the wind out of me like I was a shut bellows. I
aint got it back yet. I will never have any strength again.
Ime only fifty, but I had three years in the Army of the
Potomac ; and fighting and sleeping in the swamp and laying out all day and all night with a wound in your leg—
thats fun you got to pay for sooner or later. Ime paying

for mine now. Ime feeling very old to-night and old
men ain't no good. If Ide been younger I doubt Mary
would have shook me for Jack. Your young yet Terry
and you got a good wife, God Bless her, and youll thrive,
for your square and a good friend. But you wont never
know what it is to have the woman you loved shake you.
That hurts and it hurts just as hard even if it is your
brother she marries. Jacks only my half brother you
know but it hurt all the same. Mary married him and
hes never forgive me for the wrong he did me then. And
Mary she sides with him. Thats natural enough I suppose—hes the father of her children—but that hurts too.
Hes been doing me dirt all this winter. I know it but I
aint never let on. Now I caught him setting the kids
against me too. And theyve been friendly, both of Marys
kids have. The one named for me is a good boy and,
Terry, if you can give him a helping hand any day do it
for my sake. Ime going to pawn my watch when I leave
here to buy a pistol with. But Ill put the ticket in the
envelope with this, and some day when your feeling flush
I wish you would take it out and give it to little Danny.
I always meant him to have it.

"I ask you now for this is the last letter I will write
you and I wont never see you again. Ime smoking the
last pipe I will ever smoke and Ive drunk half of my last
glass of beer. I shall think of you when I finish it, and
it will be drinking your health and Maggies and the baby
boy your expecting.

"Ime going to quit. Ime tired, and I aint never felt so
old as I do since I had that fall an hour ago. It knocked
more out of me than wind. I was thinking Pat M'Can
here could get me a job, but he cant for fear of the civil
service. So its time I quit for good and all. Ime going
to put up my watch and get a gun. Then Ime going up
to Jacks. Mary cant refuse me a bite. Its little enough
to give me Ime thinking and its the last time Ile ask it

too. The kids are going out to a party—a sunday school
party it is. Ile see them all once more, and Ile say good-
by to them. After supper when the kids are gone I will
get out the pistol and I will put the bullet where it will
do most good. May be Jack will be sorry when its too
late may be Mary will too. I dont know. If they had
treated me white first off, I woodent need to buy no gun
now.

"Good-by now, Terry, and God Bless you all. Its time
I was going along to Marys if I want to see the kids again.

"Your old friend

"DAN MALONE."

When he had made an end of the letter he
had a pull or two at his pipe, and then he finished his beer. He took up what he had written
and read it over carefully to see if he had said
all that needed to be said. Satisfied, he folded
it and tucked it inside the envelope. After four
or five whiffs more his pipe was smoked out.
He emptied it on the table with a sharp rap, and
methodically put it back in the breast-pocket of
his coat.

Then he raised himself to his feet slowly and
carefully, not knowing just what bruised muscle
he might chance to stretch by an inadvertent
gesture. He shuffled across to the bar and paid
for his drinks, and asked the barkeeper if there
was a stamp to be had. As it happened, Tom
was able to give him one, which he stuck on the
corner of the envelope.

"Say, Mr. Malone," asked the barkeeper, " ye
don't want no tickets for the Lady Dazzlers' Co-

terie Mask and Civic Ball, to-night, do ye ? It's goin' to be the most high-toned blow-out they ever had."

" I'm not goin' to balls any more," Malone answered, " I'm too old now."

Buttoning his thin overcoat tightly across the chest, he held out his hand to Tom, to the barkeeper's great surprise.

"Good-bye," he said, " Good-bye. Maybe I won't see you again, Tom."

"Good-bye, Mr. Malone," Tom answered. "But ye'll be better in the mornin,' I'm thinkin'."

" Yes," the elder man repeated, " I'll be better in the mornin'. Yes ; I'm goin' to make sure of that, to-night."

When he opened the outer door of the saloon the damp moisture suddenly filled his lungs and he choked, but he dared not cough, as the strained muscles of his side warned him.

Two doors above the saloon was a pawnbroker's office, with the three golden balls hanging over the door, and with the unredeemed pledges offered for sale in the broad window. Into this store Malone made his way, glad to get out of the dank air, if only for a moment.

In perhaps five minutes he came forth holding in his hand the envelope addressed to the Honorable Terence O'Donnell. He paused on the threshold of the pawnshop and, by the light of the gas - jets in its window, he put the pawnticket into the letter and then closed it. In the large right-hand pocket of his thin overcoat there was something that had not been there when he entered the pawnbroker's—something irregular in shape; it was the revolver he had bought with the money advanced on his watch.

He turned down the avenue again, for there was a letter-box on the lamp-post at the corner occupied by M'Cann's saloon. The store between the pawnbroker's and the barroom was an undertaker's; and Malone, walking slowly past, saw in the window a little coffin, lined with white satin.

"It'll take a bigger one than that for me," he said. "To-night's Friday—they'll be havin' the funeral on Sunday."

At the corner he dropped the letter into the box on the lamp-post, just as there came a weird shriek from an impatient tug in the river far behind him. While he was waiting for a cable-car a lame newsboy limped up to him and proffered the evening papers with a beseeching look. Malone felt in his pocket and found only two coins, a nickel and a quarter. He gave the quarter to the newsboy. Then he lifted himself painfully on the rear platform of a cable-car, and handed the nickel to the impatient conductor. The car clanged forward again; and soon the halo about its colored lamp faded away in the murky distance.

(1895)

A GLIMPSE OF THE UNDER WORLD

IT was a little dinner indeed, a dinner for eight only; and it was given one evening in March, in a spacious and handsome dwelling in Madison Avenue, high up on the slope of Murray Hill. The wide dining-room was at the rear of the house, and it had a broad butler's-pantry extending into the yard behind. The large kitchen was under the dining-room; and under the butler's-pantry was a room of the same size which the servants used as a parlor. In one corner of this sitting-room for the domestics was the dumb-waiter which connected with the pantry above, and in another corner was a spiral staircase which allowed the butler to descend swiftly to the kitchen in case of emergency. There was a table near the window of this servants' parlor, with a battered student-lamp on it; and around the table were grouped three or four chairs.

A whistle sounded gently in the kitchen, and the Swedish cook walked leisurely to the speaking-tube and whistled back. Then she listened, and heard the butler say, "They're all here now; I've got the oysters on the table, and I'm a-goin' in now to announce dinner to the madam. So you get that soup ready—do you hear?"

The cook did not deign to make any direct reply, but, as she left the speaking-tube and went back to the range, she said, loud enough to be heard by the servants in the sitting-room adjoining, "As though I did not know anything! I will never have another place if a black man is butler."

In the room under the pantry a sharp, wiry boy was grinning. "They're allus havin' spats, ain't they, them two? If I was Cato I wouldn't let no Dutch cook sass me, even if I was a nigger, would you?"

"Who is this young cub, when he's at 'ome?" asked the clean-shaven, trim-looking young British valet.

"He's Tim," answered the Irish laundress.

"I'm Tim," said the boy, indignantly, "that's who I am, and I'm as good as you are, too, for all you belong to a lord! And you needn't put on no frills with me, neither, for when I'm a year or two older I can lick ye!—see?"

"Don't ye mind the boy, Mr. Parsons," the Irish girl intervened. "He's no call here at all, at all. He'd run of an errand belike in the mornin' and does be sthrivin' to make himself useful. That's why they kept him here the night."

"I've got just as good a right here as he has," the boy declared, "and he doesn't come here after you either, Maggie—you're not his steady. It's that French Elise he is sparkin'."

"An' greatly I care if he is! Sparkin', in

truth! Bad cess to yer impidence," said the pleasant - faced laundress, drawing herself up. "A man, is it? It's lashins and lavins of men I could have if I'd a mind."

Fortunately the cook called Tim at this juncture and gave him a chore to do; and so left the Irish girl and the young Englishman alone.

The valet had been standing until then with his hat and cane in his hand and his overcoat across his arm. Now he laid these things on the table and took his seat by the side of the comely Irishwoman.

"Mam'zelle," he began, "is a French girl, of course, and I never could abide a foreign lingo. Now it's a pleasure for me to hear you talk, Miss Maggie."

"Ah, do be aisy, now, Mr. Parsons," she returned, coquettishly.

"It's gospel truth," he rejoined. "I enjoy talkin' to you. You keep your eyes wide open and can always tell me what's goin' on!"

"Troth, can I?" replied the laundress. "I know which ind of the egg the chicken 'll be after chippin'—every time."

"Then tell me who's dinin' 'ere to-night," the valet asked.

Before she could answer the whistle sounded faintly again, and the cook immediately brought in the green-turtle soup in the handsome silver tureen, and sent it up on the dumb - waiter. Then she returned at once to the kitchen.

"It's not a big dinner," the Irishwoman explained. "There's only eight of them. There's us three, isn't there?—Mr. and Mrs. Van Allen and Miss Ethel. Then there's your lord—and I'll go bail it's Miss Ethel he's after now? He'll be the lucky man if he gets her, too; it's a sweet angel she is."

"She won't be so unlucky to 'ave 'im neither," the Englishman returned, "mark that! She'll be Lady Stanyhurst, won't she? And my lord is a fine figure of a man, too!"

"Sure it isn't under the skin of any man that ever stepped to be worthy the likes of Miss Ethel!" said Maggie, looking at Parsons out of the corner of her eye.

"There ain't any girl in the States 'ere that wouldn't be proud to 'ave my lord," the valet retorted. "There's lots of 'em settin' their caps for 'im now. He can 'ave 'is pick, 'e can."

"The sorra cap Miss Ethel 'll set for him or any man," the laundress declared. "The boy that wants her 'll have to court her."

"I 'ave reason to believe that the marriage is arranged," Parsons asserted. "I 'ope—" then he paused, and with an effort he went on again: "I hope that 'er father is a warm man? He's good to give the girl a plum at least, I 'ope? We couldn't throw ourselves away on a girl who 'adn't a plum, you know."

"An' what might a plum be?" asked Maggie.

"A plum," the young Englishman explained,

"is a 'undred thousand pounds—'alf a million dollars, isn't it?"

"It's a whole million Mr. Van Allen can give Miss Ethel," Maggie said, "and more, too, if he wanted to. By the same token, they do be after tellin' me he has one big building downtown somewhere — I don't know — where the tenants pay him a hundred thousand dollars a year; an' they pay it, too, regular, an' nivver an eviction from one year's end to the other."

The whistle shrilled out again, and the cook made haste to place on the dumb-waiter the dish containing the fillets of sea-bass.

A few minutes later Mlle. Elise, the French maid of Miss Van Allen, entered the servants' sitting-room, and was cordially greeted by Mr. Parsons. It appeared that the Frenchwoman had been detained in Mrs. Van Allen's room relieving the guests of their wraps.

"Zat ole maid, Miss Marlenspuyk—what devil of name it is—" said Elise, "she is a true grande dame; but that Mistress Playfair—oh! I cannot suffer her! She is—how you say—made up? stuck up?"

"It's both stuck up and med up she is," the Irish laundress declared. "She's that painted her own mother wouldn't know her. An' as for stuck up, her manners is that bad there isn't none of her girls will stay in her house the second month; they gets their bit of money and they goes. Sure my brother is coachman there, and it's seven years he's had the place."

"How can he rest zere," asked the French maid, "if she is so stuck up?"

"Ah, my brother is a steady lad, and they get on very well," Maggie returned. "He knows his place, and she knows her place, too. She never says nothin' to him, and he never says nothin' to her. An' it's a good job he has, an' he don't mean to let go of it. He keeps a still tongue in his head, Danny does; but there's months when, with his wages and with his board-wages and with what he makes on the feed, the place is worth more than a hundred dollars to him."

"It's as much as a man's place is worth sometimes to accept the commission you're entitled to," the valet remarked.

"Ah, but Danny's the boy!" the laundress responded, shrewdly. "It's too much he knows about Mrs. Playfair for him to lose the job; trust him for that! As long as he wants that place he can have it an' welcome; she won't never say nothin' to him."

"Is she a widow or is she divorced, zis Mistress Playfair?" asked the French maid.

"She's the wan an' the other," said the laundress, with a laugh. "Mr. Playfair, he took and died a week after the trial, barrin' a day."

"What's this I 'ear about your Mr. Van Allen and Mrs. Playfair?" Parsons inquired.

"Is there anything between them, do you think?"

The whistle was heard again, and the cook passed before them with a saddle of mutton; and for the moment the valet's question remained unanswered.

"Who is it they have to dinner, after all?" the laundress inquired. "There's our three and your lord and Miss Marlenspuyk and Mrs. Playfair—but that's sure only six. There was to be eight all out, I'm thinkin'. It's two more men they must have."

"I heard his lordship say that he expected to meet the Lord Bishop of Tuxedo," the Englishman remarked.

"And madame say zat ze judge would be here," said the French maid.

"Judge Gillespie?" asked the valet, with a certain interest.

"Yes," the Frenchwoman answered, "the Judge Gillespie. What does that make to you zat you jump like zat?"

"Oh, nothin', nothin' at all," returned Parsons, settling himself back in his chair with a snigger.

"Out with it!" cried the Irish girl. "Don't be grinnin' all night there like a stuck pig! Out with it—I see it's on tho end of your tongue."

"But yes—but yes," urged the maid, "what is it you have to laugh?"

"Really," the valet began, "I don't know that I ought to say anything 'ere in this 'ouse, you know — house, I mean. But I 'ave been told that this 'ere Judge Gillespie is a very great friend of Mrs. Van Allen's. Mind, I don't say there's anything wrong in it, you know. I only tell you what I 'ave 'eard tell myself in society 'ere and there. You see this ain't the only 'ouse I visit in New York, not by a long shot it ain't. And knowin' I visit 'ere, why, naturally, you see, my other friends tell me the news, you know — the news about the goin's on 'ere, you know."

The Irish laundress and the French maid looked at each other for a moment, and then both laughed.

"It's not outside they get the first news, is it?" the laundress inquired.

Apparently the maid was also going to make a remark, but she changed her mind as the cook again came to the dumb-waiter with the dish of little silver saucepans containing terrapin.

The valet was somewhat puzzled by the failure of his two attempts to open the family cupboard of the host and hostess for an inspection of the skeletons it might contain.

"I don't know how she has them seated at the table," Maggie declared.

"Of course, his lordship took her in," the Englishman declared. "A earl 'as precedence of a judge or a bishop."

"I'd like to have a look at that lordship of

yours," the Irishwoman said, as she rose to her feet. "I'll slip up the stairs there, and maybe I can get a glimpse of 'em through the door an' no one a ha'p'orth the wiser. Is it a young man your lordship is ?"

"His lordship is a young man yet," the valet replied.

"I know what that means," the laundress answered. "If he's a young man yet, I'll go bail he hasn't a hair between him an' heaven. An' to think that our Miss Ethel here is to take up with a poor hairless cratur like that. Well, well, there's no accountin' for tastes ! Maybe I'll marry a Dutchman myself one of these days."

And with that she began to climb the spiral staircase in the corner of the room.

"What sort of a man is he, your milord ?" asked the Frenchwoman.

"He is not a bad sort at all," the Englishman answered. "Your young lady might do worse than 'ave 'im, you know—have him, I mean. I won't say but that 'e's been a bit fast in 'is time, you know ; but that's nothin' to her now, is it ? 'E's sowed his wild oats long ago, and 'e's ready to marry now and settle down."

"He is zen—*défraîchi*—how you say—worn ? your milord ?" the Frenchwoman went on. "And mademoiselle is an angel of candor. Zey would give her *le bon Dieu* wizout confession."

"Angel or no angel," returned Mr. Parsons, "there isn't any better catch in the three king-

doms than 'is lordship to-day. 'E's a earl, isn't
'e ? And then there's the castle ! Your young
lady wouldn't be in a 'urry to let 'im go if she'd
only seen the castle, now !"

" Mademoiselle has seen ze castle," was the
answer.

" Well, I'll be damned !" said the valet.

" But yes," the French maid explained. " Last
summer, in London, your milord was presented to
mademoiselle, and he began to make his court.
Fifteen days after, when we were at Leamington,
mademoiselle and I, we go see your castle."

" It's a tip-topper now, ain't it ?" he asked.
" There's sometimes twenty and thirty of us in
the servants' 'all, and there's goin's on, and larks,
and all manner of sport. If this match comes
off, now, between 'is lordship and your young
lady, will you come with her or stay here with
her mother ?"

" Never of the life do I quit mademoiselle,"
the Frenchwoman responded.

" Then I'll 'ope to 'ave the honor of introducin'
you into the best society at the castle whenever
you come over," urged Mr. Parsons.

The Irish laundress now began to descend the
spiral stairs. The cook also came into the room
and went towards the dumb-waiter, carrying a
silver platter, on which shook and shone a dozen
little jellied cones.

" An' what might that be in thrimbles like
that ?" asked the Irishwoman, with curiosity.

"*Pâté de foie gras en aspic*," the cook responded, curtly, sending up the dish and then returning silently to the kitchen.

"Patti's photograph?" repeated the laundress.
"Do ye mind the impidence of her, tellin' me a
lie like that?"

The English valet looked at the French maid
and laughed. Then he explained, patronizingly:

"Patty de four grass, as we call it in French—
not Patti's photograph. It's a delicacy, and it's
made of goose livers."

"Then why couldn't that Dutch cook have
said so?" the laundress asked, indignantly.
"I've as good a right to know about a goose as
ever she has. I misdoubt she was that poor
where she came from they had never the grass
of a goose to their cabin."

"Did you see 'is lordship?" asked the valet.

"I did that," the Irish girl replied, "an' what
did I tell you about him? His head has grown
through his hair! There's been good and bad
harvests since he was young, I'm thinkin'—and
it's mighty quare he looks about his eyes, too.
It 'll be a poor day for Miss Ethel when she marries a bald-headed ould runt like that, for all he's
a lord!"

"Oh, I say, Miss Maggie; you must not speak
so disrespectful of his lordship," Parsons insisted; "really, now, you mustn't."

"It's that Mrs. Playfair 'ud be the match for
him, I'm thinkin'," said Maggie. "It's a bold-

faced creature she is, an' no more clothes on her than ain't decent anyway. And then, how she looked at Mr. Van Allen and then at the bishop; and how she talked—I'd no patience with her. Do ye mind what it was I heard her say now ?"

"How could we know what you 'eard her say ?" the valet responded, impatiently.

"Sure, amn't I tellin' ye ?" the Irish girl returned. "She was talkin' to the bishop, and she says, says she. 'The judge is a better man than you, bishop,' she says, 'leastwise he makes more people happy,' she says. 'How so ?' says the bishop, says he. 'This way,' she says; 'when you marry a couple you make two people happy,' she says, 'an' when the judge divorces a couple he makes four people happy,' she says. Miss Ethel and the old lady with the white hair, they said nothin', but the rest of them laughed."

What further fragments of the conversation at the dinner-table up-stairs Maggie had been able to gather during her brief visit to the butler's-pantry could not then be made known to the other domestics, for Tim came slouching into the sitting-room.

"Say, Maggie," he began, "didn't you hear that ring at the bell ? That's your feller—I seen him. He's out at the gate now."

"Is it the letter-man you mean ?" asked Maggie, adjusting her hair as she passed the looking-glass.

"Ah, go on," returned Tim, impatiently,

"what t'ell are you givin' us ?   How many fellers do you want, say ?"

After Maggie had chased Tim out of the room, the Swedish cook went to the dumb-waiter once more to send up the four smoking canvas-backs that lay luxuriously on their cushions of fried hominy.

The French maid and the English valet continued to chat, discussing chiefly the personal peculiarities of the members of the households in which they had served. His former masters Parsons was willing enough to find fault with, but Lord Stanyhurst he seemed to think it a point of honor to defend. Mrs. Van Allen the Frenchwoman had no high opinion of, nor of Mr. Kortright Van Allen ; but of their daughter, Miss Ethel Van Allen, she could not say too much in praise.

"I told that wild Irish girl that the marriage was arranged," said Parsons, "and I'm sure I 'ope so with all my heart, for 'is lordship needs money badly—I don't mind tellin' you, mam'-zelle, 'e 'asn't paid me my wages this six months, not that I'd demean myself by askin' for them. But is it really settled, after all ?—that's what I'd like to know."

"I zink so," the Frenchwoman responded ; "you see, mademoiselle is not happy here.   Monsieur and madame are at drawn knives.   Zey have not spoken since two years."

"Mr. and Mrs. Van Allen don't speak to each

other ?" asked Parsons, with great interest. "But they must be speaking to each other there at dinner now."

"Oh, at dinner, yes," the French maid explained; "in the world, yes, zey talk zemselves. But at ze house, never a word. Zat is so sad for mademoiselle, is it not? It is not remarkable zat she marry herself with anybody to get out of ze house."

"Oh, ho!" rejoined the valet, "I see, I see! But if that's the way she's been brought up, you know, I don't believe she will 'it it off with 'is lordship."

"If he makes her not happy, your milord—" began the maid, forcibly, "but he must. He must render her happy, for she will have nobody to go to after ze marriage except her husband."

"Whatever do you mean by that?" asked Parsons, a little suspiciously.

"I know what I mean," she responded. "Monsieur and madame only attend till mademoiselle is married, and zen zey are divorced. Zey don't tell me zat, no—but I know."

"Yes," the valet admitted, "it ain't so very 'ard to find out a thing like that."

"And I know more yet," added the French maid. "I am not blind, am I? I can see that two and two make four, is it not? Zen, I tell you zat after ze marriage of mademoiselle, monsieur and madame are divorced, zat is one zing. Zen madame will marry zat Judge Gillespie, and monsieur will marry zat Madame Playfair—you see !"

"That would be a rum start, now, wouldn't it ?" was the only comment of Parsons.

At this moment the portly form of Cato, the black butler, was seen descending the staircase in the corner of the room.

As soon as the aged negro's white head was visible he paused, and leaning over the light iron railing he addressed himself to the young Englishman.

"Misto' Parsons," he said, solemnly, "yo' lord knows a good thing when he gets it, sah ! He tasted my celery salad, and he said to Mrs. Van Allen that he hadn't never eaten no better salad than that, sah, and I don't believe he never did, neither !"

So saying he slowly withdrew up-stairs again, as the cook advanced to the dumb-waiter carrying the Nesselrode pudding.

(1896)

A WALL STREET WOOING

IT had poured all the night before, and even now, at three o'clock in the afternoon, the air had the washed clearness that follows a warm rain. Fortunately the sun had shone forth before the church bells summoned the worshippers to kneel in front of the marble altars, banked high with scentless white flowers. It was Easter, and the first of April also ; and, furthermore, the first warm Sunday of the spring. So the young men and maidens who clustered about the doors of the churches that afternoon were decked out in fresh apparel—the young men in light overcoats, and the maidens in all the bravery of their new bonnets.

In the corner of one of the cable-cars which were sliding along under the skeleton of the elevated railroad there sat a young man looking at his neighbors with begrudging interest, and pulling at the ends of an aggressive black mustache. Filson Shelby was not yet at home in the great city, and he knew it, and he silently protested against it. He was forever on the watch for a chance to resent the complacent attitude of city folks towards country people. Yet the metropolis had so far conquered him

that his hat and his shoes and his clothes were
city made.

It was six months now since the young Southwesterner had left his native village, and already
he thought that he knew New York pretty well,
from Harlem where he boarded to Wall Street
where he worked. He was sure that he was well
informed as to the customs of New-Yorkers, although the New-Yorkers changed their customs
so rapidly that it was not so easy to be certain
about this.

There were white flowers blossoming in the
parlor windows of many of the houses in Fifty-
third Street, through which the cable-car was
passing, and as the car clanged around the curve
and started on its way down Seventh Avenue it
grazed the tail of a florist's wagon, the box of
which was piled high with palms. Filson Shelby
was aware that it was now a practice of New-Yorkers to give one another potted plants at Easter.

He had been told also that the habit no longer
obtained of paying calls on Sunday afternoon ;
and none the less was he on his way down to
Wall Street to take out for a walk the one girl
in New York who seemed to him to have the unpretending simplicity of the girls of the South-
west. What did he care, he asked himself, whether or not it was fashionable to call on girls Sunday
afternoon ? What right had the New-Yorkers,
anyhow, to assume that their way of doing things
was the only right and proper way ?

Having propounded these questions to himself, he answered them with a smile, for he had a saving sense of humor, and even a tendency towards self-analysis, and he had long ago detected his own pride in living in New York. In his earliest letters home he had expressed his delight in that he was now at the headquarters of the whole country; and he had written these letters on broad sheets of paper bought in the German quarter, and adorned with outline views of the sights of the city, picked out in the primary colors. He had sent missives thus decorated not only to his family and to his old friends, but even to mere acquaintances of his boyhood, for whom he cared little or nothing, except that they should know him to be settled in the metropolis. He could not but suspect that if he were now to go back to the village of his birth, he would seem as stuck-up to the natives as the New-Yorkers had seemed to him the first few weeks he was in the city.

The car slipped down Seventh Avenue, and stumbled into Broadway, and sped along sometimes with a smooth swiftness and again with a jerky hesitation. Gayly dressed family groups got on and got off, and the car had almost emptied itself by the time it came to Madison Square. Filson Shelby was greatly interested in the manners of two handsomely gowned girls who sat opposite to him, and who did not know each other very well. It struck him that one of them

—the prettier of the two, as it happened—was a little uneasy in the other's company, and yet pleased to be seen with her. To his regret, both of them alighted at Grace Church, leaving only half a dozen people in the long car as it started again on its journey down-town.

He set down the plainer of the two as a member of the strange society known as the "Four Hundred," about which he had heard so much since he had been reading the Sunday papers. If he were right in this ascription, and if he were to judge by this sample, the girls of the Four Hundred were not a very good-looking lot, for all they were so stylishly dressed. It struck him, too, that this girl's manners were somehow offensive, although he could not state precisely where the offence lay.

He was glad that the one girl in New York whom he knew at all well had the easy good manners which spring from a naturally good heart. She was as well educated as the two girls who had just left the car; perhaps better, for she was going to graduate from the Normal College in two or three months; and yet she was unaffected and unassuming. As he phrased it in his mind, "she didn't put on any frills." He could chat with her just as easily as he used to talk to the girls who had gone to school with him at home. And yet when he considered how unlike she was really to these friends of his childhood he wondered why it was he and she had got along so

well, and his thoughts went back to the occasion
of his first meeting with her.

The car was now speeding swiftly down Broadway, obstructed by no carriages, no carts, no
trucks, no wagons, and no drays. Below Astor
Place the sidewalks were as bare as the street itself was empty. The shades were down in the
windows of the many-storied buildings which
towered above the deserted thoroughfare, and
the flamboyant signs made their incessant ap-
peals in vain. For a mile or more it was almost
as though he were being carried through the
avenues of an abandoned city. The one evidence
of life, other than the cars themselves, was an
infrequent bicyclist "riding the cable slot" up
from the South Ferry. If only he had first arrived in New York in the restful quiet of a Sunday, so the young Southwesterner found himself
thinking, perhaps the metropolis might not have
seemed to him so overwhelming. As it was, it
had been a shock to him to be plunged suddenly
into the vortex of the immense city.

A telegrapher in the little town near which
he was born, Filson Shelby had gone beyond his
duty to oblige a New-Yorker who had chanced
to be detained there for a fortnight, and the
New-Yorker had repaid his courtesy by the
proffer of a position as private operator in the
office of a Wall Street friend. The young man
had accepted eagerly, having no ties to bind him
to his home; and yet he had felt desperately

homesick more than once during his first three
months in New York. Indeed, it was not until
he had come to know Edna Leisler that he had
reconciled himself to the great town, which was
so crowded, and in which he was so alone. He
was slow to form friendships, but he had made
a few acquaintances.

It was one of these casual acquaintances who
had taken him one day to the top of an old office
building not far from the Stock Exchange. Here
the janitor lived, and was allowed to use one of
the rooms allotted to him as a lunch-room. The
janitor's wife was a good cook, and Filson Shelby
returned there again and again. One Saturday,
when the room happened to be more crowded
than usual, the rawboned and ruddy Irish girl
was unable to serve everybody, and some time
after he had given his order Filson Shelby was
waited upon by a young lady in a neat brown
dress. He was observant, and he saw a red spot
burning on each cheek, and he noted that the
lips were tightly set. It seemed to him that she
was acting as waitress unwillingly, and yet at
the same time that she was doing it of her own
accord. He did not like to stare at her, and yet
he could hardly take his eyes from her while she
was in the room. She was not beautiful exactly,
for she was but a slim slip of a girl, and she had
coppery hair; and he had always been taught
that red hair was ugly. Yet something about
her took his fancy; perhaps it was her inde-

pendent manner, perhaps it was rather her perky self-possession ; perhaps, after all, it was the humorous expression which lurked in her eyes and at the corner of her mouth.

He had lingered over his luncheon that noon as long as he could, and then he was rewarded. The man who had first brought him there entered and took a seat beside him. When the young lady in brown came for his order the newcomer shook hands with her cordially, and called her "Miss Edna."

"She used to go to school with my sister," he explained to the young Southwesterner. "She's up at the Normal College now, and I've never seen her here in the dining-room before. But she has a holiday, and I suppose she thought she ought to help her mother out. It's her mother who cooks, you know—and boss cooking it is, too, isn't it ?—real home sort of flavor about it."

Filson Shelby had still delayed his departure ; and as Edna Leisler brought bread and butter, and went back again to the kitchen, his friend's chatter had streamed along.

"Red-hot hair, hasn't she ?" was the next remark. "If there was half a dozen more of her you'd think it was a torchlight procession, wouldn't you ? But it suits her style, don't it ? Fact is, she's the only red-haired girl I ever saw I didn't hate at sight."

It seemed as though he had expected Filson to respond to this, and so the young Southwesterner hesitated, and cleared his throat, and admitted that her hair was red.

"Well, it *is* just," the other returned. "I guess her barber has to wear asbestos gloves, eh? But she's a good girl, Edna is, if she is a brand from the burning. My sister used to be very fond of her, and I like her myself, though she isn't in our set exactly. I'll introduce you, if you like?"

The cable-car now came to a halt sharply to set down passengers for Brooklyn by way of the bridge, but Filson Shelby was wholly unconscious of this. He was busy with the recollection of that winter day when he had stood up with bashful awkwardness and had heard Edna Leisler say that she was pleased to meet him. He had the memory also of the next Saturday, when he had gone back to the little low eating-room under the roof in the hope of seeing her again, and of the unaffected frankness of her manner towards him when he met her on the stairway.

He remembered how simply she had accepted his invitation to go to Central Park to lunch on Washington's Birthday, the first holiday when they were both free, and he remembered, too, what a good time they had up there. It was on that Washington's Birthday that he had first found out that in the eyes of some people red hair was not a blemish, but a beauty. The omnibus in which they came down-town had been so crowded that they were separated, and he heard

one well - dressed man say to his companion :
"Did you ever see such stunning hair as that
girl has ?   It is like burnished copper—except
when the sun glints on it, and then it's like spun
gold."

Hitherto he had been willing to overlook her
aggressive locks in consideration of her good
qualities, but thereafter he came rapidly to accept the view of the well-dressed man in the omnibus, and to look upon her red hair as a crown
of glory.   She did not seem any more attractive
to him than she did at first meeting, but he
knew now that other men might be attracted
also.   He wondered whether there were any other
men whom she knew as well as she knew him.
It seemed to him that they had taken to each
other at the start, and they were now very good
friends indeed.   But there was no reason why
she should not have other friends also.

The current of his retrospection was not so
sweeping that he could not follow the course of
the cable-car in which he was seated, and just
then he saw the brown spire of Trinity Church
and heard the clock strike three.   He signalled
to the conductor, and the car stopped before the
church door and at the head of Wall Street.

As he stood looking down the crooked street,
washed white by the rain and looking clean in
the April sunshine, he asked himself why he was
going to meet Edna Leisler—and especially why
it was his heart had slowed up at the suggestion

that perhaps other men were as attentive to her
as he was.   He was not in love with her, was he?
That she had made New York tolerable to him
he was ready to admit, and also that he liked her
better than any girl he had ever met.   But if he
was jealous of her, did not that prove that he
loved her?

These were the questions he propounded as
he walked from Broadway to the old building
on the top floor of which the Leislers lived.
When Edna Leisler came down-stairs to meet
him, with her new Easter hat, he knew the an-
swers to these questions; he knew that he would
be miserable if he were to lose the privilege of
her society; he knew furthermore that he had
loved her since the first day he had seen her,
even though he had not hitherto suspected it.
He knew also that he would never have a better
chance to tell her that he loved her than he
would have that afternoon; and while they were
shaking hands he made up his mind that before
he took her back to her mother's he would get
her promise to marry him.

With this resolve fixed, he took refuge in the
commonplace.

"Am I late?" he asked.

"Five minutes," she answered.   "I didn't
know but what you were going to April-fool
me."

"Oh, Miss Edna," he cried, "you know I
wouldn't do that!"

"I didn't think you would really," she laughed back. "And I felt sure I could get even with you if you did."

Thus lightly chatting, they came to the corner of Broad Street.

"Shall we go down to the Battery?" he suggested, thinking that he might find a chance there to say what was in his heart.

"Yes," she assented; "it 'll be first-rate to get a whiff of the salt breeze. It's as warm as spring to-day, isn't it?"

In front of the Stock Exchange, and for two or three blocks below, Broad Street was absolutely bare, except for a little knot of men working over a man-hole of the electrical conduit. The ten-story buildings lifted themselves aloft on both sides of the street, without any evidence of life from window or doorway; they were as silent and seemingly empty as though they belonged to a deserted city of the plains. Barrooms in cellars had bock-beer placards before their closed portals. On the glass panel of the swing-door which admitted the week-day passer-by to the Business Men's Quick Lunch there was wafered the bill of fare of the day before, but the door itself was closed tight. So were the entrances to more pretentious restaurants.

But as Filson Shelby and Edna Leisler went on farther down - town, Broad Street slowly changed its character. There were not so many office buildings and more retail shops; there

were a few wholesale warehouses; there were
even cheap flat - houses; and there were more
signs of life. Children began to fill the roadway and the sidewalks. There were boys on tri-
cycles, and there were Little Mothers pushing
perambulators in which babies lay asleep. There
were girls on roller-skates; and one of these, a
tall, lanky child, had a frolicsome black poodle,
which pulled her quickly along the sidewalk.

Seeing some of these things, and not seeing
others, and being taken up wholly by their own
talk, the young Southwesterner and the New
York girl passed through Whitehall Street and
came out on the Battery. They walked to the
edge of the water, and looked across the waves
to the Statue of Liberty holding her torch aloft.
An Italian steamer full of immigrants was just
coming up from Quarantine. The afternoon was
clear, after the rain of the night before, and yet
there was a haze on the horizon. The huge
grain - elevators over on the Jersey shore stood
out against the sky defiantly.

A fringe of men and women sat on the seats
around the grass - plots and along the sea-wall.
Many of the women had children in their arms
or at their skirts. Most of the men were reading the gaudily illustrated Sunday newspapers;
some of them were smoking. The sea - breeze
blew mildly, with a foretaste of warm weather.
The grass-plots were brownish-gray, with but the
barest touch of green at the edges, and there was

never a bud yet on any of the skeleton trees.
None the less did every one know that the winter
was gone for good, and that any day almost the
spring might come in with a rush.

As Filson Shelby looked about him he saw
more than one young couple sitting side by side
on the benches or sauntering languidly along the
winding walks, and he knew that he was not the
only young fellow who felt the stirring of the
season. No one of the other girls was as good-
looking as Edna, nor as stylish ; he saw this at
half a glance. With every minute his desire
grew to tell her how dear she was to him, and
still he put it off and put it off. Once or twice
when she spoke to him he left her remark unanswered, and then hastily begged her pardon for
his rudeness. He did not quite know what he
was saying, and he feared that she must think
him a fool. He was restless, too, and it seemed
to him quite impossible to ask her to marry him
in such an exposed place as the Battery.

"Suppose we go up to Trinity Church ?" he
suggested. "It's always quiet enough in the
graveyard there."

"Isn't it quiet enough here ?" she asked, as
they turned their footsteps away from Castle
Garden.

"It isn't really noisy, I'll admit," he responded ; "but I get mighty tired of those elevated
trains snorting along over the back of my head,
don't you ?"

5

She gave him a queer little look out of the corner of her eye, and then she laughed lightly.

"Oh, well," she replied, "if you think Trinity Church Yard is a better place, I don't mind."

Then her cheeks suddenly flamed crimson, and she turned away her head.

They were now crossing the barren space under the elevated railroad, and, as it happened, the young man did not see her swift blush.

As they skirted the oval of Bowling Green the girl nodded to a gray-coated policeman on guard over the little park.

"Who's that?" asked the young man, acutely jealous, although he saw that the officer was not less than fifty years old.

"That's Mr. O'Rourke," she explained. "He's Rose O'Rourke's father. She was graduated from the Normal College only two years ago, and then she went on the stage. She's getting on splendidly, too. She played Queen Elizabeth last year —and didn't she look it? I'm sure she's a great deal handsomer than that old Queen was."

"But that old Queen," he returned, "wasn't the daughter of a sparrow-cop—that's what you call them, don't you?"

"*I* don't call them so," she responded, "for I think it's vulgar to talk slang."

"But the boys do call a park policeman a sparrow-cop, don't they?" he persisted.

"The little boys do," she answered, "but I know Mr. O'Rourke doesn't like it."

"I can understand that," he replied. "If I had Queen Elizabeth for a daughter, I think I should want to be a king myself."

"Well," the girl went on to explain, "Rose did want him to give up his appointment. She said she was earning enough for her father not to work. But he wouldn't, for all she urged him. She's a kind girl, is Rose, and not a bit stuck-up. She came up to the college last year and recited for us. You should have heard her do 'Curfew shall not ring to-night'; I tell you she was splendid."

"I don't believe she did it any better than you could," he declared.

"Oh, don't you?" she returned, heartily; "that's only because you didn't hear her. And she was very nice to me, too. She complimented me on my piece."

"What did you speak?" he asked.

"Oh, I always choose something fiery and patriotic. I spoke 'Sheridan's Ride' first, and then, when the girls encored me, I spoke 'Old Ironsides'—but I like 'Sheridan's Ride' best; and Rose O'Rourke said I got more out of it than anybody she had ever heard. But then she always was so complimentary."

"I reckon she knows it's lucky for her you don't go on the stage," the lover asserted. "It would be a cold day for her if you did. I haven't seen her, but I'm sure she isn't such a good looker as you are!"

"Thank you for the compliment," the girl answered. "If we weren't here in Broadway, in front of Trinity Church, I'd drop you a courtesy. But you wouldn't say that if you had seen her, for she's as pretty as a picture."

"Do you mean that she is as fresh as paint?" he asked.

"That's real mean of you," she retorted, "for Rose doesn't need to paint at all, even on the stage; she has just the loveliest complexion."

"She's not the only girl in New York who has a lovely complexion," he declared; and again the color rose swiftly on her cheek, and then as swiftly faded.

They had now come to the gates of Trinity Church, and they saw a little stream of men and women pouring in to attend the afternoon service.

"You must not be down on Rose," the girl said, as they turned away from Broadway and began to ramble slowly amid the tombstones. "She's a good friend of mine. She said she'd get me an engagement if I'd go on the stage—"

"But you are not going to?" he broke in, earnestly.

"I'd love to," she answered, calmly. "But I'm too big a coward. I'd never dare stand up before the people in a great big theatre and feel they were all looking at me."

"I'm glad you're not going to," he declared.

"It would be too delightful for anything!"

she asserted; "but I'd never have the courage. I know I wouldn't, so I've given up the idea. I'll finish my course at the college, and get my diploma, and then I'll be a teacher—that is, if I can get an appointment. But it isn't easy if you haven't any influence; and father doesn't take any interest in politics, and he doesn't know any of the trustees of this district, and I can't see how I'm ever to get into a school. Now Mr. O'Rourke could help me if he wanted—"

"The sparrow-cop?" interrupted the young Southwesterner. "Why, what has he got to do with the public schools?"

"Mr. O'Rourke has a great deal of influence in this ward, I can tell you that," she returned. "He has a pull on more than one of the trustees. If he were to back me, I'd get my position sure! And maybe I had better go to Rose and ask her for her father's influence."

They were now almost in the centre of that part of the church-yard which lies above the church, and behind the monument to the American prisoners who died during the British occupancy of New York. The afternoon service was about to begin, and the solemn tones of the organ were audible where they stood.

It seemed to Filson Shelby that the time had come for him to speak.

He swallowed a lump in his throat, and began.

"Miss Edna," he said, hesitatingly, "why do you want to be a school-teacher?"

"To earn my living, to be sure!" she answered, calmly enough, although the color was rising again on her cheeks.

"But you don't need ever so many scholars to earn your living, do you?" he asked, gaining courage slowly.

"What do you mean?" she returned, forcing herself to look him in the face.

"I mean," he responded, "that I don't see why you couldn't earn your living just as well by having only one scholar—"

"Only one scholar?" she echoed.

"Yes—only one scholar," he declared; "but you could take him for life. And you could teach him everything that was good and true and beautiful—and he would work hard for you, and try and make you happy."

The color ebbed from her cheeks, but she said nothing. The low notes of the organ were dying away, and on the elevated railroad just behind the young couple a train came hissing along wreathed in swirling steam.

"I'm not worthy of you, Edna; I know that only too well; but you can make me ever so much better if you'll only try," he urged. "I love you with my whole heart—that's what I've been trying to say. Will you marry me?"

She raised her eyes to his and simply answered, "Yes."

An hour later, as they were going through the dropping twilight down Wall Street to the old office building, on the top floor of which she lived with her parents, they were still talking of each other, of their united future, and of their separate past.

When they came to the door and stood at the foot of the five flights of stairs that led up to the janitor's apartment, they had still many things to say to each other.

What seemed to Filson Shelby most astonishing was that he should now be engaged to be married, when that very morning he was not even aware of his love for her. And being a very young fellow, and, moreover, being very much in love, he could not keep this astonishing thing to himself, but must needs tell her.

"Do you know, Edna," he began, "that I must have been in love with you a long while without knowing it ? Isn't that most extraordinary ? And it was only this morning that I found it out !"

Standing on the stairs above him, and just out of his reach, she broke into a merry little laugh, and the tendrils of red hair quivered around her broad brow.

"What are you laughing at ?" he asked.

"Oh, nothing," she answered, and then she laughed again. "At least, not much. It is only because men are so much slower to see things than women are."

"What do you mean ?" he asked again.

"Well," she returned, laughing once more, and retreating two or three steps higher up the stairs, "I mean that you say you only found out this morning that you were in love with me—"

"Yes ?"

"Well," she continued, making ready for flight, "I found it out more than two months ago."

(1895)

A SPRING FLOOD IN BROADWAY

AS he came down the steps of his sister's little house, that first Saturday in May, he saw before him the fresh greenery of the grass in Stuyvesant Square and the delicate blossoms on its sparse bushes and the young leaves on its trees ; and he felt in himself also the subtle influences of the spring-tide. The sky was cloudless, serene, and unfathomably blue. The sun shone clearly, and the shadows it cast were already lengthening along the street. The gentle breeze blew hesitatingly. He heard the inarticulate shriek of the hawker bearing a tray containing a dozen square boxes of strawberries and walking near a cart piled high with crates. When he crossed Third Avenue he noticed that a white umbrella had flowered out over the raised chair of the Italian boot-black at the corner. A butcher-boy, with basket on arm, was lingering at a basement door in lively banter with a good-looking Irish cook. A country wagon, full of growing plants, crawled down the street while the vender bawled forth the cheapness of his wares.

There were other signs of the season at Union Square—the dingy landaus with their tops half open, the flowers bedded out in bright profusion, the aquatic plants adorning the broad basin of the fountain, the pigeons wooing and cooing languidly, the sparrows energetically flirting and fighting, the young men and maidens walking slowly along the curving paths and smiling in each other's faces. To Harry Grant, just home from a long winter in the bleak Northwest, it seemed as though man and nature were alike rejoicing in the rising of the sap and the bourgeoning of spring. It was as though the pulse of the strong city were beating more swiftly and with renewed youth. Harry Grant felt his own heart rejoice that he was back again amid the sights he loved, within a stone's-throw of the house where he was born, within pistol-shot of the residence of the girl he was now going at last to ask to marry him.

It was nearly a year since he had last seen her, but he knew she would greet him as cordially as she had always done. That Winifred was a good friend of his he knew well enough ; what he did not know at all was whether or not the friendship had changed to love on her part also. He could hardly recall the time when he had not known her. He could distinctly remember the occasion when he had first told her that he intended to marry her when he was grown up— that was on a spring day like this, and he was seven and she was five, and they were playing together in Gramercy Park while their nurses fol-

lowed them slowly around the enclosure. Now
he was twenty-three and she was twenty-one;
and in all these sixteen years there had been no
day when he had not looked forward to their
marriage. Of course, when he had grown to be
a big boy and had been sent away to boarding-
school, he had been ashamed to talk about such
things. But when he went to college he had
gazed ahead four years and almost fixed on the
day he intended to propose.

Then his father had died, and the family af-
fairs were left in inexplicable confusion. His
uncle had offered to pay Harry's way through
Columbia, but he was in a haste to be independent, to make his own path, to have a position
which he could ask Winifred to share. He found
a place at once in the office of a great dry-goods
house; and he had been so successful there that
one of their customers had offered him induce-
ments to go out to a swiftly growing city in the
new Northwest. Two years had Harry Grant
spent out there—two years of hard work amid
men who were all toiling mightily and who were
capable of appreciating his youthful energy.
Now he was back again in New York to act as
the Eastern representative of the chief capitalist
of the Northwestern city, an old man, who liked
Harry, and who saw how useful his address and
his character might be. The position was oner-
ous for a man so young; but it was honorable
also, and the salary was liberal even from a New

York standpoint. At last he was again able to look at life from the point of view of a New-Yorker. At last he was ready to ask her to share his life.

He was in no hurry for the moment, as he could not make sure of finding her at home until nearly five o'clock, and it was now barely four by the transparent dial which Atlas bore on his back in the jeweller's upper window on the opposite side of the square. He crossed Broadway at Fourteenth Street, and there he was caught up at once and swept along by the spring-flood rolling up from down-town that beautiful afternoon in May. The windows of the florists' were lovely with Easter lilies and fragrant with branches of lilac. The windows of the confectioners' were gay with gaudy Easter eggs and with elaborate chocolate rabbits. Young girls pressed giggling through the doors to stand packed beside the soda-water fountains. Elderly men lingered at the street corners to stare at the young women.

Within an hour or two at the most Harry Grant intended to ask Winifred to be his wife, and as he saw the dread question so close before him he could not but wonder what the answer would be. Winifred liked him—that much he felt sure about. Whether she loved him, even a little, that he could not venture to guess. She had sturdy common-sense and she was self-reliant, he knew well, and yet he could not help fearing that perhaps the influence of her grandmother had been more powerful than he wished. It was possible, of course, that the restless and ambitious old lady had inoculated her young granddaughter with some of her own dissatisfaction.

As Harry's circumstances had changed since they were boy and girl together, so had Winifred's. Her father had died also, and then her grandfather, leaving a very large fortune to his widow, and Winifred had gone to live with her grandmother, Mrs. Winston-Smith. (It was her grandmother who had put the hyphen into the name, and who had insisted on its adoption by the son and the granddaughter.) That Mrs. Winston-Smith did not like him, Harry Grant knew only too well, or, at least, that she did not approve of him as a possible suitor for the hand of Miss Winston-Smith. She thought that her granddaughter ought to make a brilliant marriage. She had been heard to say that in England Winifred would have no difficulty in marrying a title. She had taken her granddaughter to London the season before, and they had been presented at court, to go afterwards on a round of country-house visits, returning late to finish the summer at Lenox.

All this Harry knew from the newspapers; but what Winifred had thought of it all he did not know, for he had not seen her since the day before her departure for England. And that interview itself had been in the presence of the grandmother and of two or three casual callers. Really he had not had chance of speech with the woman he had loved for three years—ever since Mrs. Winston-Smith had asked him to dinner one night, only to take him into the library and to tell him that she saw that he was attracted by Winifred, and no wonder, but that he must give up the hope of winning her. Mrs. Winston-Smith was some sixty-years old at the time of this talk with Harry Grant, and she was a very stately dame, with no lack of manner, but she could, if she chose, express herself with absolute frankness and directness. On that occasion she had seen fit to be perfectly plain-spoken. She had told him that Winifred had been used to luxury and could not do without it, and that if Winifred married against her wishes she would give all her money to the new cathedral, cutting the girl off without a cent. She asked Harry if he did not think it would be very selfish of him to press his suit when its success would mean the misery of the woman he pretended to love. She reminded him that his own income was meagre, and that he had no prospects. If, then, Winifred had no money, how could she as his wife have all the luxuries to which she was accustomed, and which had now become necessities? Of course she did not admit that Winifred was in any way interested in him. In fact, she hoped and trusted that the girl's affections were in no way engaged; and she relied on Mr.

Grant's good sense and on his unwillingness to be so brutally selfish. After all, Winifred was a mere child, and had seen nothing of the world as yet.

Harry Grant had made no promises to Mrs. Winston-Smith, but he had felt the force of some of her arguments. Plainly he had no right to ask the woman he loved to give up everything for his sake; and as plainly he had no wish to live on any money her grandmother might give her. He meant, more than ever, to win her for his wife; but he saw clearly that he must make himself independent first. To be able to give her a home not unworthy of her he had worked hard all these years. At last he had succeeded, and he was in a position to ask her to marry him without at the same time asking her to surrender the most of the little comforts which made her life easy. With the salary he had now he could make her comfortable, even if her grandmother chose to take offence and cut her off without a cent. There was no false pride about the young fellow, and he did not pretend to himself that he did not care whether or not the grandmother carried out her threat. He was well aware that life would be very much pleasanter if Mrs. Winston-Smith should accept the situation and make the best of it, and give her granddaughter an adequate allowance.

Then, as these thoughts ran through his head, he smiled at his own fatuity in taking Winifred's

6

consent for granted in this summary fashion.
What Mrs. Winston-Smith said or did mattered
little.   What was of vital importance was Winifred's own answer to his question.   He could not
but recognize that to call on a young lady after
a year's separation and to ask her in marriage,
suddenly, without warning, was an unusual proceeding.   And yet that was just what he was
going to do ; and he found himself musing over
schemes for getting her away from her grandmother and from any chance visitors.   He tried
to devise a means of luring her into the library
or of coaxing her into the conservatory.   He
cared not how soon they might be interrupted ;
he knew what he had to say, and he was prepared
to say it briefly.   Five minutes would be time
enough — five minutes, if he could but have
them clear.   When a man has been wanting for
years to be able to put a simple question, it ought
not to take him long to say the needful words ;
and he knew that Winifred would not keep him
waiting for his answer.   Whether it was to be
yes or no, she would know her own mind, and
be ready and willing to accept him at once or to
reject him with as little hesitation.

He had been keeping pace with the throng
that was sweeping massively up-town, but as the
fear seized him that, after all, he had little right
to think she might love him, he lengthened his
stride in futile impatience to get his answer
sooner.   He glanced up at Tiffany's clock, then

almost over his head, and he slackened his speed
as he saw that it was not yet five minutes past
four. He had at least half an hour to wait before he could hope to find her at home.

Then, most unexpectedly, he was favored with
fortune. The foremost of the carriages drawn
up in Fifteenth Street alongside the jeweller's
was a handsome coupé, in which a young lady
was sitting alone. As Harry Grant drew near
to the corner his glance fell on this coupé, and
at that moment the young lady looked up. He
saw that it was Winifred. As their eyes met a
swift blush bloomed in her face, and faded as
speedily. She smiled and held out her hand and
laughed happily as he sprang to the door of the
carriage.

"Winifred !" he cried.

"Harry !" she answered.

"I didn't expect to see you here !" he declared.

"Is that the reason you are here, then ?" she
returned.

He made no reply. He could not take his
eyes from her. In his delight at seeing her again
he had nothing to say.

"Well ?" she asked, when she thought he had
stared enough.

"Well," he answered, "I couldn't help it.
You are prettier than ever."

Again a flush flitted across her face, fainter
this time, and fleeting sooner.

"That's a very direct compliment, don't you think?" she retorted, withdrawing her hand, which he had kept clasped in his own. "And you are looking well, too. Your life out West there is good for you. I don't wonder you prefer it to this noisy old New York of ours."

"But I don't prefer it," he declared, hotly. "A week of New York is worth a year of the whole wide West put together. And I've done with all that now. I've come back here for good now—"

"Have you really?" she responded, as he hesitated, having so much to say that he did not know where to begin.

"I got back this morning," he explained. "and I was coming to see you this afternoon. I've—I've so many things to tell you."

She looked at him for a second, and then she glanced away, as she said : "You will have to talk very fast, then, if you have so many things to tell me. We are going to sail on Tuesday morning, and this afternoon we are off to Tuxedo for over Sunday."

"You sail on Tuesday?" he cried, despairingly. "Just when I have come back on purpose to see you again !"

"You didn't telegraph grandma that you were coming, or she might have made other arrangements," the young woman retorted, with a little laugh.

"And if you are going to Tuxedo to-night,"

"'WINIFRED!' HE CRIED"

he continued, paying no heed to this ironic suggestion, "then you won't be at home this afternoon?"

"No," she answered; "we shall be back just in time to dress and get away to the train. Grandma has two or three errands to do first—she's inside there arranging about some silver things she wants to take over with us."

"But I must see you to-day," he pleaded.

"Aren't you seeing me now?" she returned, as the blush rose again and fell.

"But I've got something I want to say to you!" he urged.

"Won't it keep till Monday afternoon?" she asked, with another light laugh; but beneath the levity there was more than a hint of feeling.

"No," he declared; "it won't keep an hour longer, for it's been kept too many years already. I've come here on purpose to tell you something —and I must do it to-day!"

"If it's something you want to tell grandma—" she began, as if to gain time.

"But it isn't," he returned, leaning his head almost inside the open window of the carriage. "It's you I want to talk to—not to your grandmother."

"Then," said she, with a subtle change of manner, "if it is something you don't want grandma to hear, don't try to say it now, for here she comes."

Harry Grant gave a hasty glance behind him,

and he recognized the stately figure of Mrs. Winston-Smith in conversation with one of the salesmen just inside the door of the great store.

"Winifred," he said, pleadingly, taking her hand again, "where can I see you again, if only for a minute—only a minute? That's enough for what I want!"

Winifred looked at him and then down at her fingers. She hesitated, and finally she answered:

"I think I heard grandma say she was going to the florist's before she went home—that florist in Broadway near Daly's, you know. She has a lot of things to order there, and I shall sit in the carriage."

"I'll take the cable-car and be there waiting for you," he responded.

"Don't let grandma see you," she cried; "that is—well—"

Then she sank back on the cushions of the carriage, for Mrs. Winston-Smith was about to leave the store.

Harry Grant had caught sight of the old lady in time. He stepped away from the carriage, and, passing behind it, crossed to the other side of the street without giving Winifred's grandmother a chance to recognize him.

He waited on the opposite corner until Mrs. Winston-Smith took her place in the coupé beside her granddaughter, and until the carriage was turned and had started towards Fifth Avenue.

Then he crossed the broad space nearly to the

edge of the park and jumped on the first car that came rushing around the curve. The platform was crowded, but he took no heed of the men who were pressed against him.

His thoughts were elsewhere and his heart was full of hope; it was attuned to the gladness of the spring-time. He did not see the young men and maidens who flocked thickly up Broadway; he saw Winifred only; he saw her face, her eyes, her smile of welcome. He was to see her again, at once almost, and he could tell her then how he loved her, and he could ask her if she would not try to love him. What if the only chance he should have was in the street itself? Only the proposal itself was of importance, the place mattered nothing. Perhaps the unconventionality of the proceeding even added zest to it. There was unconventionality in the frankness with which she had made the appointment. It was this frankness partly which made his heart leap with hope, and partly it was the welcome he thought he had read in her eyes when their glances met first.

The car sped on its way, stopping at almost every corner to take on and to let off men and women, who brushed against Harry Grant and whom he did not see, so absorbed was he in going over every word of his brief dialogue with the girl he loved. On the sidewalks were thick throngs of brightly dressed women looking into the windows of the shops, where were displayed brilliant parasols and trim yachting costumes and summer stuffs in lightsome colors.

As the car crossed Fifth Avenue he saw the carriage of Mrs. Winston - Smith only a block away. He recognized the coachman upright on the box, and then all at once he wondered what the coachman must have thought of his talk through the open window, and of his abrupt appearance. He smiled — indeed he laughed gently—for what did he care what the coachman might think, or anybody else ? It was what she thought which was of importance, and nothing else mattered at all. And again he was seized with impatience to see her once and to tell her that he loved her, and to get her answer. The car was going swiftly, but it seemed to him to crawl. The coachman on the avenue was driving briskly, but Harry Grant was ready to rebuke the man for his sluggishness.

At last the car passed the door of the florist's Winifred had described. Its window was filled with azaleas massed with an artistic instinct almost Japanese. Harry Grant rode to the corner above and walked back very slowly, loitering before a shop window, but wholly unconscious of the spring neck-wear therein displayed. Two minutes later he saw Mrs. Winston - Smith's carriage coming down Twenty-ninth Street. It turned into Broadway and stopped before the florist's wide window. Mrs. Winston-Smith got out and ordered the coachman to wait at the corner.

She had disappeared inside the florist's before the coupé drew up in the side street.

As the coachman reined in his horses Harry Grant stepped up to the open window.

"Winifred—" he began.

"Oh !" she cried, "you are here already ?" and again the blush crossed her face.

"Winifred," he repeated, leaning his head inside the carriage, "I may have only a minute to say what I have to say, and I know this isn't the right place to say it, either, but I have no choice, for I may not have another chance. I have waited so long that I simply must speak now."

He paused for a moment. She said nothing, but she rubbed the back of her glove as though to wear away a speck of dirt.

"Winnie," he went on, "what I want to say is simple enough. I love you. Surely you must know that ?"

"Yes," she answered, raising her eyes to his, "I know that."

"Then it's easier for me to go on. You know me; you know all about me; you know all my faults, or most of them anyway; you know I love you. Do you think you could ever love me a little in return ? I will try so hard to deserve it. I've been working ever since I was seventeen to make money enough to be able to ask you to marry me. I've got a good position now, one that I'm not ashamed to ask you to share. Will you ? Will you marry me, Winnie ?"

Before she could make any answer, Harry Grant heard the voice of Mrs. Winston-Smith behind him saying to the coachman, "Home!"

He stepped back and found himself face to face with her.

"It's Mr. Grant, isn't it?" she said, with a haughty inclination of her head. "It's very good of you to amuse Winifred while I was in the shop. I'd ask you to come and have a cup of tea with us, but we are off to Tuxedo. And we sail on Tuesday; perhaps Winifred told you."

She stood there, expecting him to open the carriage door for her. It was the least he could do, and he did it. But he could find no words to respond to her conventional conversation. He looked at Winifred, and he saw that the color was deepening on her cheeks, and that her eyes were very bright.

"Grandma," she said, when at last Mrs. Winston-Smith was seated beside her—"Grandma," she repeated, loud enough for the young man to hear as he stood by the open window, "Harry has asked me to marry him—and you came out just before I had time to tell him that I would!"

(1895)

THE VIGIL OF McDOWELL SUTRO

FOR the third time that afternoon the young man stood before the window of the post - office to ask the same question and to receive the same answer:

"Has any letter come for McDowell Sutro?"

"No."

This time he persisted, for he could not take no for an answer at that late hour of the day.

"Are you sure?" he asked, urgently.

"Certain sure," was the answer that came through the window.

"Will there be another mail from California to-night?" he inquired, clutching a last hope.

"Not to-night," responded the clerk.

The young man stood there for a second, staring unconsciously into the window, and not seeing anybody or anything. Then he turned slowly to go.

The clerk knew that look on the face of men who asked for letters, and he had a movement of kindness.

"Say, young feller!" he called, brusquely.

McDowell Sutro faced about instantly, with a swift flash of hope.

"If you're expecting money in that letter,

241

maybe it's registered," suggested the clerk.
"Ask over there in the corner."

"Thank you," the young man answered, grate-
fully; and he walked to the window in the corner with expectation again lighting his face.

But there was no registered letter for McDowell Sutro, and there could none arrive before
the next morning. And as the handsome young
Californian left the post-office he knew that he
had hardly a right even to hope that the letter
he was asking for should ever arrive.

He stepped out on Fifth Avenue; and though
a warm June wind blew balmily up from Washington Square, his heart was chill within him.
He shivered as he wondered what he was to do
now. He knew no one in New York, and he
had not a cent in his pocket.

In his youth he had expected to inherit a fortune, and so he learned no trade and studied no
profession. He had taught himself how to be
idle elegantly; he had never planned how to earn
his own living. Perhaps this was the reason why
he had failed to find any work to do during the
two gliding weeks since he had suddenly been
brought face to face with his final ten-dollar bill.

He had no more resources than he had friends.
His trunk, with the little clothing he owned, was
still at the boarding-house he had left ten days before; it was held by the landlady till he paid her
what he owed. His modest jewelry had been
pawned, bit by bit.

It was now about seven in the evening, and he had had no food since the coffee and cakes taken perhaps twelve hours earlier, and bought with the last dime left him after he had paid for his night's lodging.   Having walked all day, he was weary and hungry, and he had no idea how he could get a roof over his head once again or fill his stomach once more.   He had heard of men and women starving to death in the streets of New York, and he found himself inquiring if that were to be his fate.

Not guiding his steps consciously, he went up Fifth Avenue to the corner of Fourteenth Street, and then turned towards Broadway.   The long June day was drawing to an end.   Behind his back the red sun was settling down slowly.   The street was crowded with cars and with carts ; and people hurried along, eager to be with their families, and giving no attention to the homeless young man they brushed against.

When he came to Broadway it seemed to him as though the rush and the tumult redoubled, and as though the men and the women who passed him were being tossed to and fro by invisible breakers.   The roar of the city rose all about him ; it smote on his tired ears like the deafening crash of the surf after a northeaster.   He likened himself to a spent swimmer about to have the life beaten out of him by the pounding of the waves, and certain sooner or later to be cast up on the beach, a stripped and bruised corpse.

So vividly did he picture this that involuntarily he straightened himself and drew a long breath. He was a good-looking young fellow, with a graceful brown mustache curling over his weak mouth. As he stood there, erect as though ready to fight for his life, more than one woman passing briskly along the street let his figure fill her eye with pleasure.

The cable-cars whisked around the curves before him, and beyond them he beheld the green fairness of Union Square. The freshness of its foliage as he saw it through the darksome twilight attracted him. He crossed cautiously, keeping a sharp lookout for the cars, and smiling as he noted how careful he was of his life, now he did not know how he was to sustain it.

As he stood at last in the verdant oasis in the centre of the square, suddenly the electric light whitewashed the pavement, and his unexpected shadow lay black and sprawling under his feet. He looked up, startled, and he saw the infinite arch of the sky curving over him—clear, cloudless, and illimitable. The faint sickle of the new moon hung low on the horizon. A towering building thrust its thin height into the air, and the yellow lights in its upper windows seemed like square panels inlaid in the deep blue of the sky. The beauty of the moment lifted him out of his present misery, and he was glad to be alive. The plash of the fountain fell on his ears and charmed them. The broad leaves of the

aquatic plants swayed languidly as a gentle breeze
blew across the surface of the water.

With a sigh of relief, McDowell Sutro dropped
upon one of the park benches. Until he sat down
he did not know how tired he was. His feet
ached, and his stomach cried for food. And yet
he was stout of heart. "If I've got to spend a
night *à la belle étoile*," he said to himself, "I
could have no better luck. There are beautiful
stars a-plenty this evening. It's like that night
in Venice when Tom Pixley and I took the two
Morton girls out in our gondolas, and their aunt
couldn't find us. I remember we had had a good
dinner at Florian's, with an immense dish of *ri-
sotto milanese*—so big we had to leave some. I
wish I had the chance again. I could finish it
now if it was twice as much."

Over on Fourth Avenue, behind the eques-
trian statue of George Washington, there was a
Hungarian restaurant, and from his bench at the
edge of the grass McDowell Sutro could see the
table right in the window at which an old man
and a young woman were having dinner. He
could follow every movement of their hands; he
could count every mouthful they ate. At last
he could bear it no longer, and he changed his
seat to a bench nearer Broadway. Here he found
himself facing another eating-room, in the broad
windows of which many kinds of food were al-
luringly displayed. Men came out and lingered
in the door-way long enough to light a cigarette.

7

When McDowell Sutro noted this, the craving for tobacco seized him. A smoke would not stay his stomach, but it would be a solace none the less. He rose to his feet and felt in all his pockets, in the vain hope that his fingers might touch some overlooked fragment of a cigar. There was something at the bottom of one of the pockets of his coat, but it mocked him by revealing itself as a match. He sank down on the bench and turned his eyes away from the restaurant, for he could not bear to gaze on the cakes and pies piled up behind the plate-glass, or to observe the smoke curling up from the lips of men who had eaten and drunk abundantly.

There was a bar-room under the hotel on the corner of Broadway, and every now and then two or three men pushed inside the swinging doors, to reappear five or ten minutes later. Farther down Broadway stood a theatre, and there was now a throng about its broad door-way. Another theatre faced the square, gay with prismatic signs and besprinkled with electric lights. McDowell Sutro watched men and women step up to the box-office of this place of amusement and buy their tickets and disappear within. He wondered why these men and women should have money to spare on a show, when he had not enough to pay for a meal and a night's lodging.

Perhaps it was the fatigue of his useless day, and perhaps it was the hypnotic influence of the revolving lights before the variety theatre, which caused the lonely young man to fall asleep. How long he slept he did not know, nor what waked him at last. But he had a doubtful memory of a human touch upon his body, and three of his pockets were turned inside out. When he discovered this, he laughed outright. The attempt to rob him then struck him as the funniest thing that had ever happened.

He must have slept for two or three hours at least, for the appearance of the square had changed. It was no longer evening; it was now night. While he looked about him he saw the doors of the theatre in Broadway pushed open, and the audience began to pour forth. A few moments later little knots of the play - goers passed him, still laughing with remembrance of the farce they had been witnessing. In another quarter of an hour the people began to come out of the other theatre, the variety show on the square, and the lights that flared above the doorway went out, all at once.

It was nearly midnight when two men sat down on the bench of which McDowell Sutro had been the sole occupant hitherto. They were tall and thin, both of them; they were clean - shaven; their clothes were shabby; and yet they carried themselves with an indescribable air, as though they were accustomed to brave the gaze of the world.

"No," said the elder of the two, continuing

their conversation, "she's no good. She has a figure like a flat-iron and a voice like a fog-horn, hasn't she? Well, there's no draft in that, is there? She's a Jonah, that's what she is, and she'd hoo-doo any show. Why, the last time I was on the road she tried to queer my act. I called her down right there and then, and when the star backed her up, I was going to give my two weeks' notice; and I'd have done it, too, but I was playing cases then, and I didn't want to come back here walking on my uppers. But if I had quit, they'd have closed in a month, I tell you! They didn't know who was drawing the money to their old show; but I did! You ought to have been in the one-night towns on the oil circuit and heard me do Shamus O'Brien. That used to fetch 'em every night— I tell you it did! And it used to make her tired!"

"Did you ever see me play Laertes?" asked the younger. "I did it first in 'Frisco in '72, when Larry Barrett came out there. Well, while I was on the stage with him, Hamlet didn't get a hand. I've got a notice here now that said I was the Greatest Living Laertes."

"I played Iago once with Larry Barrett," said the first speaker, "and I gave them such a realistic impersonation they used to hiss me off the stage almost."

"Have a cigarette?" asked the other, holding out a package.

"Don't care if I do," was the answer.   "I've got a match."

"That's lucky, for I haven't," said the owner of the cigarettes.

"Well, I haven't, after all," the elder actor had to confess, after a vain search in his pockets.

"Let me provide the match," broke in McDowell Sutro.   "I've only one, but it's at your service."

"Thank you," was the response.   "Can I not offer you a cigarette?"

"I don't care if I do," the young man answered, involuntarily repeating the phrase he had just heard, as he thrust out his hand eagerly.

The first whiff of the smoke was like meat and drink to him; and in the sensuous enjoyment of the luxury he almost neglected to respond to the remark addressed to him.   But in a minute he found himself chatting with the two actors pleasantly.   Although they had been to California more than once, they knew none of his friends; but it cheered merely to hear again the names of familiar landmarks.   There was more than a suggestion of haughtiness in the way they both condescended to him; but he did not resent this, even if he remarked it.   Human companionship was sweet to him; and to drop into a chat with casual strangers on a bench in Union Square at midnight, even this diminished the desolation of his loneliness.

The talk lasted perhaps a quarter of an hour,

and then the two other men rose to go.   Mc-
Dowell Sutro stood up also, as though he were
at home and they were his guests.

"Come over and have a drink," said the elder
of the two.

And again the young man answered, "I don't
care if I do."

He would rather have had food than drink,
but he could not tell two strangers that he was
hungry.

As they passed before the statue of Lafay-
ette and crossed the car tracks, he wondered
whether the saloon where they were going to
was one of those which set out a free lunch.

When they entered the bar-room his eyes swept
it wolfishly, and then fixed themselves at the
end of the counter, where there were broad
dishes with cheese and crackers and sandwiches.
He could hardly control himself ; he wanted to
rush there and snatch the food and devour it.
But shame kept him standing near the door with
the two actors, though his gaze was fastened on
the dishes only a few feet from him.

The barkeeper set the bottle before them, and
they poured out the liquor.   Then they looked
at each other and said, "How !"

The elder actor half finished his drink at a
single gulp.   As he set down his glass he caught
McDowell Sutro staring at the free lunch.

"That's not a bad idea," he said, moving along
the bar — "not half bad.   I'll take a sandwich

myself. I feel a bit hollow to-night. I got three encores after I gave them the 'Pride of Battery B,' and I need something to build me up. Have a sandwich?"

"I don't care if I do," responded the hungry man, as his fingers closed on the bread. Yet when he took the first mouthful it almost choked him.

Five minutes later he had said good-night to his two chance acquaintances and he was again back in the square. The scant food he had been able to take lay hard in his stomach, and the liquor he had drunk, little as that was also, was yet enough to make his head whirl. He did not walk unsteadily, although he was conscious that it took an effort for him to carry himself without swerving.

The bench on which he had been sitting was now occupied by four very young men in evening dress, who were gravely smoking pipes, as though they were trying to acquire a taste for this novel pastime. So he went to the centre of the square, where he stood for a while looking at the aquatic plants and listening to the spurtle of the fountain.

All the seats around the fountain were occupied by men and women, most of whom seemed to have settled themselves for the night, as though they were used to sleeping there. McDowell Sutro found himself speculating whether he, too, would soon be accustomed to spending his nights in the open air, without a roof over him.

One solid German had fallen into a slumber so heavy that his snore became a loud snort. Then a gray-coated policeman waked the sleeper by smiting the soles of his feet with the club.

"This park ain't no bedroom," said the policeman, "and I ain't goin' to have you fellows goin' to sleep here either ! See ?"

After walking three or four times around on the outer circle of the little park, the young man found a vacant seat on a bench near the corner of Broadway and Seventeenth Street. The brilliantly lighted cable-cars still glided swiftly up and down Broadway with their insistent gongs, but they were now fewer and fewer; and the cross-town horse-cars passed only two or three an hour. The long day of the city was nearly over at last, and for the two or three hours before dawn there would be peace and a cessation of the struggle.

As he sat back on the bench, sick with weariness, the occupant of the seat next to him aroused herself. She was an elderly woman, with grizzled hair.

"I beg your pardon—if I waked you up ?" said the young man.

"You did wake me up," she answered, "but I forgive you. It's only cat-naps I get anyway nowadays. I haven't stretched my legs out between the sheets and had my fill of sleep for a month of Sundays. And I'm a glutton for sleeping if I've the chance. But I'm getting used to sitting up late," and she laughed without bitterness. " What time is it now ?" she asked.

McDowell Sutro involuntarily lifted his hand to the pocket of his waistcoat, and then he dropped it quickly. Blushing, he answered, " I don't know—I—"

" Time's up, isn't it ?" she returned, with a laugh of understanding. " I haven't got my watch with me either; I left it in my other clothes at my uncle's. But Mr. Tiffany is a kind-hearted man, and he keeps a clock all lighted up for us to see. Your eyes are younger than mine—what time is it now ?"

McDowell Sutro looked intently for half a minute before he could make out the hour. At last he answered, " It's almost half-past one, I think."

" Then I've a couple of hours for another nap before the sparrows wake us all up," she returned. " Is it the first night you have come to this hotel of ours ?"

" Yes," he replied.

" I thought so," she continued, " by your feeling for your watch. You'll get out of the way of doing that soon."

His face blanched with fear that she might be predicting the truth. Would the time ever come when he should be used to sleeping in the open air ?

The old woman turned a little, so that she could look at him.

"It's a handsome young fellow you are," she went on ; "there's more than one house in town where they'd take you in on your looks — and tuck you up in bed, too, and keep you warm."

"Perhaps I'm better off here," he remarked, feeling that he was expected to say something.

"This isn't a bad hotel of ours, this isn't," she returned ; "it's well ventilated, for one thing. Of course you can go to the station-house if you want. I don't. I've tried it, and I'd sooner sleep in the snow than in the station-house, with the creatures you meet there. This hotel of ours here keeps open all night ; and it's on the European plan, I'm thinking—leastwise you can have anything you can pay for. When the owl-wagon is here, you can get a late sup-per—if you have the price of it. I haven't."

"Neither have I," he answered.

"Then there's two of us ready for an invite to breakfast," she responded, cheerily. "If any one asks us, it's no previous engagement will make us decline, I'm thinking."

He made no answer, for his heart sank as he looked into the future.

"Are you hungry now ?" she asked.

"Yes," he answered, simply.

"So am I," she replied, "and I can't get used to it. Hunger is like pain, isn't it ? It don't let go of you ; it don't get tired and let up on you. It's a stayer, that's what it is, and it keeps right on attending strictly to business. Sometimes, when I'm very hungry, I feel like committing suicide, don't you?"

"No," he responded—"at least, not yet; I haven't had enough of life to be tired of it so soon."

"Neither have I," was her answer. "Sometimes I'm ready to quit, but somehow I don't do it. But it would be so easy; you throw yourself in front of one of those cable-cars coming down Broadway now—and you'll get rapid transit to kingdom come. But they don't sell excursion tickets. Besides, being crunched by a cable-car is a dreadful mussy way of dying, don't you think? And to-day's Friday, too—and I don't believe I'd ever have any luck in the next world if I was to commit suicide on a Friday."

"This isn't Friday any longer," he suggested; "it's Saturday morning."

"So it is now," she rejoined; "then we'd better be getting our beauty-sleep as soon as we can, for the flower-market here will wake us up soon enough, seeing it's Saturday. And so, good-night to you!"

"Good-night!" he responded.

"And may you dream you've found a million dollars in gold, and then wake up and find it true!" she continued.

"Thank you," he replied, wondering what manner of woman his neighbor might be.

She said nothing more, but settled herself

again and closed her eyes. She was dressed in
rusty black, and she had a thin black shawl over
her head. She had been a very handsome woman—so she impressed the young man by her side
—and he was wholly at a loss to guess how she
came to be here, in the street, at night, without
money and alone. She seemed out of place there;
for her manner, though independent, was not
defiant. There was no rasping harshness in her
tones; indeed, her talk was dashed with jovial-
ity. Her speech even puzzled him, although he
thought that showed her to be Irish.

Turning these things over in his mind, he fell
asleep. He dreamed the same dream again and
again—a dream of a barbaric banquet, where
huge outlandish dishes were placed on the table
before him. The savor of them was strange to
his nostrils, but it brought the water to his
mouth. Then, when he made as though to help
himself and stay his appetite, the whole feast
slid away beyond his reach, and finally faded
into nothing. The dream differed in detail
every time he dreamed it; and the last time the
only dish on the board before him was a gigantic
pasty, which he succeeded in cutting open, only
to behold four-and-twenty blackbirds fly forth.
The birds circled about his head, and then returned to the empty shell of the pasty, and
perched there, and sang derisively.

So loudly did they sing that McDowell Sutro
awoke, and he heard in the trees above him and

behind him the chirping and twittering of count-less sparrows.

He recalled what the old woman had said—that the birds would wake them up. Probably they had aroused her first, for the place on the bench next to him was empty.

He rose to his feet and looked about him. It was almost daybreak, and already there were rosy streaks in the eastern sky. A squirrel was running up and down a large tree in the middle of the grass-plot behind the bench on which he had been sleeping. In the open space at the northern end of the square there were a dozen or more gardeners' wagons, thick with growing flowers in pots, and men were arranging these plants in rows upon the pavement. Another heavy wagon, loaded with roses only, rolled across the car track and disturbed a flock of pigeons that swirled aloft for a moment and then settled down again. A moist breeze blew up from the bay, and brought a warning of rain to come later in the day.

The sleepers on the other benches here and there throughout the square were waking, one by one. McDowell Sutro saw one of them go to the drinking-fountain and wash his hands and face. He followed this example as best he could. When he had made an end of this his eye fell on Tiffany's clock, which told the hour of half-past four. A few minutes later the first rays of the sun began to gild the cornices of the tall

buildings which towered above the Lincoln
statue.

Within the next hour and a half the cable-
cars began to pass down-town more frequently,
and the cross-town cars from the ferries also
came closer together. The gardeners' wagons
and the plants taken from them filled the broad
space at the upper end of the square. Milk-carts
rattled across the car tracks that bounded the
square on all four sides. The signs of the coming day multiplied, and McDowell Sutro noted
them all, one after another, with unfailing interest, despite the gnawing pain in his stomach.
It was the first time he had ever seen the awaken-
ing of a great city.

He walked away from Union Square as far as
Fifth Avenue and Twenty - third Street, and
again as far as Third Avenue and Fourteenth
Street; but he found himself always returning
to the flower-market. At last a hope sprang up
within him. Among the purchasers were ladies
not strong enough to carry home the heavy pots,
and perhaps he might pick up a job. This was
not the way he wanted to earn his daily bread,
but never before had he felt the want of the daily
bread so keenly.

When he came back to the line of gardeners'
wagons he found other men out of work also hanging about in the hope of making an honest penny;
and more than once he saw one or another of
these others sent away, burdened with tall plants.

At last he took his courage in his hand, and went up to a little old lady whom he had seen going from row to row. She had bright eyes and a gentle manner and a kindly smile. He asked her, if she bought anything, to let him carry it home for her. She looked at the handsome young fellow, and her glance was as shrewd as it seemed to him sympathetic.

"Yes," she answered, "I think I can trust you."

A minute or two later she bargained with a Scotch gardener for two azaleas in full bloom. Then she turned to McDowell Sutro:

"Will you take those to the Post-Graduate Hospital, corner of Second Avenue and Twentieth Street, for half a dollar?"

"Yes," he answered, eagerly.

"Very well," she responded. "They are for the Babies' Wards. Say that they are from Miss Van Dyne. The Babies' Wards, you understand? And here is your money. I've got to trust you; but you have an honest face, and I don't believe that you would rob sick children of the sight and smell of the flowers they love."

"No," said McDowell Sutro, "I wouldn't." He picked up the heavy pots, and held one in the hollow of each arm. "The Babies' Wards of the Post-Graduate Hospital, from Miss Van Dyne? Is that it?"

"That's it," she answered, with her illuminating smile.

He walked off with the plants. Having the money in his pocket to break his fast, it seemed as though he could not get to the hospital swiftly enough. But when he had handed in the flowers, and was on his way back again to the square, he remembered suddenly the woman who had sat by him on the bench, and who had been hungry also. He had fifty cents in his pocket now, and in the window of an eating-house on Fourth Avenue he saw the sign, "Regular Breakfast, 25 cts." He had money enough to buy two regular breakfasts, one for himself and one for her.

He made the circle of the little park three times, besides traversing it in every direction, and then he had to confess that she was beyond his reach.

So he went to the restaurant alone, and had a regular breakfast all to himself.

When he came forth he felt refreshed, and the people who were now hurrying along the streets struck him as happier than those he had seen in the gray dawn. The long sunbeams were lighting the side streets. The workmen with their dinner-pails were giving place to the shop-girls with their luncheons tied up in paper.

The roar of the great city arose once more as the mighty tide of humanity again swept through its thoroughfares.

He went back to the gardeners' wagons, believing that he might earn another half-dollar. But when he saw other men waiting there hungrily, he turned away, thinking it only fair to give them a chance too.

He found a seat in the sun, and looked on while the flower-market was stripped by later purchasers. He wondered where the plants were all going, and then he remembered that the same flowers serve for the funeral and for the wedding. For the first time it struck him as strange that the plant which dresses a dinner-table to-day may gladden a sick-room to-morrow, and be bedded on a grave the day after.

At last he thought the hour had come when the post-office would be open again, and he set off for Fifth Avenue and Thirteenth Street.

When he reached the station he checked his walk. He did not dare go in, although the doors were open, and he could see other men and women asking questions at the little square windows. What if his questions should meet with the same answer as yesterday ? What if he should have to spend another night in Union Square ?

He nerved himself at last and entered. As he approached the window the clerk looked at him with a glance of recognition.

" McDowell Sutro, isn't it ? Yes—there *is* a letter for you. Overweight, too—there's four cents extra postage to pay."

The young man's hand trembled as he put down the quarter left after paying for his regular breakfast. He seized the envelope swiftly, and

8

almost forgot to pick up his change, till the clerk reminded him of it.

He tore the letter open. It was from Tom Pixley; it contained a post-office order for fifty dollars; and it began:

"MY DEAR MAC,—Go and see Sam Sargent, 78 Broadway, and he will get you a place on the surveyor's staff for the new line of the Barataria Central. I'm writing to him by this mail, and—"

But for a minute McDowell Sutro could read no further. His eyes had filled with tears.

(1895)

AN IRREPRESSIBLE CONFLICT

THE summer sun had blazed down all day on the low wooden roof of the old shed lately used as an ice-cream saloon, and now hastily altered to accommodate a post of the Salvation Army. Placards at the wide doorway proclaimed that All were Welcome, and besought the stranger to Come in and be Saved. The tall tenements that lined the side-streets east and west had emptied their hundreds of inhabitants out into the avenue that evening, and the sidewalks were thronged with men and women languid from the heat of the day, and longing for the lazy breeze that sometimes creeps into the city with nightfall; but few of them cared to enter the stifling hall where the song-service was about to begin, and that night especially there were many counter-attractions out-doors. Already were the rockets beginning to burst far above the square where the fireworks were to be displayed; and now and again a boy (who had more than boyish self-control) produced a reserve pack of fire-crackers, and dropped them into a barrel, and capered away with delight as the owner of the barrel was called to his door by the rattle of their explosion.

A pale and thin young woman, in the uniform

of the Salvation Army, stood wearily in the entrance, proffering the *War Cry* to all those who came near. She looked as though she had been pretty when she was a girl. Now she was obviously worn and weak, like one recovering from a long illness. High up over her head appeared a shower of colored stars shot forth from a bomb; and then she remembered how she had seen the fireworks on the last Fourth of July, only a year before, lying on her bed which Jim had pulled to the window before he went down to conduct the meeting. She had lain there peacefully with her two-weeks-old baby in her arms, and it had seemed to her as though the glowing wheels that revolved in the air, and the curving lines of fire that rose and fell again, were but a prefiguration of a golden future where all would be splendor and glory. How that vision had faded into blackness in the months that followed!—when the baby sickened because they had not proper food for him, and when Jim broke down also; and she had had to get up, feeble as she was, and nurse them both until they died, one after another. When she let herself think of those days of despair, she had always to make a resolute effort if she did not wish to give way and go into a fit of sobbing that left her exhausted for the next twenty-four hours.

She mastered her rising emotion and turned for relief to the duty of the moment. For five minutes no one had bought a paper from her, and the time had come to go into the hall to take part in the service of song.

She pushed inside the swinging-door and found that perhaps a score of visitors had gathered, and that already half a dozen members of the Salvation Army had taken their seats at the edge of the low platform at the end of the shallow hall. Captain Quigley was standing there, with his shiny black hair carefully curled and his pointed beard carefully combed. He was waiting, ready to begin, with his accordion in his hands.

She wondered why it was that she was always sorry to have Captain Quigley lead the service. She would not deny that he led well, giving a swing to the tunes he played that carried all the people off their feet ; he sang sweetly and he spoke feelingly. But she did not altogether like his manner, which was almost patronizing ; and then he had a way of bringing her suddenly into his remarks and of calling her forward needlessly. Even after her two years' service she shrank from personalities and from self-exhibition. Yet there was no doubt that he meant to be kind to her, and she knew that he had allowed her special privileges more than once. With motherly kindness Adjutant Willetts had asked her only a week before if she really liked Captain Quigley, telling her that if she did not like him, she ought to be careful not to encourage him, and since that talk with the adjutant her distaste for the captain had been intensified.

It was as though Captain Quigley had been waiting for her to appear, for he began to speak as soon as he saw her. In a high nasal voice and with an occasional elided aspirate, he welcomed those present and told them he was glad that they had come. He asked them all to take part in singing the grand old hymn, "There Is a Fountain Filled with Blood." He set the tune with his accordion, and lined out the first stanza and led in the singing. Only three or four of the chance visitors joined in the song, the burden of which was borne by the members of the Salvation Army.

Then the captain told his hearers that there was a new *War Cry* published that very morning full of interesting things, and containing the words of the songs they would all sing later, so he wanted everybody in the hall to buy one, that they could all follow the music.

The thin young woman with the saddened face began to move down the aisles offering her papers right and left.

"That's the way, Sister Miller," called out the captain, as though to encourage her ; but she winced as she heard her name thus thrown to the public. " I want you all to buy Sister Miller's papers, so that she can come up here and join us in the singing. You don't know what a sweet voice Sister Miller has—but we know."

He continued to talk thus familiarly as she made the circuit of the seats. When she had taken her place on the platform by the side of Adjutant Willetts, who smiled at her with maternal affection in her eye, then suddenly the captain changed his tone. "Now we will ask the Lord to bless us—to bless us all, to bless this meeting. I don't know why any of you have come here to-night, but I do know this : if you have come here for God's blessing, you will get it. If you have come here for something else, I don't know whether you will get it ; but if you have come here for that you will surely get it. God always gives His blessing to all who ask for it. Brother Higginson, will you lead us in prayer ?"

The men and women on the platform fell on their knees, and the most of those scattered about the hall bowed their heads reverently, while Brother Higginson prayed that the blessing of God might descend upon them that night. Sister Miller had heard Brother Higginson lead in prayer many times and she knew almost to a word what he was likely to say, for the range of his appeal was limited ; but she always thrilled a little at the simple fervor of the man. It annoyed her, as usual, to have the captain punctuate the appeal of Brother Higginson with an occasional "Amen ! Amen !" or "Hallelujah !"

After the prayer there was another gospel song, and then the captain laid aside his accordion and took up a Bible. He read a passage from the Old Testament describing the advance

of the Children of Israel into the desert, guided
by a pillar of cloud by day and a pillar of fire
by night.   He held the book in his hand while
he expounded his text.   The Children of Israel
had their loins girded to fight the good fight, he
said.   That is what every people has to do ; the
Israelites had to do it, the English had to do
it, the Americans had to do it.   They all knew
what the Fourth of July stood for and how well
Americans fought then, more than a hundred
years ago; and so saying he seized the flag which
had been leaning against the wall behind him,
by the side of the blood-red banner of the Salvation Army.

As he was waving the Stars and Stripes Sister
Miller felt her dislike accentuated, for she knew
that the captain was an Englishman who had
been here but a few years, and it seemed to her
mean of him to be taking sides against his native
land.   She wondered if he was really ignorant
enough to think that one of the great battles of
the Revolution had been fought on the Fourth of
July.

Then her mind went back to her girlhood, and
she recalled the last celebration of the Fourth
that had taken place in the old school-house at
home the summer before she graduated.   She
remembered how old Judge Standish read the
Declaration of Independence with a magnificent
air of proprietorship, as though he had just
dashed it off.   Other incidents of that day came

floating back to her memory as she sat there in
the thick air of the little hall, and she ceased to
hear Captain Quigley calling urgently on all those
present to be Soldiers of God.   In her ears there
echoed, instead, the pleading words of young
Dexter Standish, telling her that he was going to
the Naval Academy and that he wanted her to
wait for him till he should come back.   She had
given her promise, and why had she not kept her
word ?   Why had she been foolishly jealous when
she heard that he was the best dancer in his class
at Annapolis, and that all the Baltimore girls
were wild to dance with him.   She had long ago
discovered that her reason for breaking off the
engagement was wholly inadequate ; and, in her
folly, she had not foreseen that Dexter could not
leave the Academy and come to her and explain.
If only he had presented himself and told her he
loved her she would have forgiven him, even if
he had really deserved punishment.   But he was
a cadet, and he would not have a leave of absence
for another year.   Before that year was out, she
had married James Miller, a theological student,
who soon threw up all his studies in his religious
zeal to join the Salvation Army, as though craving martyrdom.   Jim had loved her, and he had
thought she loved him.   It was with a swift pang
of reproach that she found herself asking whether it was not better for Jim that he had died
before he found out that his wife did not love
him as he loved her.

With the ingenuity that came of long experience, Captain Quigley had ended his address with a quotation from "Onward, Christian Soldiers," and Sister Miller was roused from her reverie to take part in the chorus. When they had sung three stanzas the captain stopped abruptly and turned to the gray-haired woman who sat beside Sister Miller, and called on Adjutant Willetts to say a few words of loving greeting to the souls waiting to be saved.

To Sister Miller it was a constant delight to be with the adjutant, to be comforted by her motherly smile and to be sustained by her cheerful faith. There was a Quaker simplicity about Sister Willetts, and a Quaker strength of character that the wan and worn Sister Miller had found she could always rely upon. And another characteristic of the elder woman's endeared her also to the younger : her religious fervor was as fresh as it was sincere, and she gave her testimony night after night with the same force and the same feeling that she had given it the first time. Too many of the others had reduced what they had to say to a mere formula, modified but little and delivered at last in almost mechanical fashion. But Sister Willetts stood forward on the platform and bore witness to her possession of the peace of God which passeth all understanding; and she did this most modestly, with neither shyness nor timidity, merely as though she were doing her duty gladly in declaring what God had done for her.

When the adjutant had made an end of speaking and had taken her seat by the side of the pale young woman, who smiled back at her again, Captain Quigley grasped his accordion once more.

"Now you shall have a solo," he said. "Sister Miller will sing that splendid old hymn, 'Rock of Ages.' Come, Sister Miller."

Her voice had no great power, but it sufficed for that little hall. She did not like to stand forward conspicuously, but the singing itself she always enjoyed. Sometimes she was almost able to forget herself as she poured out her soul in song.

On that Fourth of July evening she had not more than begun when she became conscious that somebody was staring at her with an intensity quite different from the ordinary gaze of curiosity to which she was accustomed. She obeyed the impulse, and looked down into the eyes of Dexter Standish fixed upon her as though he had come to claim possession of her at once.

So unexpected was this vision, and so enfeebled was her self-control, that her voice faltered, and she almost broke off in the middle of a line.   But she stiffened herself, and though she felt the blood dyeing her face, she sang on sturdily. Her first thought was to run away—to run away at once and hide herself, somewhere, anywhere, so that she were only out of his sight. He had not seen her for six years and more, and in those weary years she had lost her youth and her looks. She knew that she was no longer the pretty girl he had loved, and she shrank from his scrutiny of her faded features and of her shrunken figure.

She could not run away and she could not hide; she had to stand there and let him gaze at her and discover how old she looked and how worn. She met his eyes again—he never took them from her—and it seemed to her that they were full of pity. She resented this. What right had he to compassionate her? She drew her thin frame up and sang the louder in mere bravado. Yet she was glad when she came to the end, and was able to sink back into the seat by the side of Sister Willetts.

The captain spoke up at once, and said that the time had come to take up a collection. Let every man give a little, in proportion to his means, no more and no less. Would Sister Willetts and Sister Miller go about among the people to collect the offerings?

As she picked up her tambourine she turned impulsively to the elder woman.

"Let me go to those near the platform, please," she begged. "Won't you take the outside rows?"

The adjutant looked down on her a little surprised, but agreed at once.

The younger woman went only a few steps down the aisles, keeping as far away from him as possible. Whenever she glanced towards him she found his eyes fixed upon her, following her everywhere ; and now it was not pity she thought she saw in his look, but love—the same love she had seen in those eyes the last time they two had stood face to face.

When the tambourines had been extended towards everybody in the hall, the two women went back to the platform and the adjutant counted up the money—coppers and nickels, most of it, and not two dollars in all.

The captain kept on steadfastly. He gave out another hymn. When that had been sung, he turned to a portly man who had come in late and who was sitting on the platform behind Brother Higginson.

"Brother Jackman," he asked, with unction, "how is your soul to-night ? Can't you tell us about it ?"

While the portly man, standing uneasily with his hands on the chair before him, was briskly setting forth the circumstances of his assured salvation, Sister Miller was silent on the platform.

She could not help seeing Dexter Standish, who was straight in front of her. She noted how erect he was, and how resolutely his shoulders were squared. She saw that he was older, too ; and she observed that his face had a masterful look, wanting there the last time she had seen him.

He had always been a fine-looking fellow, and

the training at Annapolis had done him good. He was no mere youth now, but a man, bronzed and bearded, and bearing himself like one who knew what he wanted and meant to get it. She realized that the woman he chose to guard from the world would be well shielded. A weary woman might find rest under the shelter of his stalwart protection. Involuntarily she contrasted the man she had promised to marry with the man she had married—the manly strength of the one with the gentle weakness of the other. Then she blushed again, for this seemed to her disloyalty to the dead. Jim had been very good to her always ; he was the father of her child ; he never did any wrong. But the thought returned again—perhaps if he had had more force of character the child need not have died as it did.

Brother Jackman was rattling along glibly, but Sister Miller did not heed him. She did not hear him even. She did not hear anything distinctly during the rest of the service. She rose to her feet with the rest of them, and she sat down again automatically, and she knelt like one in a trance. When the meeting was over and the people began to disperse she saw that he did not move. He stood there silently, waiting for her to come to him, ready to bear her away. Without a word Sister Miller knew what it was her old lover wanted ; he wanted to pick up their love-story where it had been broken off four years before.

When the hall was nearly empty he started towards her.

She turned to the gray-haired woman by her side.

"Tell me what to do," she cried. "He is coming to take me away with him."

Sister Willetts saw the young man advancing slowly, as those last to go made a path for him.

"Is he in love with you, too?" she asked.

"Yes," the younger woman answered.

"And do you love him?"

"Yes—at least, I think so. Oh yes!"

"And is he a good man?" was the last question.

"Yes, indeed," came the prompt reply, "the best man I ever knew!"

The sturdy figure was drawing nearer and the elder woman rose.

"If you love him better than you love your work with us, go to him, in God's name," she said. "We seek no unwilling workers here. If you cannot give yourself to the service joyfully, putting all else behind you, go in peace—and may the blessing of God be with you!"

She bent forward and kissed the younger woman and left her, as Dexter Standish came and stood before her.

"Margaret," he said, firmly, "I have come for you."

Without a word she stepped down from the platform and went with him.

9

When they came to the door a hansom happened to pass and he called it.

"Where are you taking me?" she asked, glad to be under the shelter of his devotion and ready to relinquish all right to decide upon her future for herself.

"To my mother," he answered, as he lifted her into the vehicle. "She's at a hotel here. She'll be glad to see you."

"Will she?" the girl asked, doubtfully.

"Yes," was the authoritative answer, "she knows that I have always loved you."

(1897)

THE SOLO ORCHESTRA

THE air was thick and heavy, as it sometimes is in the great city towards nightfall after a hot spell has lasted for ten days. There were sponges tied to the foreheads of the horses that wearily tugged at the overladen cross-town cars. The shop-girls going home fanned themselves limply. The men released from work walked languidly, often with their coats over their arms. The setting sun burned fiery red as it sank behind the hills on the other side of the Hudson. But the night seemed likely to be as hot as the day had been, for the leaves on the trees were motionless now, as they had been all the afternoon.

We had been kept in town all through July by the slow convalescence of our invalid, and with even the coming of August we could not hope to get away for another ten days yet. The excessive heat had retarded the recovery of our patient by making it almost impossible for her to sleep. That evening, as it happened, she had dropped off into an uneasy slumber a little after six o'clock, and we had left her room gently in the doubtful hope that her rest might be prolonged for at least an hour.

I had slipped down-stairs and was standing on the stoop, with the door open behind me, when I heard the shrill notes of the Pan-pipes, accompanied by the jingling of a set of bells and the dull thumping of a drum. I understood at once that some sort of wandering musician was about to perform, and I knew that with the first few bars the needful slumber of our invalid would be interrupted violently.

I closed the door behind me softly and sprang down the steps, and sped swiftly to the corner around which the sounds seemed to proceed. If the fellow is a foreigner, I thought, I must give him a quarter and so bribe him to go away, and then he will return every evening to be bought off again, and I shall become a subscriber by the week to the concerts I do not wish to hear. But if the itinerant musician is an American, of course I can appeal to him, as one gentleman to another, and we shall not be troubled with him again.

When I turned the corner I saw a strange figure only a few yards distant—a strange figure most strangely accoutred—a tall, thin, loose-jointed man, who had made himself appear taller still by wearing a high-peaked hat, the pinnacle of which was surmounted by a wire frame-work, in which half a dozen bells were suspended, ringing with every motion of the head. He had on a long linen duster, which flapped about his gaunt shanks encased in tight, black trousers.

"THE AIR WAS THICK AND HEAVY"

Between his legs he had a pair of cymbals, fastened one to each knee. Upon his back was strapped a small bass-drum, on which there was painted the announcement that the performer was "Prof. Theophilus Briggs, the Solo Orchestra." A drumstick was attached to each side of the drum and connected with a cord that ran down his legs to his feet, so that by beating time with his toes he could make the drum take part in his concert. The Pan-pipes that I had heard were fastened to his breast just at the height of his chin, so that he could easily blow into them by the slightest inclination of his head. In his left hand he held a fiddle, and in his right hand he had a fiddle-bow. Just as I came in sight, he tapped the fiddle with the bow, as though to call the attention of the orchestra. Then he raised the fiddle; not to his chin, for the Pan-pipes made this impossible, but to the other position, not infrequent among street musicians, just below the shoulder. Evidently I had just arrived in time.

He was not a foreigner, obviously enough. It needed only one glance at the elongated visage, with its good-natured eyes and its gentle mouth, to show that here was a native American whose parents and grandparents also had been born on this side of the Atlantic.

"I beg your pardon for interrupting you before you begin," I said, hastily, "but I shall be very much obliged indeed if you would kindly

consent to give your performance a little farther
down this street—a little farther away from this
corner."

I saw at once that I had not chosen my words
adroitly, for the kindly smile faded from his lips,
and there was more than a hint of stiffness in
his manner as he responded, slowly :

"I don't know as I quite catch your meaning," he began. "I ain't—"

"I'm sorry to have to ask you to go away," I
interrupted, wishing to explain; "I'd like to
hear your concert myself ; but the fact is, there's
a member of my family slowly recovering from
a long sickness, and she's only just fallen asleep
now for the first time since midnight."

"Why didn't you say so at first ?" was Profess-
or Briggs's immediate response, and the genial
smile returned to his thin face. "Of course, I
don't want to worry no one with my music. And
I'd just as lief as not go over the other side of
the city if it will be any more agreeable to a sick
person. I know myself what it is to have sickness in the house ; there ain't no one knows what
that is better than I do—no one don't."

"It is very kind of you, I'm sure," I said, as
he walked back with me to the corner.

"Oh, that's all right," he returned. "It don't
make any differ to me. Now you just show me
which house it is, so I can keep away from it."

I pointed out the door to him.

"The third one from the corner, is it ?" he repeated. " Well, that's all right. And I am much obliged to you for telling me about it, for I should have hated to wake up a sick person ; and these pipes and this drum ain't exactly soothing to the sick, are they ?"

Then the smile ripened to a laugh, and after I had thanked him once more and shaken hands, he turned back and walked away, accompanied by the bevy of children who had encircled us expectantly ever since I had first spoken to him.

Before daybreak the next morning a storm broke over the city, and the heavy rain kept up all day, cooling the streets at last and washing the atmosphere. With the passing of the hot wave sleep became easier for us all. Men walked to their offices in the morning with a brisker step, and the shop - girls were no longer listless as they went to their work. Our invalid improved rapidly, and we could count the days before we should be able to take her out of the city.

The rain-storm had brought this relief on a Thursday, and the skies did not clear till Friday evening. The air kept its freshness over Saturday and Sunday.

On the latter day, towards nightfall, I had taken my seat on the stoop, as is the custom of New-Yorkers kept in town during the summer months. I had brought out a cushion or two, and I was smoking my second after-supper cigar.

I felt at peace with the world, and for the moment I had even dispensed with the necessity of thinking. It satisfied me to watch the rings of tobacco-smoke as they curled softly above my head.

Although I was thus detached from earth, I became at last vaguely conscious that a man had passed before the house for two or three times, and that as he passed he had stared at me as though he expected recognition. With his next return my attention was aroused. I saw that he was a tall, thin man, of perhaps fifty years of age, with a lean face clean-shaven, plainly dressed in black, and in what was obviously a Sunday suit, so revealing itself by its odd wrinkles and creases. As he came abreast of me, he slackened his gait and looked up. When he caught my eye he smiled. And then I recognized him at once. It was Professor Theophilus Briggs, the Solo Orchestra.

When he discovered that I knew him again he stood still. I rose to my feet and greeted him.

"I thought this was the house," he began, "but I wa'n't sure for certain. You see, my memory ain't any longer than a toad's tail. Still, I allowed I hadn't ought to disremember anything as big as a house—now had I ?" and he laughed pleasantly. "And I thought that was you, too, setting up there on the porch," he went on, cheerfully. "And I'm glad it is, because I wanted to see you again to ask after the lady's health. Did she have her sleep out that evening? And how is she getting on now?"

I thanked him again for his considerate action the first time we had met, as well as for his kindly inquiries now, and I was glad to give him good news of our patient. Then I recognized the duties of hospitality, and I asked my visitor if he would not "take something."

"No, thank you," he returned—"that is, if there ain't no offence. Fact is, I've quit. I don't look on the wine when it is red now, for it biteth like an adder and it stingeth like a serpent, and I don't want any more snakes in mine. I've had enough of them, I have. Croton extra dry is good enough for me now, I guess; and I ain't no use now for a happy family of blue mice and green rats and yellow monkeys. I've had whole menageries of them, too, in my time— regular Greatest Show on Earth, you know, and me with a season ticket. But it's like all these continuous performances, you get tired of it pretty soon—leastways, I did, and so I quit, and I don't touch a drop now."

"Sworn off?" I suggested, as I made room for him on the cushion by my side.

"Oh no," he said, simply, as he sat down; "I hadn't no need to swear off. I just quit; that's all there was to it."

"Some men do not find it so very easy to give up drinking," I remarked.

"That's so, too," he answered, "and I didn't

either, for a fact. But I just had to do it, that's all. You see, I'd given drinking a fair show, and I'd found it didn't pay. Well, I don't like no trade where you're bound to lose in the long-run—seems a pretty poor way to do business, don't it? So I quit."

This seemed to call for a commonplace from me, and I was equal to the occasion. "It's easier to get into the way of taking a drop now and then than it is to get out of it."

"I got into it easy enough, I know that," he returned, smiling genially. "It was when I was in the army. After a man has been laying out in the swamp for a week or so, a little rum ain't such a bad thing to have in the house."

Then it was that for the first time I noticed the bronze button in his coat.

"So you were in the army?" I said, with the ever-rising envy felt by so many of my genera-tion who lived through the long years of the Civil War mere boys, too young to take part in the struggle.

"I was a drummer-boy at Gettysburg," he an-swered; "and it warn't mighty easy for me, either."

"How so?" I asked.

"Well, it was this way," he explained. "Fa-ther, he was a Maine man, and he was a sea-cap-tain. And when mother died, after a spell father he up and married again. Now that second wife of father's she didn't like me; and I didn't like

her either, not overmuch. I guess there warn't
no love lost between us. She liked to make a
voyage with father now and then, and so did
I. We was both with him on a voyage he
made about the time the war broke out. We
cleared for Cowes and a market, and along in
the summer of '62 we was in the Mediterranean.
It was towards the end of that summer we
come into Genoa, and there we got a chance at
the papers, all filled chock-full of battles. And
it didn't seem as though things was going any too
well over here, either, and so I felt I'd like to
come home and lend a hand in putting down the
rebellion. You see, I was past fourteen then,
and I was tall for my age—'most as tall as I am
now, I guess. I was doing a man's work on the
ship, and I didn't see why I couldn't do a man's
work in helping Uncle Sam, seeing he seemed to
be having a hard time of it. And I don't mind
telling you, too, that she had been making me
have considerable of a hard time of it, too ; and
there warn't no way of contenting her, she was
so all-fired pernicketty. There was another ship
in the harbor near us, and the captain was a sort
of a kind of a cousin of mother's, and so I
shipped with him and we come straight home
from Genoa to Portsmouth. And when I wanted
to enlist they wouldn't have me, saying I was too
young, which was all foolishness. So I went for
a drummer-boy, and I was in the Army of the
Potomac from Gettysburg to Appomattox."

" You were only a boy even when the war was over," I commented.

"Well, I was seventeen, and I felt old enough to be seventy," he returned, as a smile wrinkled his lean features. " At any rate, I was old enough to get married the year after Lee surrendered, and my daughter was born the year after that— she'd be nearly thirty now if she was living to-day."

"Did you stay in one of the bands of the regulars after the war ?" I asked, wondering how the sailor-lad who had become a drummer-boy had finally developed into a solo orchestra.

"No," he answered. "Not but what I did think of it some. But after being at sea so long and in the army, camping here and there and always moving on, I was restless, and I didn't want to settle down nowhere for long. So I went into the show business. I'd always been fond of music, and I could play on 'most anything, from a fine-tooth comb to a church-organ with all the stops you please. So I went out with the side-show of a circus, playing on the tumbleronicon."

" The tumbleronicon ?" I repeated, in doubt.

" It's a tray with a lot of wineglasses on it and goblets and tumblers, partly filled with water, you know, so as to give different notes. Why, I've had one tumbleronicon of seven octaves that I used to play the 'Anvil Chorus' on, and always got a double encore for it. I believe it's what they used to call the 'musical glasses'—but tumbleronicon is what it's called now in the profession."

I admitted that I had heard of the musical glasses.

"It was while I was playing the tumbleronicon in that side-show that I met the lady I married," he went on. "She was a Circassian girl then. Most Circassian girls are Irish, you know, but she wasn't. She was from the White Mountains. Well, I made up to her from the start, and when the circus went into winter-quarters we had a lot of money saved up and we got married. My wife hadn't a bad ear for music, so that winter we worked up a double act, and in the spring we went on the road as Swiss Bell-ringers. We dressed up just as I had seen the I-talians dress in Naples."

Again I asked for an explanation.

"Oh, you must have seen that act?" he urged, "though it has somehow gone out of style lately. It's to have a fine set of bells, three or four octaves, laying out on a table before you, and then you play tunes on them, just as you do on the tumbleronicon. There's some tunes go better on the bells than on anything else—'Yankee Doodle' and 'Pop Goes the Weasel.' It's quick tunes like them that folks like to have you pick out on the bells. Why, Mrs. Briggs and I used to do a patriotic medley, ending up with 'Rally Round the Flag,' that just made the soldiers' widows cry. If we could only have gone on, we'd have been sure of our everlasting fortunes. But Mrs. Briggs went and lost her health after our daughter was born the next summer. We kept thinking all the time she'd get better soon, and so I took an engagement here in New York, at Barnum's old museum in Broadway, to play the drum in the orchestra. You remember Barnum's old museum, don't you?"

I was able to say that I did remember Barnum's old museum in Broadway.

"I didn't really like it there; for the animals were smelly, you know, and the work was very confining, what with two and three performances a day. But I had to stay here in New York somehow, for my wife wa'n't able to get away. The long and short of it is, she was sick a-bed nigh on to thirty years—not suffering really all the time, of course, but puny and ailing, and getting no comfort from her food. There was times I thought she never would get well or anything. But two years ago she up and died suddenly, just when I'd most got used to her being sick. Women's dreadful uncertain, ain't they?"

I had to confess that the course of the female of our species was more or less incalculable.

"My daughter, she died the year before her mother; and she'd never been sick a day in her life—took after me, she did," Professor Briggs went on. "She and her husband used to do Yankee Girl and Irish Boy duets in the vaude-villes, as they call them now."

I remarked that variety show, the old name for entertainments of that type, seemed to me more appropriate.

"That's what I think myself," he returned, "and that's what I'm always telling them. But they say vaudeville is more up to date—and that's what they want now, everything up to date. Now I think there's lots of the old-fashioned things that's heaps better than some of these new-fangled things they're so proud of. Take a three-ringed circus, for instance—what good is a three-ringed circus to anybody, except the boss of it ? The public has only two eyes apiece, that's all—and even a man who squints can't see more than two rings at once, can he? And three rings don't give a real artist a show; they discourage him by distracting folk's attention away from him. How is he to do his best if he can't never be certain sure that the public is looking at him?"

Here again I was able to express my full agreement with the professor.

"I'd never do in a three-ring show, no matter what they was to give me," he continued. "And I've got an act nearly ready now that there's lots of these shows will be wanting just as soon as they hear of it. I"—here he interrupted himself and looked up and down the street, as though to make sure that there were no concealed listeners lying in wait to overhear what he was about to say—"I don't mind telling you about it, if you'd like to know."

10

I declared that I was much interested, and that I desired above all things to learn all about this new act of his.

"Well," he began, "I think I told you awhile ago that my granddaughter's all the family I got left now ? She's nearly eight years old, and as cunning a little thing as ever you see anywhere—and healthy, too, like her mother. She favors me, just as her mother did. And she takes to music naturally—can't keep her hands off my instruments when I put them down—plays ' Jerusalem the Golden' on the pipes now so it would draw tears from a graven image. And she sings too—just as if she couldn't help it. She's a voice like an angel—oh, she'll be a primy donny one of these days. And it was her singing gave me the idea of this new act of mine. It's *Uncle Tom's Cabin* arranged just for her and me. I do Uncle Tom and play the fiddle, and she doubles Little Eva and Topsy with a lightning change. As Little Eva, of course, she'll sing a hymn—' Wait Till the Clouds Roll By,' or the 'Sweet By-and-By,' or something of that sort ; and as Topsy she'll do a banjo solo first, and then for the encore she'll do a song and dance, while I play the fiddle for her. It's a great scheme, isn't it ? It's bound to be a go !"

I expressed the opinion that it seemed to me a most attractive suggestion.

"But I've made up my mind," he went on, "not to bring her out at all until I can get the right opening. I don't care about terms first off, because when we make our hit we can get our own terms quick enough. But there's everything in opening right. So I shall wait till fall, or maybe even till New Year's, before I begin to worry about it. And in the meantime my own act in the street goes. The Solo Orchestra is safe for pretty good money all summer. You didn't hear me the other evening, and I'm sorry —but there's no doubt it's a go. I don't suppose it's as legitimate as the tumbleronicon, maybe, or as the Swiss bells—I don't know for sure. But it isn't bad, either ; and in summer, wherever there's children around, it's a certain winner. Sometimes when I do the 'Turkish Patrol,' or things like that, there's a hundred or more all round me."

"From the way the little ones looked at me the other evening, when I asked you to move on," I said, "it was obvious enough that they were very anxious to hear you. And I regret that I was forced to deprive myself also of the pleasure."

He rose to his feet slowly, his loose-jointed frame seeming to unfold itself link by link.

"I tell you what I'll do," he responded, cordially ; "isn't your lady getting better ?"

I was able to say that our invalid was improving steadily.

"Well, then," he suggested, "what do you say to my coming round here some evening next

week ? I'll give a concert for her and you, and
any of your friends you like to invite ? And you
can tell her there isn't any of the new songs
or waltzes or marches or selections from operas
she wants I can't do. She's only got to give it
a name and the Solo Orchestra will play it."

Of course I accepted this proffered entertainment ; and with that Professor Briggs took his
leave, bidding me farewell with a slightly conscious air as though he were accustomed to have
the eyes of a multitude centred upon him.

And one evening, in the middle of the week,
the Solo Orchestra appeared on the sidewalk in
front of our house and gave a concert for our
special benefit.

Our invalid had so far regained her strength
that she was able to sit at the window to watch
the performance of Professor Briggs. But her
attention was soon distracted from the Solo Orchestra itself to the swarm of children which
encompassed him about, and which took the
sharpest interest in his strange performance.

" Just look at that lovely little girl on the stoop
opposite, sitting all alone by herself, as though
she didn't know any of the others," cried our
convalescent. " She's the most elfinlike little
beauty I've ever seen. And she is as *blasée*
about this Solo Orchestra of yours as though it
was *Tannhäuser* we were listening to, and she
was the owner of a box at the Metropolitan."

When the concert came to an end at last, as

the brief twilight was waning, when the Solo Orchestra had played the "Anvil Chorus" as a final encore after the "Turkish Patrol," when Professor Theophilus Briggs, after taking up the collection himself, had shaken hands with me when I went down to convey to him our thanks, when it was so plainly evident that the performance was over at last that even the children accepted the inevitable and began to scatter—then the self-possessed little girl on the opposite side of the way rose to her feet with dignity. When the tall musician, with the bells jingling in his peaked hat, crossed the street, she took his hand as though he belonged to her. As he walked away she trotted along by his side, smiling up at him.

"I see now," I said ; "that must be his granddaughter, the future impersonator of the great dual character, Little Eva and Topsy."

(1896)

THE REHEARSAL OF THE NEW PLAY

WHEN Wilson Carpenter came to the junction of the two great thoroughfares, he stood still for a moment and looked at his watch, not wishing to arrive at the rehearsal too early. He found that it was then almost eight o'clock, and he began at once to pick his way across the car-tracks that were here twisted in every direction. A cloud of steam swirled down as a train on the elevated railroad clattered along over his head ; the Cyclops eye of a cable-car glared at him as it came rushing down-town ; from the steeple of a church on the corner, around which the mellow harvest-moon peered down on the noisy streets, there came the melodious call to the evening service ; over the entrance to a variety show a block above a gaudy cluster of electric lights illuminated the posters which proclaimed for that evening a Grand Sacred Concert, at which Queenie Dougherty, the Irish Empress, would sing her new song, "He's an Illigant Man in a Scrap, My Boys." As the young dramatist sped along he noted that people were still straggling by twos and threes into the house of worship and into the place of entertainment ; and he could not but contrast swiftly this Sunday

evening in a great city with the Sunday evenings
of his boyhood in the little village of his birth.

He wondered what his quiet parents would
think of him now were they alive, and did they
know that he was then going to the final rehearsal of a play of which he was half author.
It was not his first piece, for he had been lucky
enough the winter before to win a prize offered
by an enterprising newspaper for the best one-act
comedy ; but it was the first play of his to be produced at an important New York house.   When
he came to the closed but brilliantly lighted entrance of this theatre, he stood still again to read
with keen pleasure the three - sheet posters on
each side of the doorway.   These parti-colored
advertisements announced the first appearance
at that theatre of the young American actress,
Miss Daisy Fostelle, in a new American comedy,
" Touch and Go," written expressly for her by
Harry Brackett and Wilson Carpenter, and produced under the immediate direction of Z. Kilburn.

When the author of the new American comedy
had read this poster twice, he took out his watch
again and saw that it was just eight.   He threw
away his cigarette and walked swiftly around the
corner.   Entering a small door, he went down a
long, ill-lighted passage.   At the end of this was
a small square hall, which might almost be called
the landing-stage of a flight of stairs leading to
the dressing-rooms above and to the property-

room below.   This hall was cut off from the
stage by a large swinging-door.

As Carpenter entered the room this door swung
open and a nervous young man rushed in. Catching sight of the dramatist, he checked his speed,
held out his hand, and smiled wearily, saying,
"That's you, is it ? I'm so glad you've come !"

"The rehearsal hasn't begun, has it ?" Carpenter asked, eagerly.

"Star isn't here yet," answered the actor, "and
she's never in a hurry, you know. She takes her
own time always, Daisy does. I know all her
little tricks. I've told you already that I never
would have accepted this engagement at all if I
hadn't been out since January. I don't see myself in this part of yours. I'll do my best with
it, of course, and it isn't such a bad part, maybe ;
but I don't see myself in it."

Carpenter tapped the other on the back heartily and cried : "Don't you be afraid, Dresser ;
you will be all right ! Why, I shouldn't wonder
if you made the hit of the whole piece !"

And with that he started to open the door that
led to the stage.

But Dresser made a sudden appeal : "Don't
go away just as I've found you. I've been wanting to see you all day. I've got to have your
advice, and it's important."

"Well ?" the dramatist responded.

"Well," repeated the young actor, "you know
that bit of mine in the third act, where I have

the scene with Jimmy Stark ?   He has to say to
me, 'I think my wife's mind is breaking,' and I
say, 'Are you afraid she is going to give you a
piece of it ?'   Now, how would you read that ?"

After the author had explained to the actor
what seemed to him the obvious distribution of
the emphasis in this speech, he was able to escape
and at last to make his way upon the stage.

The scene of the first act of "Touch and
Go" was set, and the stage itself was brilliantly
lighted, while the auditorium was in absolute
darkness.   It was at least a minute before Carpenter was able to discern the circle of the balcony, shrouded in the linen draperies that pro-
tected its velvet and its gilding from the dust.
Here and there in the orchestra chairs were little
knots of three or four persons, perhaps twenty
or thirty in all.   The proscenium boxes yawned
blackly.   Although it was a warm evening in the
early fall, the house struck Carpenter as chill
and forbidding.   He peered into the darkness
to discover the face he was longing to see again.

Two men were talking earnestly, seated at a
table in the centre of the stage near the footlights.   One of these was a short man, with
grizzled hair and a masterful manner.   This was
Sherrington, the stage-manager who had been
engaged to produce the play.   The other was
Harry Brackett, Carpenter's collaborator in its
authorship.

Just as the new-comer had made out in the

dark house the group he was seeking and had bowed to the two ladies comprising it, Harry Brackett caught sight of him.

"Well, Will," he cried, "the Stellar Attraction is late, as usual—and we've got lots of work before us to-night, too. Sherrington isn't at all satisfied with the way they do either of the big scenes in the second act; and we've got to look out and keep them all up to their work if we want this to be anything more than a mere 'artistic success.'"

"'Artistic success!'" said Sherrington, emphatically; "why, there's money in this thing of yours—big money, too, if we can get all the laughs out of those two scenes of Daisy's in the second act. But it will take good work to get out all the laughs there ought to be, legitimately—and we've got to do it! Every laugh is worth a dollar and a half; that's what I say."

"The two scenes in the second act?" inquired Carpenter. "The one with Stark and the one with Miss Marvin, you mean?"

"The one with Marvin will be all right, I think," said the stage-manager.

"I'm not so sure of that," Harry Brackett interjected; "you insisted on her being engaged, Will, but she is very inexperienced, and I don't know how she'll get through that long scene."

"Miss Marvin is very clever," Carpenter declared, eager to defend the girl he was in love with; "and she will look the part to perfection!"

"Looking is all very well," Brackett responded, "but it is acting she will have to do in that scene in the second act."

"And she will do it too," asserted the stage-manager. "You see, she's got her mother here to-night, and there isn't a sharper old stager anywhere than Kate Shannon Loraine."

"That's so," Harry Brackett admitted; "I suppose Loraine can show her daughter how to get out of that scene all there is in it."

"Shannon 'll see the whole play to-night," said Sherrington, "and she'll be able to give Marvin lots of pointers to-morrow. The little girl will be all right; it's Daisy I'm more afraid of in that scene. It ought to be played high comedy, 'Lady Teazle,' way up in G—and high comedy isn't altogether in Daisy's line."

"That can't be helped now," Brackett replied; "and if the Stellar Attraction can't reach that scene it's the Stellar Attraction's own fault, isn't it? You remember, Will, how she kept telling us all the time we were writing the play that she wanted as high-toned a part as we could give her. We gave it to her, and now she's just got to stretch up to it, if she can."

"I am not afraid of that scene," Carpenter declared, "for I've always doubted whether she could really do high comedy, and that scene is written so that it will go almost as well if it's played broadly. You know there are two ways of doing Lady Teazle."

" There are no two ways about Daisy's being a great favorite," said the stage-manager. " She's accepted, and that's enough. After all, I don't suppose it matters much how she takes that scene ; high or broad, the public will accept her. The part fits her like a glove, and all we've got to do is to keep everybody up to concert-pitch and get all the laughs we can. You took my advice and cut that talky scene in the third act, and now the whole act will go off like hot cakes —see if it don't. I tell you what it is, I'll teach you two boys how to write a real farce before I've done with you !"

Harry Brackett was standing almost behind Sherrington as the stage - manager made this speech. He winked at Carpenter.

" Yes," he said, a moment later, " I think it is a pretty good piece of the kind, and I hope it will fetch them. At any rate, I don't believe even our worst enemies will praise it for its ' literary merit.' "

Carpenter laughed a little bitterly. " No," he assented, " we've got it into shape now, and I doubt if anybody insults us by saying that ' Touch and Go ' is ' well written.' "

" Do you remember our joke while we were working on it last winter, Will ?" asked Harry Brackett. Then turning to Sherrington he explained : " We used to say that the managers wouldn't ' touch' it, so the people couldn't ' go.' "

" It's harder to touch the manager than it is

to make the public go," added Carpenter. "I believe that any fool can write a play, but that only a man of great genius ever succeeds in getting his play produced."

A handsome young woman with snapping black eyes walked on the stage briskly.

"Here's the Stellar Attraction at last," said Harry Brackett; "now we can get down to business."

"Am I late?" the handsome young woman asked, as she came forward. "Everybody waiting for me?"

"You are just twenty minutes late, my dear," said the stage-manager, looking at his watch, "and we are all waiting for you."

"That's all right, then," she replied, laughing lightly; "we've got all night before us, haven't we?"

The prompter clapped his hands and called out "First act!" Two clean-shaven men of indefinite age who had been sitting in the wings rose and came forward. Mr. Dresser joined them, and his manner suggested a certain increase of his ordinary nervous tension. A well-preserved elderly lady left her seat on one side of the aisles under the proscenium box and came through the door which led from the auditorium to the stage. She was followed by a slight, graceful girl, a blonde with clear gray eyes.

"Mrs. Castleman — Miss Marvin," said the prompter, seeing them; "now we are all ready."

And then the serious business of the rehearsal began. Mrs. Castleman came down to the centre of the stage and took up a newspaper and read the date of it aloud, and remarked that it was just five years since master and mistress had parted in anger, adding that neither of them had put foot inside the old house in all the five years, and yet it was not an hour from New York. Then one of the minor actors, an awkward young fellow, one of the two who had been standing in the wings, entered with a telegram, which he gave to Mrs. Castleman. She tore it open and read it aloud ; the master would arrive early that evening. Then Miss Marvin, the girl with the clear blue eyes, came forward with an open letter in her hand and told Mrs. Castleman that the mistress of the house would be home again at last late that afternoon. And thus the rehearsal went on gravely, every one intent upon the business in hand. The speeches of the actors were interrupted now and then by the stage-manager. "Take the last scene over again," he might command, whereupon the performers would resume their places as before and begin again. "Don't cross till he takes the stage, my dear. And when he says, 'What is the meaning of this ?' don't be in a hurry. Wait, and then say your aside, 'Can he suspect ?' in a hoarse whisper. See ?"

Finally there was a jingle of sleigh-bells, and the orchestra, beginning faintly and slowly, soon

11

worked up to a swift *forte*, and then Miss Daisy Fostelle made her first appearance through the broad door at the back of the stage. Finding that she had taken everybody by surprise, she smiled sweetly, and said, " You didn't expect me, I see—but I hope you are all glad to see me once more."

A thin, cadaverous man with a heavy, black mustache here stepped forward to face the wife he had not seen for five years. " We are all glad to see you once more," he had to say, "very glad indeed, and we are gladder still to see that you seem to be in such excellent health and such high spirits ! The separation has not dimmed the brightness of your eyes, nor—" Here the tall, gaunt actor stopped and hesitated. "I don't know what's the matter with that speech," he said, impatiently, "but I can't get it into my head. I never had such tricky lines !"

The prompter gave him the word he needed, and no one else paid any attention to this outbreak.

The two authors were seated at the table in the centre of the footlights, and Harry Brackett whispered to Carpenter : "Stark is getting the big head, isn't he ? The idea of a mere cuff-shooter like that taking himself seriously !"

Then there followed an important scene in which the wife gave her husband a witty and vivacious account of all her doings during the five years of their separation, ending with the startling announcement that she had spent six weeks in South Dakota and had there procured a divorce from him! But there is no need to disclose here in detail the plot of "Touch and Go," as the new American comedy unfolded itself scene by scene. As the end of the act approached Sherrington pressed the actors to play more briskly so as to bring the curtain down swiftly on an unexpected but carefully prepared tableau.

When the act was over the stage manager had the final passages repeated twice, to make sure of its going smoothly at the first performance; and then the stage was cleared so that the scene might be set for the second act.

Carpenter watched the graceful, gray-eyed girl go back into the dim auditorium and take a seat beside her mother; and his heart thumped suddenly as he found himself wondering when he would dare to tell her that he loved her and to ask her to be his wife. Then he also left the stage and dropped into the chair behind mother and daughter.

"It was very good of you to come this evening, Mrs. Loraine," he began. "I feel as if having your daughter act in this play of mine will bring me luck somehow."

"The idea!" said Miss Marvin, smilingly.

"Mary had told me how clever the piece was," the elder actress responded, "but it is really better than she said. The dialogue is very brilliant at times, and the characters are excellently contrasted—and, what is more important, the whole thing will act! The parts carry the actors; they've got something to do which is worth while doing. It will go all right to-morrow night!"

"It's a beautiful piece," Mary Marvin declared, "and I think my part is just lovely!"

And before he could say anything in fit acknowledgment, Mrs. Loraine went on: "Yes, Mary's part is charming. And I think she will play it very well, too!"

"I'm sure of it!" he cried, unhesitatingly.

"I think there is more in it than I thought at first," said Mary's mother, "now I've seen the play, and I'll go over Mary's part with her to-night and show her what can be done with it. I'm waiting for that scene in the second act with Fostelle. I think that Mary ought to share the call after that. In fact, I'm not sure that she can't take the scene away from Fostelle."

"Oh, mother," the daughter broke in, "that would never do! I should get my two weeks' notice the next morning, shouldn't I? And I don't want to be out of an engagement just at the beginning of the season when all the companies are made up."

"Are you sure that the ghost will walk every week with this Fostelle company, if you strike bad business for a month or so?" asked Mrs. Loraine, with a suggestion of anxiety in her voice.

"I think Zeke Kilburn is all right," the dramatic author responded; "he made a pile of money last year on that imported melodrama, the 'Doctor's Daughter'; and, besides, he has a backer."

Mrs. Loraine laughed gently, showing her beautifully regular teeth. She was still a handsome woman, with a fine figure and a crown of silver hair.

"A backer?" she rejoined; "but who backs the backer? I've heard your friend, Mr. Brackett, there, say that a jay and his money are soon parted."

Carpenter answered her earnestly. "I really think Kilburn is pretty solid, but I suppose that a great deal does depend on the way that the play draws. They've got open time here in New York, and if 'Touch and Go' catches on they can stay here till Christmas. So it comes down to this, that if our piece is a go the ghost will walk regularly."

"I hope it will make a hit," Mrs. Loraine answered, "for your sake, too. You haven't sold it outright, have you?"

"No, indeed," the young dramatist replied. "Harry Brackett is too old in the business for that. We've got a nightly royalty, with a percentage on the gross whenever it plays to more than four thousand dollars a week. We stand to make a lot of money—if it makes a hit. What do you think of its chances, Mrs. Loraine?"

"The first act is all right," she responded. "That's the most I can say now. But come and ask me after I've seen the third act and I'll tell you what I think, and I believe I can then prophesy its fate pretty well."

By this time the scene of the second act had been set. It represented a stone summer-house on the top of a hill overlooking the Hudson just below West Point. It was picturesque in itself, and it was ingeniously arranged to provide opportunities for effective stage business.

Carpenter accompanied Miss Marvin back to the stage when the time drew nigh for the second act to begin.

As he was passing through the door between the auditorium and the stage, he found himself face to face with Dresser, who was fidgeting to and fro.

"Oh, Mr. Carpenter," he cried, "I'm so glad to see you! I want to ask your opinion about this. After all, you know, you wrote the play, and you ought to be able to decide. In my scene with Marvin in this act, am I really in love with her then, or ain't I? Sherrington says I am, but I think it's a great deal funnier if I'm not in love with her then — it helps to work up the last act better. Now what do you think? Sherrington insists that his way of playing it is more dramatic. Well, I don't say it ain't, but it isn't half as funny, is it?"

After Carpenter had given his opinion upon

this question, Dresser allowed him to escape. But he had not advanced ten yards before he was claimed by Mrs. Castleman.

"Mr. Carpenter," the elderly actress began, in her usual haughtily dignified manner, "how do you think I ought to dress this part in the first act ? She's a house-keeper, isn't she ? So I suppose I ought to wear an apron."

The young dramatist expressed his belief that perhaps an apron would be a proper thing for the house-keeper to wear in the first act.

"But not a cap, I hope ?" urged Mrs. Castleman.

Carpenter doubted if a cap would be necessary.

"Thank you," said Mrs. Castleman. "You see, I have always hitherto been associated with the legitimate, and I really don't quite know what to do with this sort of thing." Then she suddenly paused, only to break out again impetuously : "Oh, I beg your pardon, Mr. Carpenter, really I did not mean to imply that this charming play of yours is not legitimate—"

The dramatic author laughed. "You needn't apologize," he declared ; "I'm inclined to think that 'Touch and Go' is so illegitimate now that its own parents can't recognize it !"

At last the rehearsal of the second act began, the two authors sitting at the little table with the stage-manager.

Sherrington consulted them once or twice in regard to the omission of a line here and there.

"Cut it down to the bone when you can—

that's what I say," he explained; "what you cut out can't make people yawn."

But once he stopped the rehearsal to suggest that a speech be written in. "You've got to make that complication mighty clear," he declared, "and this is the place to do it, I think. If you want them to understand that Dresser here is going to mistake Marvin for Fostelle in the next scene, you had better give him another line now to lead up to it."

The two authors consulted hastily, and Carpenter, drawing out a note-book and a pencil, hurriedly wrote a sentence, which he showed to Brackett.

"That'll do it," said Sherrington; and he read it aloud to Dresser, who borrowed Carpenter's pencil and wrote in the line on the manuscript of his part, wondering aloud whether he should ever remember it on the first night.

A few minutes later Sherrington again interrupted the actors to insist that the sunset effect should be adjusted carefully to accompany the spoken dialogue.

"I want a soft, rosy tinge on Fostelle in this scene," he explained.

"Quite right," laughed the black-eyed star; "that ought to be becoming to my style of beauty."

"And I want it to contrast with the blue moonlight in the scene with Marvin," said the stage-manager.

"Quite right again," Miss Daisy Fostelle commented.   "I'll take the centre of the stage, and you will order calciums for one!"

"We had better go back to your entrance, I think," Sherrington decided, "and take the whole scene over."

The actors and actresses obediently resumed the positions they had occupied when Miss Daisy Fostelle made her first appearance in that act. The cue for her entrance was given, and she came forward with a burst of artificial laughter.

"That laugh was very good," Sherrington declared—"better than it was last time; but you must make it as hollow as you can.   Remember the situation : your best young man has gone back on you and you are trying to keep a stiff upper-lip—but your heart is breaking all the same.   See ?"

The star repeated the laugh, and it was more obviously artificial.

"That's it, my dear," said the stage-manager. "Now keep it up till you cross, and then drop into that chair there, and then you let the laugh die away into a sob."

The star went back to the rustic gate by which she had entered, laughed again, and came forward ; then she crossed the stage, sank upon a seat, and choked with a sob.

Carpenter stepped forward and whispered into Sherrington's ear, whereupon Miss Fostelle sat upright instantly and very suspiciously asked,

"What's that ?   I'd rather have you say it out loud than whisper it !"

The young dramatist explained at once.

"I was only suggesting to Sherrington that perhaps it would be better if that seat were turned a little so that you were not so sideways : then the audience would get a full view of your face here."

"It would be a pity to deprive them of that, I'll admit," said the mollified actress, as she and the stage - manager slightly turned the rustic chair.

Then she dropped into the seat and repeated her sob.

Miss Marvin stepped upon the stage, and remarked to space, "What a lovely evening, and how glorious the sunset !" Then she stood silently watching.

Miss Daisy Fostelle sobbed again, and, in tones heavy-laden with tears, she said, "What have I to live for now ?" Looking back at the other actress she remarked, in her ordinary voice, "You will give me time to pick myself up here, won't you ?" Then she went on, in the former tear-stained accents, "What have I left to live for now ?   My heart is broken !   My heart is broken !" Again she resumed her every-day tones to ask the stage-manager : "Is that all right ?   Am I far enough around now ?"

Thus they came to perhaps the most important scene of the play—that between the Stellar Attraction (as Brackett liked to call her) and the girl Carpenter was in love with.   Both actresses were well fitted to the characters they had to perform.   Carpenter, who had no liking for Daisy Fostelle, was a little surprised at the judgment and skill with which she carried off the *bravura* passages of her part; and he was not a little charmed with the delicate force the gentle Mary Marvin revealed in the contrasting character.

And so the rehearsal proceeded laboriously, Sherrington directing it autocratically, ordering certain scenes to be played more rapidly and seeing that others were taken more slowly, so that the spectators might have time to understand the situation.   Now and then either Carpenter or Brackett made a suggestion or a criticism, but both yielded to Sherrington, if he was insistent. The stage-manager kept the whole company of actors up to their work, and imposed on them his understanding of that work, much as the conductor of an orchestra leads his musicians at the performance of a symphony.

When the whole act had been rehearsed, and the final scene was repeated three or four times until it ran like well-oiled clockwork, the stage was cleared so that the scenery of the third act might be set.

Sherrington accompanied Miss Marvin through the door behind the proscenium box into the dark auditorium.

"You will play that scene very well," he said, "but you've got to have confidence."

"It is a beautiful part, isn't it?" she responded, with enthusiasm. "I never had a part I could enjoy playing so much."

Carpenter was about to leave the stage to tell Mary what a delight it was to him to hear her speak the words he had written, when his collaborator tapped him on the shoulder. As he turned Harry Brackett whispered in his ear:

"Look out for the Stellar Attraction. I'm afraid she has just dropped on Marvin's part. If she once suspects that the little girl may get that scene away from her, she can make herself mightily disagreeable all round. I guess we had better go up and tell her she is a greater actress than Charlotte Cushman."

Carpenter laughingly answered: "Take care she doesn't drop on you! It would be worse if she thought you were guying her."

"There's no danger of that," Harry Brackett returned. "That Stellar Attraction of ours is a boa-constrictor for flattery—there isn't anything she won't swallow."

The two dramatic authors found Miss Daisy Fostelle standing in the wings and discussing with Dresser the personal peculiarities of another member of the dramatic profession.

As Carpenter and Brackett came up the actress was saying: "Why, she had the cheek actually to tell me I was more amusing off the stage than

on—the cat! But I got even with her. I told
her I was sorry I couldn't return the compliment, for she was even less amusing on the
stage than off !"

The two dramatists joined in the laugh, and
then Harry Brackett began.

"Is it your hated rival you are having fun
with ?" he asked. "Well, if she comes to see
you in this play to-morrow they'll have to put
a waterproof carpet into the private box, for
she will weep bitter tears of despair while she's
watching you in this second act of ours."

Miss Daisy Fostelle snapped her big black eyes
at him and smiled with pleasure.

"Yes," she admitted. "I don't believe she
will really enjoy that scene—and yet she'll have
to give me a hand at the end of the act."

"She'll go through the motions, perhaps,"
Brackett returned, "but she won't burst a hole
in her gloves." Then he slyly nudged his collaborator.

"The fact is," began Carpenter, thus admon-
ished, "I was just going to tell Harry Brackett
here that maybe we have made a mistake in writing you a high-comedy part like this—"

The actress flashed a suspicious glance at him,
but he went on as if unconscious of this.

"We can see now," he continued, "that you
are going to play this part so well that you will
make a great hit in it, and then the critics will
all be after you to play Lady Teazle and Rosalind.

They'll tell you that you are only wasting your talents in modern plays and that you ought to devote yourself to the legitimate."

The suspicion faded from Miss Daisy Fostelle's face and the smile of pleasure reappeared.

" That's so," Harry Brackett declared. " You will make such a hit in this part, I'm afraid, that Sheridan and Shakespeare will be good enough for you next season. Now that would be taking the bread out of our mouths !"

The actress laughed easily. " I don't think you would starve," she returned ; "and I might, maybe—if I took to the legitimate. Not that it would be my first attempt, either, for I played Ariel in the ' Tempest' when I was a mere child. And it wasn't easy, I can tell you. Ariel's a real hard part, I think ; there's a certain swing to the words, too, and you can't make up a line of your own if you get stuck, as I could in this piece of yours."

" No," Brackett confessed, solemnly, " the dialogue of ' Touch and Go ' is not as rhythmic as the dialogue of the ' Tempest.'"

"And I've played François in 'Richelieu,' too," continued Miss Fostelle. "But I don't think I really like any of those Shakespearian parts."

" No," Brackett confessed again, with fearless gravity, " François is not one of Shakespeare's best parts. It wasn't worthy of you, no matter how inexperienced you were. But Rosalind, now, as Carpenter suggests, and Beatrice—"

Carpenter here guessed from Dresser's spasmodic manner that the actor was about to intervene in the conversation, and not knowing what might be the result, the younger of the dramatists dropped out of the group and managed to draw Dresser away with him.

After they had exchanged a few words Carpenter looked into the auditorium to discover where Mary Marvin might be. He saw that she was by the side of her mother, and that Mrs. Loraine and Sherrington were still engaged in an earnest conversation. He made a movement as if to leave Dresser, whereupon the comedian begged him for a moment's interview.

"It's about that speech of mine in the third act that I want to make a suggestion," said the actor. "It's a very good speech, too, and I think I can get three laughs out of it, easy. You know the speech. I mean the one about the three old maids : ' There were three old maids in our town; one was as plain as a pikestaff, and the other was as homely as a hedge fence, and the third was as ugly as sin ; and whenever they all three walked out together every clock in the place stopped short. Their parents had christened them Faith and Hope and Charity; but the boys always called them Battle and Murder and Sudden Death.' Now, don't you think it would help to ring out the point more if the orchestra was to play ' Grandfather's Clock' very gently just as I say that ' every clock in the place stopped

short'? What do you think? That's my own
idea !"

The dramatist said nothing for a second or
two, and then told the actor to consult the stage-
manager, who was just returning to begin the rehearsal of the third act.

The new scene had been set swiftly and the
furniture was already in place. The first of the
actors to enter was the cadaverous and irritable
Stark. He began glibly enough, but soon hesitated for a word, and then broke out impatiently, regardless of the presence of the two authors :
" Oh, I can't get that line into my head ! And
I don't know what it means, either ! How can
you expect a man to speak such rubbish ?"

As before, nobody paid any attention to this
petulance, and the actor went on with his part
without further comment.

Dresser then entered, and the two men proceeded to misunderstand each other in the most
elaborate fashion. The character which Stark
represented had reason to believe that the character that Dresser represented was the uncle
of the character that Daisy Fostelle represented
and was also a soldier. In like manner Dresser
had reason to believe that Stark was the lady's
uncle and also a sailor. They addressed each
other, therefore, in sailor talk and in soldier
talk ; and the fun waxed fast and furious. At the
height of the misunderstanding Daisy Fostelle entered unexpectedly and found herself instant-

ly immeshed in the humorous complication, with no possibility of plausible explanation.

Once the stage-manager reminded Dresser that he had omitted a phrase. "You left out 'Confound it, man!'" he said.

"I know it," the actor explained, "but I wanted to save it to use in my next speech. It goes better there—you see if it does not."

And Sherrington decided that "Confound it, man!" was more effective in the later speech; so the transposition was authorized, to Dresser's satisfaction.

The stage-manager had this important scene of mutual misunderstanding between Stark and Dresser and Daisy Fostelle repeated twice, until every word fell glibly and every gesture seemed automatic. And so the rehearsal went to the end, Sherrington applying the finishing touches, and seeming at last to be fairly well satisfied with the result of his labors.

The final lines of the comedy were, of course, to be delivered by the star; but when the cue was given to her Miss Fostelle simply said "Tag!" everybody being aware that it is very unlucky to speak the last speech of a play at a rehearsal—as unlucky as it is to put up an umbrella on the stage, or to quote from "Macbeth."

"That will do," said the stage-manager; "I think it will be all right to-morrow night."

And with that the rehearsal concluded and the company began to disperse.

12

"I hope it is all right," Harry Brackett remarked to Carpenter, "and I think it is. But I shall have a great deal more confidence after the man in the box-office shakes hands with me cordially, say, next Wednesday or Thursday, and inquires about my health. He'll know by that time whether we've got a good thing or not!"

Carpenter helped Miss Marvin to put on her light cape. Then, after her mother had joined them, they said good-night to the others and left the theatre together.

When they came out into the warm night the street was quieter than it had been when Carpenter entered the theatre. There were fewer cablecars passing the door, and the trains on the elevated road in the avenue were now infrequent. The lights had been turned out in front of the variety show across the way, and evidently the grand sacred concert was over. The moon had sunk, and before they had gone a block the bell of the church tolled the hour of midnight.

The young man who was walking by the side of Mrs. Loraine broke the silence at last.

"Well," he asked, "what do you think of the play now?"

"I think it is a good piece of its kind," the elder actress answered—"a very good piece of its kind; and it is well staged; and it will be well acted, too. Sherrington knows how to get his best work out of everybody. Yes, it will be a success."

"Is it good for three months here now?" the young author asked, "and for the rest of the season on the road?"

"Oh yes, indeed," replied Mrs. Loraine; "yes, indeed. It's safe for a hundred nights here at least!"

They paused at the corner to wait for a cable-car, and Sherrington joined them.

This gave Carpenter a chance to lead the daughter away from the mother half a dozen steps.

"I'm so glad mother thinks the play will go," the girl began. "And mother is a very good judge, too. You ought to make a lot out of it."

The young dramatist felt that he had his chance at last.

"I've wanted to make money mainly for one reason," he returned; "I wanted to ask you to take half of it."

"Half of it?" she echoed, as though she did not understand.

"Oh, well—all of it," he responded, swiftly; "and me with it."

"Mr. Carpenter!" she cried, and her blushes made her look even lovelier than before.

"Won't you marry me?" he asked, ardently.

"Oh, I suppose I've got to say yes," she answered, "or else you'll go down on your knees here in the street!"

(1896)

A CANDLE IN THE PLATE

LITTLE Miss Peters had given a last look to the dinner-table with its effective decoration of autumn leaves, and she had made sure that the cards were in their proper places. She had glanced at herself in the mirror of the music-room as she passed through, and she had smiled to see the little spot of color burning in her cheek. She had taken her place modestly behind her employer, the portly hostess, and she had seen the guests arrive one by one. She had remarked the cheerful eagerness of the young Irishman for whose sake the company had gathered, and she had frankly admired his good looks. Now she was sitting silently in her seat at the table, and she was wondering what the stranger would think of them all.

It would not be quite fair to the worthy widow to say that Mrs. Canton's dinners were always ponderous; but it might be admitted that, although the cooking was ever excellent and the guests were selected from the innermost circle of Society, the bill of fare was monotonous and the conversation often lacked variety. That evening, however, there were several present who had not before been honored with invitations to dine in

323

that exclusive mansion.   Few people of fashion
were back in town so early in October, and it had
not been easy for Mrs. Canton to make up her
complement of guests when she found that she
had suddenly to honor a letter of introduction
Lord Mannington had given to the Honorable
Gilbert Barry, brother of Lord Punchestown.
She had heard that the handsome Irishman had
been a great success at Lenox, and that all the
girls were wild about him.   In Mannington's letter she was informed that the young man went
in for slumming and all that sort of thing, and
that he had been living in Toynbee Hall; she
was besought, therefore, to make him acquainted
with the people in New York most interested in
the elevation of the lower classes.

This sentence of Lord Mannington's letter it
was that had caused Mrs. Canton to invite Rupert de Ruyter, the novelist, for she happened to
have read one of his stories about the wretched
creatures living down in the Italian quarter, and
she was sure he would be able to tell Mr. Barry
all that the young Irishman might want to know
about the slums of New York.   She had been
fortunate enough to get the Jimmy Suydams,
too ; and she knew that Mrs. Jimmy took such
an interest in the poor, acting as patroness so
often, and all that.   Then when little Miss Peters
had come in to write the invitations and to bal-
ance the check-book and to answer the accumu-
lated notes, Mrs. Canton, having gone over the

list, looked at the pretty young secretary for a
minute without speaking, and then said, " It
won't be easy to get just the people one wants.
Why shouldn't you come, Miss Peters ? You
belong to one of those things, you know, what
do you call them—Working Girls' Clubs—don't
you ?"

"I'm a working girl myself, am I not ?" Miss
Peters answered.   " And I reckon I'm very glad
I've gotten the work to do."

" Then you can tell him anything Mr. de
Ruyter doesn't know about these sort of people.
How absurd for the younger brother of a peer to
bother himself about such things over here, isn't
it ?" Mrs. Canton had returned.   " Then that's
settled."

Although the Southern girl had not relished
the way the invitation had been proffered, she
had not declined it, glad to get a glimpse again
of the life of luxury to which she had been a
stranger since she had been earning her own
living ; and thus it was that she was sitting silently in her seat at the dinner-table that evening in October, with Gilbert Barry and Rupert
de Ruyter opposite to her.   She did not seem to
notice how the young Irishman glanced across
the table at her more than once with obvious
admiration, or how he tried to lure her into the
conversation.

It irritated Miss Peters to have Rupert de Ruyter monopolize the talk.   His rather rasping voice

sawed her nerves, and she detested the way he
thrust forward his square chin. She listened
while he chattered along, not boasting exactly,
yet managing to convey the impression that he
knew more than any one else. Now and again he
did bring forth a picturesque fact, for which he
had the kodak eye of a reporter. He had the
happy - go - lucky facility of the newspaper man,
and he rattled away with more than one absurd
misapprehension of the reality, until he reminded her of a singer with a fine voice but unable to
avoid false notes.

"I don't pretend to know New York inside-
out and upsidedown," he was saying ; "but it
is a most fascinating study, this polyglot city of
ours, and the more you push your investigations
the more likely you are to make surprising dis-
coveries.   You know we have an Italian quarter
here ?"

This was addressed, perhaps, to the British
guest, but it was Mrs. Jimmy Suydam who answered it.

"Of course we do," she said ; " haven't we all
read that thrilling story you wrote about it ?—
the story with the startling title—*A Vision of
Black Despair.*"

The author flushed with pride that so handsome a woman and so exclusive a leader of Society should thus praise one of his writings.

Mr. Jimmy Suydam leaned over to Mrs. Canton, at whose left he was sitting, and said, "I

don't see how my wife does it, do you ? She keeps up with everything, you know—reads all the books—and all that."

"I didn't mean to remind you of that little thing of mine," continued De Ruyter, with a self-satisfied air that made little Miss Peters feel as though she would like to stick a pin in him. "That's neither here nor there, though I spent two days down in the Italian quarter getting up the local color for it. But what you didn't know, any of you, I am certain, is that part of the soil of this city was imported from Italy."

"Really, now," commented the British guest, "that is very interesting, indeed. It would be from a religious motive, I suppose—just as some of the mediæval cemeteries had earth brought from the Holy Land ?"

"That would be a more romantic reason, no doubt," the story-teller explained. "But the real one is very prosaic, I fear. The Italian soil here in New York was brought over as ballast by the ships that were going to take back our bread-stuffs. There is lot after lot upon the Harlem that has been filled in with this ballast—stones mostly, but some of it is earth."

"Genoa the superb providing a foundation for imperial New York," said the young Irishman, with a little flourish—and Miss Peters guessed that De Ruyter made a mental note of the figure for future elaboration. "And has New York a volcano under the city like Naples, now ?—like every great town in Europe for the matter of that. Have you a seething mass of want and misery and discontent, such as boiled over in Paris under the Commune? That's what I'm wanting to find out."

"We have a devil's cauldron of our own, if that's what you mean," responded De Ruyter; "and we have people from every corner of the globe here now helping to keep the pot a-boiling. We have Russian Jews by the thousand, living just as they did in the Pale. We have Chinese enough to support a Chinese theatre. We have so many Syrians now that they are pre-empting certain blocks for themselves. We have Irish peasants so timid and suspicious that they won't go to the hospital when they are almost dying, because they believe the doctors keep a Black Bottle to be administered to troublesome patients."

"I should think they would be ever so much more comfortable in a roomy hospital than in their stuffy little tenement-house rooms," said Mrs. Jimmy; "and they can't get decent nursing in their own homes, can they?"

"The poor are a most unreasonable lot—and ungrateful, too," added Mr. Suydam; "that's what I think."

"They are not so badly off in their tenement-houses as you might think," explained De Ruyter. "They help each other with the children when there's sickness."

"The universal freemasonry of motherhood," commented Gilbert Barry ; and again Miss Peters suspected the story - teller of making a mental record of the phrase.

"They are impossible to understand," De Ruyter declared.

"Why ?" asked Miss Peters, suddenly, across the table, to the surprise of everybody. The young Irishman smiled encouragingly, as though he had been regretting that this pretty girl refused to talk.

"Why are they impossible to understand ?" repeated the American story - teller. "I don't know, I'm sure. They are conundrums, all of them, and I am ready to give them up."

"Isn't it because you persist in approaching them as though they were strange, wild beasts ?" the young woman went on. "You speak of them just as if they were different from us. But they are not, are they ? They have their feelings just like we have ; they fall in love and they get married and they quarrel and they die, just like we do. There is not more crime in the tenement-houses than there is in the rest of the city—not if you remember how many more people live in the tenement-houses. There isn't less joy there, or less sorrow either. There is quite as much happiness, I reckon, and a good deal more fun. They are not the lower animals ; and it just makes me mad all over when I hear them spoken of in that way. They are human beings, after all—and if you can't understand them it's because you're not ready to go to them as your equals."

"That's what I say," the Irishman agreed; "we must approach them on the plane of human sympathy—that's the only way to get them to open their hearts."

"Why should we expect them to open their hearts to us?" Miss Peters continued. "We don't open ours to strangers, do we?"

"That's quite true," admitted Barry. "Sometimes I wonder if it isn't impertinent we are when we thrust ourselves into a poor man's room. I doubt we should like him to thrust himself into ours."

"I think that is a most amusing suggestion of yours," Mrs. Jimmy declared. "I shall look forward with delight to the day when the Five Points send missionaries up to Fifth Avenue."

"What an absurd idea!" cried Mrs. Canton, in disgust.

"Come now," the Irishman returned, "I deny that the suggestion is mine; but it is not so absurd—really, it isn't. There's lots of things they can teach us. I don't know but what we have more to learn from them than they have from us—really I don't. Christianity, now—practical Christianity—'inasmuch as ye did it to one of the least of these,' and all that sort of thing—well, there's more of that among the poor than there is among the rich, I'm thinking."

"If you want to pick up picturesque bits of low life in New York," broke in De Ruyter, "you must get a chance to see a candle in the plate."

"A candle in the plate?" echoed Barry. "I've never heard of it."

"It sounds like the title of a tale of superstition transplanted from Europe and surviving here in America," said Mrs. Jimmy.

"It's not a superstition, it's only a custom," De Ruyter explained; "and whether it's a transplanted survival or not I can't say. You see I've never seen the thing myself, but I've been told about it. I hear that down in the tenement-house region, when a family can't pay the rent and the landlord puts their scant furniture out on the sidewalk, and they don't know where to lay their heads that night, then one of the neighbors takes a candle and lights it and sticks it up on a plate, and takes his stand on the sidewalk; and this is a sign to everybody that there is a family in sore distress, and so the passers-by drop in a penny or two until there is enough to pay the arrears of rent and let the poor mother and children go back."

Mrs. Jimmy Suydam laughed a little bitterly. "That sort of thing may be possible on Cherry Hill," she said, "but it would never do on Murray Hill, would it? Just imagine how absurd a broken millionaire would look standing at a street corner with a little electric light on a silver salver, expecting the multi-millionaires going by to drop in a check or two to pay his rent for him !"

"I thought I had a quaint little silhouette of metropolitan life for you," De Ruyter responded, smiling back; "but you spoil the picture if you guy it like that."

"Very curious it is," said Barry—"very curious, indeed. 'How far a little candle throws its beams.' I don't think that the custom was exported from Ireland or from England—at least, I do not recall anything analogous."

"I've heard an old Irishwoman complain that the law was harder here on the tenant than it was in the old country," Miss Peters asserted; and then she appended an imitation of the old Irishwoman's speech: "'Sure, they'd boycott the landlord there, that's what they'd do, or they'd shoot the agent, maybe; but here ye can't—there's the police, bad cess to 'em !'"

"Have you ever seen the candle in the plate ?" Barry asked her, across the table.

"Never," she answered.

"But you have heard of it ?" De Ruyter inquired.

"Never before to-night," was her reply.

"You don't mean to say you don't believe that there is any such custom ?" Mrs. Jimmy asked. "Thus all our illusions are shattered one by one."

"Of course, I don't know," the girl responded; "I haven't been working down there very long—only since last February. But it sounds like it was a fake, as we used to say in the newspaper office when I was a reporter."

Mrs. Jimmy Suydam had never met Miss Peters before, and now she examined the girl curiously, wondering what sort of being a woman was who had been a reporter and was now living among the poor, and who happened also to be dining at Mrs. Canton's.

The hostess was just then explaining to Mr. Suydam in a whisper that Miss Peters was a Southern girl of excellent family, who used to write those "Polly Perkins" articles for the *Dial* on Sunday, but who had given it up last winter, and now acted as her secretary.

"A fake?" repeated the Irishman, gleefully; "that's one of your Americanisms, isn't it? I must remember that. A fake—what does it mean exactly?"

"It means the thing that is not," De Ruyter explained, with a trace of acerbity in his voice. "Miss Peters disbelieves in the existence of the candle in the plate, and she was too polite to call my story a lie, so she said it was a fake."

"Oh, Mr. De Ruyter," was her retort, "and you used to be a newspaper man yourself once!"

"Your newspapers, now," Barry broke in, "I confess they puzzle me. They are so clever, you know, and so up-to-date, and all that; but you never know what to believe in them, do you? And then they do such dreadful things."

13

" I fear you will find few Americans prepared to defend our newspapers," said the story-teller, always a little ashamed that he had once been a reporter. "But what sort of a dreadful thing have you in mind just now?"

"Things quite inconceivable, you know," the Irishman explained ; "a thing like this, for example. A year or two ago a man gave me a copy of one of your New York papers—the *Dial,* I think it was. I read it with great interest, as one would the writing of some strange tribe of savages, don't you know ? It was so very extraordinary."

As the guest made this plain statement, little Miss Peters happened to catch the eye of the handsome Mrs. Jimmy Suydam, and they exchanged an imperceptible smile.

"What shocked me the most," Barry continued, "was a long article from some special commissioner, with headings in huge letters—"

" Scare - heads they call them," explained De Ruyter.

" Scare - heads ?" repeated the Irishman. "That's the very name for them. Scare-heads —delicious ! This article, then, had scare-heads galore, and it described how a suicide had been identified. It seems some poor girl of the working-class had got into trouble, and sooner than bring disgrace on her family she had jumped into the river here—Hudson's River, isn't it ? She had carefully arranged so that there was no

clew by which she could be traced. But she
had not counted on the devilish ingenuity of the
special commissioner, a woman, too—at least I
suppose it was a woman, since the thing was
signed 'Polly Perkins.'"

Mrs. Jimmy saw the blood rise in the cheeks
of Miss Peters, until the little Southern girl was
as red as any of the maple-leaves that decked the
cloth between the two women. She noticed that
Rupert De Ruyter was staring into his plate with
ill-concealed embarrassment, and that Mrs. Canton seemed a little uneasy.

"It seems that the poor creature's body was
sent to the Morgue," Barry continued, "and no
one claimed it, so it was buried at the cost of the
county. And there's where the diabolical cunning of this reporter was exercised. She guessed
that the girl's family would want to see the body
laid away in holy ground, and so she went to the
burying. And she hit it, for there were two
women there in deep black, the mother of the
poor wretch and the sister, not afraid to show
their bitter grief when they thought they were
unknown and unwatched. The spy tracked them
to their house and she found out their names,
and she put the whole story in the paper! I suppose it broke the mother's heart, and the sister's,
to see the dead girl's shame brought home to her
and to them when they thought it was buried in
the grave with her body. I don't deny that the
female detective showed a deal of skill; but what

a pitiful thing! To risk breaking two loving hearts—and for what purpose?"

There was a moment's silence when the Irishman asked this unanswerable question. Then Miss Peters raised her head and looked him in the eye.

"That was what is called a 'beat.' No other paper had the news," she said; "and the reporter who wrote that story got a raise of five dollars a week."

"Faith, she deserved it," Barry returned. "It was blood-money she was taking, I'm thinking."

"That's what I think now," Miss Peters replied. "I wish I had thought so then. I wrote that article, and that is one reason why I am living down there among the poor, to try and make it up to them. Of course, I can't undo the wrong I did; but I mean to do my best."

Then there was another silence, broken by Mrs. Jimmy, who turned to Mrs. Canton and asked if she was going to take a box at the horse-show.

When the ladies left the dining-room Barry took the chair by the side of Suydam.

"What's the name of that pretty little girl?" he asked. "Peters, isn't it? I say, it was awfully plucky of her to tell us that she was 'Polly Perkins,' wasn't it, now? I like her; she's a trump! And that fair hair of hers is very fetching, isn't it?"

(1897)

ERRYMOUNT MORTON walked briskly down Madison Avenue that warm November evening, when there was never a foretaste of winter in the intermittent breezes that blew gently across the city from river to river; and as he crossed the side streets one after another he saw the full moon in the east, low and large and mellow. On the brow of Murray Hill he checked his pace for a moment in frank enjoyment of the vista before him, differing in so many ways from the scenes which met his vision in the little college town of New England where he earned his living, and where he had spent the most of his life. The glow of the great town filled the air, and the roar of the city arose all about him. It seemed to him almost as though he could feel the heart of the metropolis throbbing before him. He caught himself wondering again whether he had not erred in accepting the professorship he had been so glad to get when he came back from Germany, and whether his life would not have been fuller and far richer had he come to New York, as once he thought of doing, and had he resolutely struck out for himself in the welter and chaos of the commercial capital of the country.

337

Down at the foot of the slope a cluster of electric lights spelled out the name of a trivial extravaganza then nearing its hundredth performance in the lovely Garden Theatre, and the avenue hereabouts had a strange, unnatural brilliance. High up in the pure dark blue the beautiful tower rose in air, its grace made visible by many lights of its own. The avenue was clogged with carriages, and the arcade before the theatre and under the tower was thick with men who carried under their arms folded card-board plans of the great amphitheatre, and who vociferously proffered tickets for the horse-show. So far remote from the current of fashion was Merrymount Morton that he had not been aware that the horse-show week was about to come to a glorious end. But he was familiar enough with New York to know that the horse-show was also an exhibition of men and women, and that the human entries were quite as important as the equine, and rather more interesting. He had never happened to be in the city at this season of the year ; and although he had intended to spend the evening at the College Club, he seized the occasion to see a metropolitan spectacle which chanced to be novel to him.

From one of the shouting and insistent venders he bought a ticket, and he walked through the broad entrance-hall, the floor of which slanted upwards. He passed the door of a restaurant

on his right, and he glanced down a staircase
which led to the semi-subterranean stalls where
the horses were tethered. A pungent, acrid,
stable odor filled his nostrils. Then he found
himself inside the immense amphitheatre, under
the skeleton ribs of its roof picked out with long
lines of tiny electric bulbs. Morton had a first
impression of glittering hugeness, and a second
of restless bustle. From a gallery behind him
there came the blare and crash of a brass band
playing an Oriental march; but even this did
not drown the buzz and murmur of many thousand voices. The vast building seemed to Morton to be filled with men and women, all of them
talking and many of them in motion. He found
himself swept along slowly in the dense crowd
that circled steadily around the high fence which
guarded the arena wherein the horses were ex-
hibited. This crowd was too compact for him
to approach the railing, and he could not discover for himself whether or not anything was
to be seen.

A thin line of more or less horsy fellows fringed
the fence, and seemed to be interested in what
was going on. The most of the men and women
who filled the broad promenade between the railing and the long tier of private boxes paid little
or no attention to the arena; they gave themselves up to staring at the very gayly dressed
ladies in the boxes. It struck the New England
college professor that the most of those present

made no pretence of caring for the horses, as though horses could be seen any day; while they frankly devoted themselves to gazing at the people of fashion penned side by side in the boxes, and not often placing themselves so plainly on exhibition. Some of those who were playing their parts on this narrow and elevated stage had the self-consciousness of the amateur, and some had the ease that comes of long practice. These latter looked as though they were accustomed to be stared at, as though they expected it of right, as though they were there on purpose to be seen. They seemed to know one another; and it struck Morton that they were apparently all members of a secret fraternity of fashion, with their own signs and passwords and their own system of private grips; and they wholly ignored the people who had not been initiated and who were not members of their society. They nodded and smiled brightly to belated arrivals of their own set. They kept up a continual chatter among themselves, the women leaning across to talk to acquaintances in the adjoining compartments, and the men paying visits to the boxes of their friends. Now and again some one in a box would recognize some one in the circling throng below; but for the most part there was no communication between the two classes.

To Morton the spectacle had the attraction of novelty; it was so novel, indeed, that he did not

EXPLANATIONS

quite know what to make of it. It disconcerted him not a little to see people, of position presumably, and obviously of wealth, willing thus to show themselves off, dressed, many of them, as though with special intent to attract attention. As a student of sociology, he found this inspection of Society — in the narrowest sense of the word — almost as instructive as it was interesting. At times the vulgarity of the whole thing shocked him, more especially once when he could not but hear the loud voices of one over-dressed group of women, who were discussing the characteristics of one "Willie."

"He's a wretched little beast!" cried one of these ladies.

"You mustn't say that," rejoined another, a tall woman with gray hair; "you know he's my corespondent." And at this stroke of wit the rest of the party laughed repeatedly.

But few of those on exhibition were as common as the members of this group. Indeed, Morton was struck with the fact that the most of the men and women who were being stared out of countenance were apparently people of breeding, and he wondered that they were willing to place themselves in what seemed to him so false a position. Many of the girls, for example, who wore striking costumes and extravagant hats, were themselves refined in face and retiring in bearing; they were stylish, no doubt, but they were well bred also. It seemed to Morton that style was perhaps the chief characteristic of these New York girls—style rather than beauty.

The average of good looks was high, and yet, as it happened, he was able to walk half around the huge building without seeing half a dozen women whom he was prepared to declare handsome. The girls appeared to be strong, healthy, lively, quick-witted, and charming, but rarely beautiful. They seemed to him, moreover, to be emphatically superior to the men who accompanied them, superior not only in looks, but in manners and intelligence.

Morton noted, to his surprise, that some of these men were quite as conscious of their clothes as any of the women were; and he caught also more than one remark showing that the appreciation of the women's clothes was not confined to the women themselves.

As he was nearing the Fourth Avenue end of the edifice he saw in a box just above him—for he found himself staring like the rest—a lady of striking beauty, with a look of sadness on her face, that gave place to a factitious smile when she spoke to one or another of the three or four young men who stood on the steps at the side of her chair. The face interested Morton, and it was recognized by two young men just behind him.

"Hello!" said one of them, "there's Mrs. Cyrus Poole. Smart gown, hasn't she?"

"Always has," answered the other. "Best-groomed woman in New York."

"She is pretty well turned out generally, for a fact," the first speaker responded. "But Cyrus Poole's made money enough out of the widow and the orphan this summer to pay for all the gowns his wife can wear this winter, at any rate."

It was only when Merrymount Morton had threaded his way half around the horse-show that he first saw a horse there. As he came to the Fourth Avenue end the crowd before him fell away, and a gate in the railing swung back across the promenade, while grooms led out of the arena five or six beautiful stallions. The New England college professor had a healthy liking for a fine horse, and his eyes followed these superb creatures till they were out of sight. Then in the clear space at the far end of the building he saw three coaches, one of them already equipped with its four-in-hand, while the horses were being harnessed to the others.

He stood there for a minute or two looking at them with interest. Then he turned his back, and once more began circling about the arena in the thick of the crowd, with no chance of seeing a horse again until he could get to the seat to which his ticket entitled him. He took out the bit of pasteboard and examined it again, and he saw that his place was very near the entrance, only he had gone to the right when he came in instead of to the left. By this time the men and women on exhibition in the boxes had begun to lose the attraction of novelty; and Morton walked

on as swiftly as he could make his way through
the crowd, wishing to get his seat in time to see
the competition of the coaches.

He had come almost to the foot of the little
flight of steps by which he could reach his seat
when he happened to look up, and he caught
sight of a familiar face. In a box only a score
of feet before him there sat a lady about whose
high-bred beauty there could hardly be two opinions. She was probably nearly thirty years old,
but she looked fresher than either of the girls by
her side. She wore a costume combining studied simplicity and marked individuality ; and yet
no one who saw her took thought of her attire,
for her beauty subdued all things, and made any
adornment she might adopt seem as though it
were necessary and inevitable.

There was a suggestion of stiffness in her carriage, and perhaps a hint of haughtiness ; but
when she smiled she was as charming as she was
handsome.

As his eyes first fell upon her Morton's heart
gave a sudden thump, and then beat swiftly for
a minute or two. Although he had not seen her
for nearly ten years, he recognized her instantly.
She had changed but little since they had met
for the last time. He would have known her
anywhere and at once.

And if he had been in any doubt as to her
identity, it would have been dispelled by the
conversation of the two young men who had

been walking around the arena just behind him.

"Devilish pretty Mrs. Jimmy Suydam looks to-night, doesn't she?" asked one of them.

"She's had a good summer's rest," the other answered. "She was at St. Moritz with her mother while Jimmy was off with Lord Stany-hurst."

"Drove from Paris to Vienna, didn't he?" the first speaker queried. "I'd rather do it in a sleeper—wouldn't you?"

"I don't know," the second responded. "It's very swagger to drive your own coach all over Europe with a man like Stanyhurst, who knows everybody. I guess Jimmy thought it was cheap at the price. Besides, *Punch* called him the 'Wandering Jehu,' and they thought that was a great joke over there."

"The joke was at Jimmy's expense, of course," was the next remark. "They say Lord Stany-hurst never pays a bill himself when he can get an American to do it."

"Well, Jimmy made by the bargain," the other rejoined, "and he can afford it. Old man Suydam left a good business, and Jimmy knows enough to let it alone."

There had been a congestion of the crowd in front of Morton, but now there was a path opened before him. He drew back and let the two young men pass. He could not look away from the beautiful woman in the box before him.

He wondered if he had courage to go up and speak to her. He remembered her so sharply, he recognized every turn of her head and every dainty gesture of her hands, he recalled so distinctly every word of their conversation the last time they met that it did not seem possible to him that she might have forgotten him. And yet it was not impossible. Why should she remember what he could not forget?

While he was hesitating, the party in her box broke up. One of the young ladies who were sitting with her arose and came down the steps, escorted by two young men, and as they passed Morton he caught from their conversation that they were going to the stables below to see a certain famous horse in his stall. The other young lady had changed her seat to the back of the box, where she was deep in conversation with a young man who had taken the chair beside hers. Mrs. Suydam was left alone in the front of the box.

She sat there apparently not bored with her own society, and obviously indifferent to the frank staring of the men and women who passed along the promenade a few feet below her. She sat there calm in her cold beauty, unmoved and uninterested, almost as though her thoughts were far away.

Morton made up his mind, and pressed forward again.

When he was within a yard or two of the steps

leading to her box she happened to glance down, and she caught his eye fixed upon hers. She was about to glance away, when she looked again, and then a smile of recognition lighted her face, followed by the faintest of blushes.

She bowed as Morton raised his hat, and she held out her hand cordially when he climbed the steps to her box.

"I hardly dared to hope that you would remember me, Mrs. Suydam," he said, as he shook hands gently. "It is so long since I saw you last."

"How could you think I should ever forget the pleasant month I spent in your mother's house?" she returned. "We do not have so many pleasant months in life, do we, that we can afford to let any one of them slip out of memory? You haven't forgotten me, have you? Well, then, why should I forget you and your mother and the lovely little college town?"

"That month I can't forget," he responded; "but it was a long while ago, and my existence is uneventful always, while yours is full—and then so many things have happened since."

"Yes," she admitted, "so many things have happened. I'm married, for one thing. But that hasn't made me forget how kind you all were to me. Can't you sit down here for a few minutes and give me all the news of the college and the town?"

"I shall be only too glad," he said, taking the chair by her side. "Where shall I begin?"

14

"Tell me about yourself," she commanded.

"That won't take me long," he returned. "Very little has happened to me. I was going to Germany—perhaps you remember—that fall, after you left us. Well, I went, and I stayed two years, and I took my Ph.D. there, and I came back to the old college, and they gave me a professorship—and that's all."

"That's enough, I think," she answered, looking at him frankly with her dark eyes. "You have your work to do, and you do it. I don't believe there is anything better in life than to be sure what you ought to work at and to be able to work at it."

"I suppose you are right," Morton acknowledged. "I find hard labor is often the best fun, after all. But I can get solid enjoyment out of loafing, too. I don't recall that we worked very steadily that month that you were with us, and we certainly had a very good time. At least I did !"

"And so did I," she declared, unbending a little, and with a laugh of pleasant recollection. "I enjoyed every minute of my visit. I wish I could have such good times now !"

"Don't you ?" he asked.

"Not often," she answered. "Perhaps never."

"You surprise me," he replied. "I supposed you were being entertained by day and by night, week in and week out, from one year's end to another."

"So we are," she explained.   "But being entertained isn't always being interested, is it ?"

"That's the theory, isn't it ?" he rejoined.

"It may be the theory," she confessed, "but
I'm sure it isn't the practice."

"I know that little college town of ours is remote from the path of progress," he went on,
"but sometimes we behold those messengers of
civilization, the New York Sunday newspapers.
And whenever I do get one I am certain to see
that you have been to a dinner-dance here, to a
bal poudré there.   I should judge that you lived
in an endless merry-go-round of gayety."

She smiled again, and there was no sadness
in her smile, only a vague, detached weariness.
"Dinner-dances are the fashion just now," she
said ; "and if there is anything more absurd than
the fashion it's to waste one's strength struggling
against it."

"That is very end-of-the-century philosophy,"
he commented.

"It's philosophical not to want to be left out
of things, isn't it ?" she inquired.   "Even if one
doesn't care to go, one doesn't like not to be
asked, and so one goes often when one would
rather stay at home."

"I should think that if many people had mo-
tives like that, your parties here in New York
might be rather dull," he retorted, with a little
laugh.

"They are dull," she returned, calmly. "Sometimes they are very dull. But, of course, it doesn't do not to go."

"I suppose not," he agreed.

"But I find myself wondering sometimes," she continued, "where all the dull people in society were dug up. Sometimes after a long month of dinners I get desperate and almost wish I could renounce the world. Why, at the end of last winter I told my husband that we had not spent a single evening home since we got back from Florida, and we hadn't had a single pleasant evening, not one. He didn't think it was as bad as that, and perhaps it wasn't for him either, for I don't believe the women are as stupid as the men. Of course now and then there was a dinner I thought I should enjoy, but I never did. I'd see the clever man I'd have liked to talk to ; I'd see him far down at the other end of the table, and that was all I did see of him. Some dreary old man would take me in, and then after dinner I'd have perhaps two or three little boys come up and try to pay compliments, and succeed in keeping away the men who might possibly have had something to say."

"And yet yours is the set that so many people seem to be trying so hard to enter," he suggested ; "that is, if I understand aright what I read in New York novels."

"Yes," she answered, "I suppose that's the chief satisfaction we have — we know we are envied by the people who want to visit us, and to have us visit them. I suppose the desire to get into Society fills the emptiness in many a woman's life; it gives her something to live for."

"They don't seem to have much of the stern joy that foemen feel," Morton commented. "They take life desperately hard. Over there in the other corner I saw a handsome woman, and I overheard a man call her by name—she's the wife of Cyrus Poole, the Wall Street operator. And when I saw the unsatisfied aspiration in her face, I wondered whether she was one of those social strugglers I had read about."

"Mrs. Poole?" echoed Mrs. Suydam, indifferently. "I don't know her: I've met her, of course—one meets everybody—but I don't know her. She is good-looking, and she is in the thick of the social struggle. Upward and outward is her motto—Excelsior! They used to say that all last winter you could positively hear her climb. But then they have said that of so many people! She is clever, they say, and she entertains lavishly, so I shouldn't wonder if she succeeded sooner or later; and then she will be so disappointed."

Morton smiled. "From your account," he said, "the social struggle is rather a tragedy than a comedy; and I confess it has hitherto struck me as not without a suggestion of farce."

"It is absurd, isn't it?" she returned, smiling back. "And are we not a very snobbish lot? Jimmy declares that society in New York is almost as snobbish as it is in London even."

There was a moment of silence, and then Morton asked, a little stiffly, "How is Mr. Suydam? You know I have never had the pleasure of meeting him."

"Haven't you?" Mrs. Suydam responded. "You can see him soon. He's to drive George Western's coach. There they come now!"

A trumpet sounded; a gate in the railing at the Fourth Avenue end of the building was opened; and a coach was driven into the arena. A very stout man sat on the box alone.

Mrs. Suydam raised her long-handled eye-glass and looked at the approaching coachman.

"Oh, that's not Jimmy," she said, quickly; "of course not. That's the man they call The Adipose Deposit."

The trumpet sounded again, and a second coach was turned into the arena. The four horses were beautifully matched bays. The driver was a tall, thin, youngish man, who sat impassible on the box, and gave no sign of annoyance when a wheel of the vehicle rasped the gate-post.

"That's Mr. Suydam," said the lady to whom Morton was talking, as the bays trotted briskly past them, the man on the box holding himself rigidly and handling the ribbons skilfully.

"He is quite a professional," Morton remarked.

"Isn't he?" Mrs. Suydam replied. "You know he drove the Brighton coach out of Lon-

don for three years.   He really does it very well,
they all say.   I've told him that if we ever lost our
money he would make a very superior coachman."

"Those bays go together admirably," the college professor declared, "and Mr. Suydam handles them superbly.   But how pitiful it is to see
their tails docked !"

"Oh, they do that in England," she explained,
"so it's fashionable.   But it is ugly, isn't it ?
Do you remember what a lovely long tail that
Kentucky mare had, the one I rode that day—"

Then Mrs. Suydam paused suddenly.

"Yes," answered Morton, not looking at her,
"I remember it."

Mrs. Suydam conquered her slight embarrassment and gave a light little laugh.

"How rude I have been !" she said.   "Here
I've been talking about myself and about my
husband, and I haven't asked about you.   Are
you married yet ?"

"No," he answered, and now he looked at
her, and she blushed again ; "and I am not likely ever to marry, I think.   There was only one
woman in the world for me, and I told her so,
but she didn't care for me at all, and she told me
so—and then she touched up that Kentucky
mare and rode away with my heart hanging at
her saddle-bow."

"You can find a better woman than she is,"
was her response ; "a woman who will make you
a better wife than she would ever have done."

Before Morton could reply to this, the girl and the two young men who had been in the box at first returned from their visit to the stables. The trumpet sounded again, and the judges made the drivers of the four coaches—for two more had entered after Mr. Suydam's—repeat their evolutions around the arena. And then, after protracted consultation together, the awards were made, and grooms ran to attach rosettes to the leaders of the team driven by the stout gentleman, who took the first prize, and then to the leaders of the team driven by Suydam, who took the second prize. The numbers of the winning coaches were displayed on the wide sign-boards at each end of the hall. The coaches were driven around again, and then out. The trumpets were silent for a while ; and the brass band crashed forth again.

"Jimmy won't like not getting the first prize, will he ?" asked the girl who had just returned to the box.

"I don't think it will worry him," answered his wife, with a return of her haughty manner.

She had not introduced Morton to any of the others in the box.

In the presence of so many it was impossible to resume their conversation on the old friendly basis. It seemed to Morton that since the girl and the young men had come back there was a difference in Mrs. Suydam's manner towards him ; he could not define it to himself, but he

felt it.   Perhaps she was conscious of this herself.

When he made a movement preparatory to
going, she said : " Must you go ?   I wanted you
to meet my husband.   Can't you drop in and
lunch with us to-morrow ?"

Morton thanked her and regretted that he
might have to take a midnight train, and expressed his pleasure at having met her again.
Then she held out her hand once more ; and a
minute later he was again in the thick of the
throng circling along the promenade.

Before he reached the entrance the music was
checked suddenly and the trumpet blared out,
and then the voice of a man in the centre of the
building was heard, intermittently, hopelessly
endeavoring to inform the thousands packed in
the splendid edifice that the fastest trotter in the
world would now be shown.   The crowd which
was staring steadily at the men and women in the
boxes paid little attention to this proclamation ;
to it the men and women in the boxes were far
more interesting than any horses could be, even
if any one of these could trot a mile in two
minutes without a running mate.

(1895)

IN THE WATCHES OF THE NIGHT

T was still snowing solidly as the carriage swung out of the side street and went heavily on its way up the avenue; the large flakes soon thickened again upon the huge fur collars of the two men who sat on the box bolt-upright; the flat crystals frosted the windows of the landau so that the trained nurse could see out only on one side. She sat back in the luxurious vehicle. She had on the seat beside her the bag containing her change of raiment; and she wondered, as she always did when she was called unexpectedly to take charge of an unknown case, what manner of house it might be that she was going to enter, and what kind of people she would be forced to associate with in the swift intimacy of the sick-room and for an unknown period. That the patient was wealthy and willing to spend his wealth was obvious — the carriage, the horses, the liveried servants, were evidence enough of this. That his name was Swank she also knew; and she thought that perhaps she had heard about the marriage of a rich old man named Swank to a pretty young wife a year or two ago. That he had been taken sick suddenly, and that the case might be seri-

ous, she had gathered from the note which the
doctor had sent to summon her, and which had
been brought by the carriage that was now returning with her.

She had ample time for speculation as they
drove up the avenue in the early darkness of the
last day of the year.   The Christmas wreaths
still decked the windows of the hotels, although
through the steady snow she could see little more
than a blur of reddish-yellow light as she sped
past.   There were few people in the avenue, except as they crossed the broader side streets, now
beginning to be filled with the throng of workers returning home after the day's labor.   They
passed St. Patrick's Cathedral, already encrusted
with snow whiter than its stone.   They came to
Central Park, and they kept on, with its broad
meadows on their left gray in the descending
darkness.   At last the carriage drew up before a
house on a corner—a very large house it seemed
to the trained nurse; and its marble front struck
her as cold, not to call it gloomy.   Workmen
were hastily erecting the frame of an awning
down the marble steps, and a path had been made
across the snowy sidewalk.

The footman carried her bag up the stoop and
rang the bell for her.

The door was opened promptly by a very British butler.

"This is the nurse for Mr. Swank," said the
footman.   "Is he any better?"

"''E's about the same, I'm thinkin'," the butler responded.   "This way, please," he said to
the owner of the bag, which the footman depos-
ited just inside the door.   "I'll take you up to
Mr. Swank's room, and I'll send your bag up to
you afterwards."

The trained nurse followed the butler up the
massive wooden stairs, heavy with dark carving.
She noticed that the house was now dimly lighted, and that there was a going and a coming of
servants, as though in preparation for an entertainment of some sort.

"We 'ave a dinner on this evening," the butler explained ; "only twenty-four ; but it's 'ard
Mr. Swank ain't goin' to be able to come down.
We're keepin' the 'ouse dark now, so it won't get
too 'ot at dinner-time."

Whatever the reason for the absence of adequate illumination, it made the upper hall even
more dismal than the one below—so the trained
nurse thought.

"That's Mr. Swank's room there ; and 'ere's
'is dressin'-room, that you're to 'ave—so the doctor said," the butler declared, leading the stranger into a small room with a lofty ceiling, and
with one window overlooking Central Park.   The
shades had not been drawn ; the single gas-jet
was burning dimly ; there was no fireplace ; and
a sofa on one side had had sheets and blankets
put on it to serve as her bed.

She almost shivered, the place seemed to her

so cheerless. But her training taught her not
to think of her own comfort.

"This will do very well," she asserted.

"I'll tell them to fetch up your bag," the butler said, as he was about to withdraw. "Would
you be wantin' any dinner later?"

"Yes," she answered, "I would like something to eat later—whenever it is convenient."

The butler left the room, only to reappear almost immediately.

"'Ere's the doctor now," he announced, holding the door open.

A tall, handsome man, with a masterful mouth,
walked in with a soft, firm tread.

"So this is the nurse," he began. "Miss
Clement, isn't it? I'm glad you were able to
follow my note so quickly. If you will come
into the next room, where the patient is, as soon
as you have changed your dress, I'll tell you
what I wish you to do."

With that he left her; and in less than ten
minutes she followed him into the large bedroom
on the corner of the house. It was an unusually
spacious room, with a high ceiling and four tall
windows.

There was a dull-red fire, which seemed insufficient to warm even the elaborate marble mantel.
Almost in one corner stood a large bed, with
thick curtains draped back from a canopy.

The doctor was sitting by the side of the bed
as the nurse came into the room.

"SHE ALMOST SHIVERED, THE PLACE SEEMED TO HER
SO CHEERLESS"

"This is Miss Clement, Mr. Swank," he said, in a cheerful voice, to the old man, who lay in the bed motionless. "She will look after you during the night."

Mr. Swank made no answer, but he opened his eyes and looked at the woman who had come to nurse him. She used to say afterwards that she had never felt before so penetrating a gaze.

The doctor turned to her, and in the same professionally cheery tones he said: "I sent for you, nurse, because Mrs. Swank has an important dinner to-night, and it might therefore be difficult for her to give Mr. Swank the attention he may require."

The physician was addressing the nurse, but it seemed to her that his words were really intended for the patient, whose eyes were still fixed on her.

All at once the sick man sat up in bed and began to cough violently. When the paroxysm had passed he sank back on the pillow again and closed his eyes wearily.

"I think that was not as severe as the last one," the doctor remarked ; " I can leave you in Miss Clement's hands now. Perhaps, if I happen to be up this way about midnight, I may drop in again just to see that you are getting on all right. In the mean time, nurse, you will see that he takes these capsules every two hours—he had the last at half-past five. And you will take his temperature every hour if he is awake."

15

He said good-night to Mr. Swank in the same cheering tone, and then he went to the door. The nurse knew that she was to follow him.

When they stood alone in the hall, the doctor said to her : "If there is any change in the pulse or the temperature, send for me at once. Ring for the butler, and tell him I am to be sent for ; he will know what to do. Mr. Swank has influenza only, but his heart is weak, and he needs careful attention. I shall be here again the last thing to-night."

When the nurse returned to the corner room the patient had fallen into a heavy doze, and she took advantage of this to prepare for the long vigil. She arranged her own belongings ready to her hand in the dressing-room set aside for her use. In that room she did not lower the shade, and she even stood at the window for a minute, trying to look out over Central Park, hidden from her by a swaying veil of swirling snow. The workmen had completed the canvas tunnel down the stoop to the edge of the sidewalk, and the lanterns hung inside the frame-work revealed grotesquely its striped contortions. As the nurse gazed down on it an old man without any overcoat sought a temporary shelter from the storm in the mouth of the awning, only to be ordered away almost immediately by the servant in charge.

The nurse went back into the larger room. She looked at her patient asleep in the warm bed. She wondered why life was so unequal ; why

the one man should spend the night in the snowy
street, while the other had all that money could
buy — shelter, warmth, food, attendance. She
recalled how her father used to declare that the
inequalities we see all around us are superficial
only, and that there are compensations, did we
but know them, for all deprivations, and that all
apparent advantages are to be paid for, somehow,
sooner or later. More than ever to - night she
doubted the wisdom of her father's saying. How
could there be anything but inequality between
the old man in the street there below and the old
man here in the bed ? The thing seemed to her
impossible.

As she became accustomed to the dim light of
the room she was able to note that the furniture
was heavy and black, that the carpet was unusually thick, that the walls had large paintings hanging on them, that the ceiling was frescoed in
sombre tints. On all sides of her she saw the
evidences of wealth and of the willingness to
spend it ; and yet the room and the house seemed
to her strangely uninviting, and almost repellent.
She asked herself why the sick man lying there
asleep in the huge bed had not used his money
to better advantage, and had not at least made
cheerful his own sick-room. Then she smiled at
her own foolishness. Of course the owner of the
room had not expected to be stricken down ; of
course he had no thought of illness when he had
furnished.

She moved gently about the room and tried to look at the pictures, but the illumination was insufficient. All that she could make out clearly were the names of the artists carved on tiny tablets attached to the broad frames; and although she knew little about painting, she had read the newspapers enough to be aware that pictures by these artists must have cost a great deal of money—thousands of dollars each, very likely. If she had thousands to spend, she believed that she could lay them out to better advantage than the owner of the house had done here. It struck her again as though the sick man had more than his share of the good things of life. She had not yet heard him speak, and she had not really had a good look at him; but she could not help thinking that a man who had so much, who had the means of doing so much, who was absolutely his own master, and who could spend a large fortune just as he pleased—she could not help thinking that he ought to be happy. It was true that he was ill now, but the influenza wears itself out at last; and when he was well he had so much money that he must be happier than other men—far happier than poor men, certainly.

When she came to this conclusion she was standing near the foot of the bed, looking at the man lying there asleep. It was on the stroke of half-past seven, and she had come to let him have his medicine again. Then she noticed that his eyelids were parted, and that he was looking at her.

"It is time to take one of these capsules now," she said, gently moving to his side and offering it to him.

He took it without a word, and gulped it down with a swallow of water. Then he sank back on the pillow, only to raise himself at once, as he was again shaken by a severe fit of coughing.

At last he lay back on the bed once more, still breathing heavily.

A fresh, young voice was heard at the door leading to the hall, saying, "May I come in, John?" and then a graceful young figure floated into the room with a birdlike motion.

The sick man opened his eyes wide as his wife came near him, and a smile illumined his face.

"How beautiful you are!" he said, faintly, but proudly.

"Am I?" she answered, laughing a little. "I *tried* to be to-night, because there will be the smartest women in New York at Mrs. Jimmy Suydam's dance, and I wanted to be as good as *any* of them."

The nurse had withdrawn towards the window as the wife came forward, and she did not believe that any woman at Mrs. Jimmy Suydam's, wherever that might be, could well look more beautiful than the one who now stood smiling by the side of the sick husband.

She was a blonde, this young wife of an old

man, a mere girl, and the vaporous blue dress
was cut low on a slender neck girt about by a
single strand of large pearls, while a diamond
tiara high on her shapely head flashed light into
every corner of the darkened sick-room.

"I thought I'd just run in and see how you
were before anybody came," she said, lightly.
"Dinner is at quarter to eight, you know. I
do *wish* you could be down. We shall miss you
dreadfully. Of course I sent out at the last minute and got a man to fill your place, so we shall
sit down with twenty-four all right; but then—"

Here she broke off, having caught sight of the
third person in the room.

"So this is the nurse Dr. Cheever sent for?"
she went on. "I'm sure she'll take good care of
you, John—the doctor is always *so* careful. And
if you hadn't had somebody with you I shouldn't
have liked to leave you all alone — really I
shouldn't!"

With that she circled about the bed again,
turning towards the door.

"I must be off now," she explained. "I can't
be *wasting* my time on you in this way. I really
ought to be down in the drawing-room *now;*
and first, I've got to see if the flowers are all
right on the table."

Her husband's eyes had followed her wistfully
about the room, watching every one of her easy
and graceful movements; and when at last she
slipped out of the door, it was a moment before

he turned an inquiring glance on the nurse, as
though to discover what she thought of the brilliant vision.

The nurse came to the side of the bed with
her clinical thermometer in her hand.

"You are awake now," she said, with a pleasant smile. "May I take your temperature?"

Five minutes later, when she was entering in
her note-book the high degree shown by the
thermometer, and when the patient had again
dropped off to sleep, the first guests began to arrive for the wife's dinner party.

The thick snow made the wheels inaudible,
but the nurse heard the doors of the carriages
slam as those who had been invited passed
through the canvas tunnel one after another.
In the room next to the dressing-room assigned
to her for her own use there was a rustling of
silken stuffs, and there were fragments of conversation now and again so loudly pitched as to
reach the ear of the young woman who sat silent
in the sick-chamber. Then, when all the guests
were come, the house sank again into silence,
and a tall clock in a corner of the stairs chimed
forth the hour of eight.

So long as her patient slept the nurse had
little or nothing to do; but though her body
was motionless, her thoughts were busy. She was
country-bred herself; she had left her home
in a little New England village by the sea to
make her way in the world. She had now been a

trained nurse for nearly two years; and yet, as it happened, her work had been either in hotels or in families of only moderate means. This was the first time she had been in so handsome a house or with people of so much wealth. She could not help being conscious of her surroundings, and she caught herself wishing that she too were rich. She confessed that she would like to be a guest at the dinner below. She wondered what a dinner-table for twenty-four must be. To be able to entertain as lavishly as that, and not to have to worry about the arrangement, or the cost, or anything — well, that would be an existence any woman must delight in. She felt herself capable of expanding, and of being equal to the enjoyment of any degree of luxury. She liked her occupation, for she had chosen her own calling. She had been successful in it too; and yet she was beginning to be a little afraid that she had miscalculated her strength. The work was very laborious and confining, and more than once of late she had felt overtaxed. It might be that in a year or two her reserve force would be exhausted, and she would have to give up the struggle and go back home, where she would be welcome, of course, but where she would add to the burdens her mother was already laden with.

There was an alternative, and never before had it seemed to her so tempting as when she was sitting there alone with the sick man in the darkened corner room of his great house. She

might marry. More than once she had been
asked in marriage ; and one man had asked her
more than once. He was persistent, and he still
declined to accept her refusal as final. He was
not an old man yet, although he was twice her
age. He was a rich man, even if he was not as
wealthy as the owner of the splendid but de-
pressing home where she now sat silently musing. She did not love him, that was true, and
there was no doubt about it ; but she did respect
him, and she had heard that sometimes love
comes after marriage. He could let her have
all she longed for, and he was ready to give her
everything he had. If she married him she too
could have dinners of twenty - four, and wear a
rope of pearls and a diamond tiara ; and then,
too, she could do so much good with money if
she had it.

In the course of her services in the hospital,
and afterwards among the poor, she had seen
many a case of sore distress which she had been
unable to relieve. If she had riches she could
accomplish much that was now impossible ; she
could do good in many ways ; she could relieve
suffering and aid the impoverished and help the
feeble far more adroitly and skilfully than could
any woman who had always been wealthy, and
who had not had her experience of life and of
its misfortunes and its miseries. She thought
that she knew her own character, and she believed that she had strength to withstand the

temptations which beset the rich. Thinking
herself unselfish, she held herself incapable of
keeping for herself alone any good fortune that
might come to her. And she made a solemn
resolve that if she should marry the man who
stood ready to take her to wife she would devote
to good works the greater part of her money and
of her time. She would dress as became her station, of course, and she would entertain sumptu-
ously too; but no old man should ever be turned
shivering from her door when she was giving a
dinner of twenty-four.

Her revery was interrupted half a dozen times
by the fits of coughing which shook her patient,
and which seemed to her to become more and
more frequent and more violent. At half-past
nine she gave him his medicine again, and took
his temperature once more. Then she made up
the fire, which burned badly; and she straightened the sheets on his bed, and turned the
pillows.

He soon sank to slumber again, breathing heavily and turning uneasily in his sleep. The house
was singularly still, and no sound of the dinner
party below reached the nurse in the corner room
above. When she happened to go into the dressing-room she found there awaiting her a tray
with several dishes from the dinner table. She
was glad to have something to eat, and she sat
down by the window to enjoy it. The thick, soft
snow had silenced nearly all the usual street

sounds. The carriages that went up and down the avenue were as inaudible as though they were rolling on felt. But sleighing parties became more frequent, and she found a suggestion of pleasant companionship and of human activity in the jingle of the bells. Once a fire-engine sped swiftly past the house, its usual roar deadened by the heavy snow, and its whistle shrilling forth as it neared the side streets, one after another; ten minutes later it came slowly back. The nurse was glad that there was only a false alarm, for she knew how terrible a fire would be in a crowded tenement-house on such a night.

She finished her belated dinner a few minutes after the deep tones of the clock in the hall had told her that it was ten, and that there were left of the old year but two hours more. Except when the sick man waked with a cough, the next hour was wholly eventless.

And yet, when it had drawn to an end, the nurse thought that it would count in her life as important beyond most others, for it was between ten and eleven that she made up her mind to marry the rich man who wanted her for his wife, and whom she did not love. The resolution once determined, she let her mind play about the possibilities of the future. She would not be married till the spring, of course, and they would go to Europe for their wedding-trip. Then, in the fall, she would persuade him to move to New York. He was fond of his own

town, but he would get used to the city in time;
and they could buy a new house, overlooking
Central Park—perhaps in the same neighbor-
hood as the one where she was sitting in the
hazy light of the sick-room.   She smiled unconsciously as she found herself wondering whether
her patient's beautiful young wife would call on
her if she purchased the house next door.

It was a little after eleven o'clock when she
again heard a rustling of silken stuffs in the room
by the side of hers, followed shortly by the voice
of the servant in the street below calling the carriages of the departing guests.   But some of the
diners still lingered, for it was nearly half an
hour later before the door of the sick-room
opened and the sick man's wife came gliding
in again with her languorous grace.

He fixed his eyes upon her at once, and smiled
with contentment as she came towards him.

"You've been asleep, haven't you?" she began.   "I'm so glad, for of course that's so good
for you.   We all missed you down-stairs, and
everybody asked about you and said they were
so sorry you were not there.   You must hurry
up and get well; and I'll give another dinner
like this, for it was a *great* success.   The flowers
were superb—and I don't think any of the wom-
en had a handsomer gown than I did.   And I
know all of them together hadn't as elegant dia-
monds.   I don't believe *anybody* at the dance
will have as many either."

"Sit down by me here and tell me all about the dinner," said the sick husband.

"Oh, I can't wait now," the young wife answered. "I *must* be off at once. I've simply *got* to be there in time to see the old year out and the new year in. They say Mrs. Jimmy has a surprise for us, and nobody at dinner had the slightest idea what it *could* possibly be !"

"Are you going to the dance to-night ?" asked the man in the bed ; and the nurse saw the pleading look in his eyes, even if his wife failed to perceive it.

"Of course I am," was the wife's reply. "I wouldn't miss it for *anything*. I think it's a lovely idea to have a dance on New-Year's Eve, don't you ? I *do* wish you were well enough to go, and I'm certain sure Mrs. Jimmy will ask about you—she's always *so* polite. You won't miss me—you will be asleep again in five minutes, won't you ?"

"Perhaps," he answered, still clinging to her fingers. "I'll try to sleep."

"That's right," she responded, withdrawing her hand and going towards the door. "I'll trust you to the nurse. She'll take better care of you than I should, I'm afraid. I never was *any* good when people were sick. Now goodbye. I *do* hope you'll be better when I get back. I'll come in and say good-night, of course. I sha'n't be late, either—I'll be home by three— or before four, *anyway*."

And with that she glided away, smiling back at her husband as she left the room. He followed her with his eyes, and he gazed at the door fixedly after she had gone. There was a hungry look in his face, so it seemed to the nurse, as of one starving in the midst of plenty. With the vain hope that the vision of beauty might yet return, he lay silent, but listening intently, until he heard the sharp slam of the carriage doors. Then he relaxed and turned restlessly in bed.

It was then half - past eleven, and the nurse took his temperature and administered another capsule, as the doctor had ordered. It seemed to her that he was more feverish and that he was coughing more frequently ; and even as she saw the patient sink into a broken sleep, she wished that the physician would come soon.

The arrival of the doctor was delayed till a few minutes before midnight, and the nurse had time to reconsider, once and forever, her decision to marry for money and without love. Her mind had been made up slowly and with great deliberation ; it was unmade suddenly and unhesitatingly and irrevocably. It was the sight of the mute pleading in the sick man's eyes which made her change her mind. After seeing that look she felt that it would be impossible for her to make a loveless marriage—not for her own sake only, but also for the sake of the man she should marry. If he loved her and

she did not love him, there would be no fair exchange ; she would be cheating him. When she
beheld clearly the meaning of the transaction
her honesty revolted. She had refused to marry
him more than once, and now her refusal was
final.

She stood for a moment at the window and
looked out. The snow had ceased falling, and
there was already a clearing of the clouds, which
let the moonlight pierce them fitfully. The
wind blew steadily across the broad meadows of
the Park, bending the whitened skeletons of the
trees.

Three immense sleighs filled with a joyous
and laughing party went down the avenue,
bandying songs from one sleigh to the other.
A horn was tooted repeatedly in one of the side
streets, and there were louder and more frequent whistles from the river craft on both sides
of the city. A pistol-shot rang out now and
again. It was almost midnight on the last day
of the old year; and the new year was to be
greeted with the customary chorus of wild noises.

As the nurse turned from the window the
doctor entered the room. She made her report
briefly, and she told him that the old man's
cough was worse, and that he seemed weaker.

While they were standing at the foot of the
bed, the patient was seized with another paroxysm. He sat up, shaken by the violent effort
—far more violent than any that had preceded

it.   He seemed to struggle vainly for relief, and then he dropped back limply on the pillows. The physician was at his side instantly, and laid a hand on his heart.   There was a moment of silence, and the clock on the stairs began to strike twelve, its chimes mingling with the uproar made by the pistols and the horns and the steam-whistles out-doors.

"That's what I was afraid of," said the doctor at last.   "I suspected that he had fatty degeneration of the heart."

"Is he—is he dead?" asked the nurse.

"Yes, he is dead."

But it was not for five or ten minutes that the shrill noises outside ceased.

(1895)

DATE DUE